ON THE WAY I LOST IT

Frankie Howerd

ON THE WAY I LOST IT

An autobiography

W. H. ALLEN · LONDON
A Howard & Wyndham Company
1976

PRINTED IN GREAT BRITAIN BY FLETCHER AND SON LTD, NORWICH
FOR THE PUBLISHERS, W. H. ALLEN AND CO. LTD,
44 HILL STREET, LONDON W1X 8LB
BOUND BY RICHARD CLAY (THE CHAUCER PRESS) LTD,
BUNGAY, SUFFOLK

ISBN 0 491 01807 X

For my mother and family.

For my friends.

For those not so friendly, whose assessments of me are probably the most accurate.

For the printers of this book for their seemingly inexhaustible supply of the first-person singular.

Contents

The Prologue

(Or should it be Apology?)

You may not credit this, but at regular intervals I've been asked to write my autobiography. This has been going on for about ten years now (long before the current flood of show-business books hit the market), and although I've always been flattered by the invitations I've steadfastly refused them.

There were a number of reasons:

I thought it was too egotistical.

I doubted if I could string together two coherent sentences.

I was too lazy to try.

I didn't think anyone would buy the book.

Recently the request was again made and, once more, bashful and unassuming Francis refused.

"But why not?" demanded "Thing" from the publishers. "Everybody else has."

"Precisely," replied modest, down-to-earth me. "I wouldn't exactly be blazing a trail, would I?"

"Well, pardon me for a long time," said "Thing" curtly. "I didn't realise you were something special. One day when you're feeling ordinary – do get in touch!"

I was so shocked by this untoward attack on my illusions that I borrowed a sheaf of paper (from "Thing" – why not?) and am now sitting here, pen in hand, waiting for inspiration.

Do forgive this somewhat arch opening – but inspiration and I have long since gone our separate ways, and it's not easy to effect a reconciliation.

ONE A Bump on the Head

Descriptions of my face have included comparisons with most root vegetables (usually in an advanced state of decomposition), and an entire menagerie of luckless animals; among them a disreputable bloodhound, a melancholy camel and an apologetic yak.

If any of these descriptions is accurate, I can only say that it relates to a face well serviced by the caprices of turbulence and time, for as a child, I am reliably informed, I was quite beautiful – difficult though you may find it to believe today!

I was fair-haired like my father, Frank, while my features reflected the delicacy of my mother, Edith: a short, slim, very pretty woman with jet-black curls that gave her an almost gypsy-like quality. Her family were, in fact, Scots – very Presbyterian, very disciplinarian – but they came to England, and during the First World War my mother was working at the Rowntree chocolate factory in York where she was wooed and won by Sergeant Frank Howard, a regular soldier in the Royal Artillery.

I was born after the war in a poorish area of the city near the River Ouse (during a snowstorm, my mother told me), and was christened Francis Alick. I have only one personal memory of York, but it may account for much in my later life: falling down the stairs and landing on my head.

I recall it sufficiently vividly to be able to re-live precisely five tumbles as my head hit various stairs – then an almighty *bang!* at the bottom.

I don't know how it happened. Had it occurred a few years later, a push might have been a reasonable – and justifiable – explanation, but I don't think I was much of a problem baby. I fancy I just wandered, and apart from any permanent damage to the few brain cells I possessed, the only other effect was to leave me with a permanent dread of heights: to this day I get vertigo when the heels of my shoes are repaired.

However . . .

When I was two and a half my father was posted to Woolwich, so we moved to Eltham in Kent where my brother, Sidney, and my sister Bettina (Betty) were to be born. I was too young to remember my brother's birth, but I remember Betty's. Told by an aunt that I had a new sister, I was most resentful: instead of sharing my mother's love with my brother, I reckoned that I'd now get only a third of it. (I was quite good at maths at the age of five.)

Anyway, in those days Eltham, if not exactly a village, was certainly in the Green Belt, yet to be swallowed by the ugly, shapeless sprawl of London. Our terrace house in Arbroath Road was in a working-class area of the town, but it had a nice garden and was near the Nine Fields, so called because that's what they were – nine fields. They've gone now, sacrificed for a housing estate. Nor will posterity make mass pilgrimages to the early home of F. Howerd – that also went to help make way for a housing estate. All that's left of those childhood landmarks is the cemetery.

So my earliest memories of Eltham are mainly of fields, and I developed a great passion for the countryside. This was due not only to the proximity of the Nine Fields, but also because I was an incredibly shy and withdrawn child, and away from the family I loved wandering on my own. I'd take solitary walks and, paradoxically, despite the dread of heights that made my stomach turn at the sight of a ladder, I'd climb trees – just to be alone in my own private, dream world.

An indication of my shyness was provided by my very first introduction to show-business at the age of about four. My parents took me to a working-men's club where the kids were supposed to go on stage and "do something" for a bag of sweets: recite a nursery rhyme, sing a song, or dance. What I did was somewhat more original – I screamed, demonstrating a lung power Shirley Bassey would envy. Petrified with fear, I yelled and shouted, howled and cried – and ruined the evening for everyone. (Still, I did get the sweets, and without any work – something I've tried to repeat ever since, with singular lack of success. And, considering the fights I later had to get *on* the stage, my struggle at the age of four to get *off* it had a quality of mad irony.)

So there was no evidence of stage-struck precociousness – yet! On the contrary, there was this excruciating shyness, although the stammer that was to plague me in later years – until I learned to capitalise on it – was not yet evident. Not that it was ever a b-b-b-but sort of impediment: simply that when I was frightened or under stress, and in an unfamiliar environment, I'd gabble and garble. Always a very fast talker, I'd repeat words and run them together when this terror came upon me.

"Why-why-why . . . Um . . . Why-why-why did-did-did the chicken crosser-crosser-crosser road" may be an over-simplification, but it gives an indication of what was to happen when I was scared – which was to be depressingly often, as you will see.

But – as you will also see – it was all part of the absurd mess that became Frankie Howerd.

I say that my parents took me to that working-men's club. It's odd to use the plural, for I seldom saw my father in those days. Ill health, brought about by the war, meant his transfer from the Royal Artillery to the Education Corps, and his duties took him all over Britain. So I knew little of him, and any closeness of parental relationship had to be with my mother. Most people have a mother and father: I seemed to have only a mother. For the first years of my life – until my father left the Army – we were virtually a one-parent family, and when my father was finally invalided out, he came into my life almost as a stranger. My mother was the one I'd known during the formative years, so Dad seemed to be something of a gate-crasher. It was nobody's fault: it's just the way these things happen. But the result was a singular lack of rapport, and in a sort of way I positively resented his "intrusion" in the relationship I had with my mother. Mine was far from an isolated instance of this sort of situation: there are always fathers who have to spend more time away than at home, and the effect on the children is almost invariably traumatic.

My father was essentially a practical man, and my brother Sidney (now a rather senior gentleman with the Post Office) took after him in this respect. Betty and I were more attuned to our mother's personality: to her way-out sense of humour and her love of the theatre. Indeed, my first impression of show-business (apart from that disaster at the working-men's club) was of my mother singing snatches from the musical comedy successes of the day.

Anyway, the time came for me to go to elementary school – Gordon School, named after General Gordon of Khartoum. Being so nervous and shy made the first months there agonising; and fear of authority made me conscientious to the point of stupidity (in any case, discipline in those days was backed by a liberal use of the cane!). When, during one school holiday, we were set three hundred sums to do, I struggled through the lot – and discovered I was the only pupil who'd bothered to do so. Yet my years at General Gordon were not unhappy once I'd settled down and made friends.

The recall of childhood is always fragmented: isolated occasions and incidents for one reason or another remain vivid, despite the erosion of time on the powers of recall. Empire Day was one example, when the school would parade before parents and local dignitaries, and after speeches the children would sing "Jerusalem". (I still get a lump in the throat when I hear it, evoking, as it does, memories of childhood.) I'd look around for my mother, hoping that she could see me, and pleased to be in the limelight as long as I was protected by the anonymity of being just one face in the mass chorus. (My great ego trips were yet to come!)

Another crystal-clear memory, and one of much greater importance in terms of my later development, is of the first of our regular Boxing Day visits to the pantomime.

My mother took the three of us to the Woolwich Artillery Theatre and we queued for eightpenny seats in the gallery. The normal price was sixpence, but Boxing Night was the traditional opening date, so they upped the price, and we had to walk the long distance there and back so as not to make too big a hole in my mother's very tight budget.

The panto's principal boy was Nora Delaney (and was to be in most of the years that followed) and for me, aged six, it was love at first sight. (Her real-life Prince Charming proved to be Prince Littler, who ran the theatre with his brother, Emile – and for whom, of course, I was to work in later years.)

So there I sat in what seemed to be this huge theatre (when I later performed there I realised that it was, in fact, quite tiny) absolutely hypnotised by the fairyland magic of *Cinderella*: make-believe to an adult, but to a small boy a splendid reality of a world in which everything was beautiful and glamorous, and poverty was a comedy rewarded with riches. It was an exciting, glittering, over-the-rainbow world, and I instantly wanted to become a part of it: not specifically as an actor or comedian or singer or anything else, but just in order to escape to wonderland.

So after this visit to the panto I began to dream of the theatre. I'd make scenery, put it in a cardboard box through the side of which I'd stab a tiny hole, and so create peep-shows. I'd also borrow my mother's tea tray, build curtains from rags supported on sticks, and for actors make cut-outs from *Film Fun*. I'd create the stories for these characters – needless to say I was always the hero – and put on performances for my mother and baby sister. But not my brother: even as a toddler he showed no great enthusiasm for my idiot world of fantasy.

Living next door at this time were the Smiths. Their daughter Ivy was a year older than me (although today we argue about which way the differential works) and I bullied her into joining me in a great venture: a two-child concert party. Now this may seem out of character in terms of my being so shy and nervy, but it wasn't. In fact it was inspired by those very defects of character, for that night at the panto had given me a glimpse of a magic world in which shyness and nerves did not appear to exist (little did I know!) and in which I'd be popular and applauded. So, despite my trembles and trepidations, I was determined to have a try.

Ivy and I put on these primitive concerts in my back garden for the local kids, charging them a farthing admission fee (not enquiring too closely where the farthings came from in that poor neighbourhood) and with a wardrobe unofficially borrowed from our parents.

It was during the third or fourth of these Saturday matinées that my mother came round the back and asked what was going on.

"We're giving a concert," I replied.

"Who are these children?"

"From round and about," I told her, adding with some pride that each had paid a farthing to attend.

But instead of the expected praise, I was rewarded with a thump.

"*A farthing!*" my mother cried. "A farthing! How dare you rob these poor children? Give the money back immediately!"

Rob? I was affronted, even at that early age, for I assumed that if I charged a farthing, and kids paid, I just had to be worth it. Yet here was my mother suggesting I was Baby-Face Howard, Con Man.

So entrance to the concerts was now free, but I was to learn that my mother's words reflected a basic rule for any form of entertainment: always try to make sure that you do give value for money.

Because of my shyness and loneliness, I took well to Sunday School at the Church of St Barnabas. It gave me a feeling of belonging; some comforting communal security. And although it would be stretching things to describe Sunday School as a form of show-business, there was a sort of theatrical presentation about its organised programme of events: the vicar's sermon, the lantern slides, the communal hymn singing, the Bible story. I loved it, and in consequence became extremely religious, going on to join the Band of Hope, the Cubs, the Society for the Propagation of the Gospel – I joined everything religious in sight.

Possibly my mother, because of her own religious background, had vague hopes that I'd become a vicar – but my own, new, ambition aimed much higher: I decided to become a saint. No, that isn't a misprint – a saint. Why? Because Heaven seemed to offer an even happier world than the theatre. Naïve? Maybe – but it's the truth. I really thought in those pre-teen years that if I lived a good, pure life in the service of God I could end up as Saint Francis of Eltham, and go to Heaven. And after all, what is Heaven if it isn't this world without this world's miseries: its poverty and sickness and stammering shyness? So I decided to become a saint.

Oh well, it was a nice idea at the time . . .

Do I hear you ask how I lived up to that boyhood dream? Let me put it this way: as far as that particular aspiration is concerned, I'm rather like a footballer in the second half of a match who sees that his side is twenty goals down . . . I've accepted that it's one game I've lost.

Now you may not need much formal education to become a saint, but you do to become a vicar, so my mother urged me to study hard and try to win one of two London County Council scholarships that were offered at Shooter's Hill Grammar School. And I did win one; not because I was any cleverer than my brother and sister – I wasn't – but I was the one offered the opportunity, and succeeded by sheer hard slog. My best subject was maths – which is surprising, to say the least, when I think what a lousy businessman I turned out to be. My worst subject was geography (which a psychologist might put down to my extraordinary insularity) but which is also ironic in that I am now an inveterate traveller.

Anyway, Shooter's Hill was considered to be something of a posh school, where you learned Latin and things. It was also a new school, and I went there on the first day that it opened.

Another powerful memory: that very first day at school. Getting there meant a three-quarters-of-an-hour walk through the fields and woods (a bus was too much of a luxury), and I was petrified every step of the way: the transfer from General Gordon meant that once again I was leaving surroundings where I had become known and was accepted (and which were therefore safe because of their familiarity) in exchange for the terrifying question-mark of a strange unknown. It was to take me a full year to settle in among the middle-class, fee-paying lads at Shooter's Hill. The situation was in no way helped by the fact that in those days "scholarship boy" had a positive ring of charity about it. But when my curiosity value wore off and I was accepted (as, of course, I was desperately anxious to be) my school-mates proved to be a great bunch of lads, and I became very happy there. . . . Except for one shaming incident.

I had a great crush on a girl called Sheila and would write her florid (if innocuous) love letters. One day the draft of one such letter was found and pinned to the school notice-board. I was made to look foolish, for writing to girls was not considered manly! Cricket and cold baths were the masculine ways to spend your life when you were a pre-teenager at Shooter's Hill. (Although I never took to cold baths, I could be quite good at cricket. I once achieved every bowler's dream: six wickets in six balls and was chaired off the field. But at other times, if I wasn't relaxed,

I could almost be guaranteed to bowl wide enough to break a pavilion window. Very erratic, I was. Still am, come to think of it: when I have a flop it's usually spectacular!)

I went to church regularly, and at thirteen became a Sunday School teacher. I was happy teaching, despite my diffidence, for being religious I was anxious to serve. Every Monday night I'd go with other teachers to the home of the vicar and he would brief us on the subject of instruction for the following week. He was a nice and good man, and I'd feel terribly ashamed for feeling so incredibly bored by his lectures. I remember how I'd look at him, trying to be attentive, but with my mind wandering to films and music and the theatre. Even in those days I had the capacity to look at one thing and think of another (already my saintly ambitions were wearing a trifle thin), but it proved to be of great help in later life – during a long run, when words, movements and gestures became automatic, actors need the capacity to portray intense drama while wondering what's for supper!

I'd teach at Sunday School every week, but because I paid little attention to the vicar I'd never remember his briefings. So I'd make up stories: not, alas, about splendid Biblical happenings, but of Robin Hood, Morgan the Pirate and Sexton Blake. I had a great gift for invention in those days, and although my stories had nothing to do with the Christian faith (or maybe because of it), I was the most popular Sunday School teacher in Eltham. In his ignorance of what was happening, the vicar, poor soul, put it down to my goodness – and in later years, when the odd sins crept in, I was to feel dreadfully guilty about it all: I thought I'd let God down in some way.

These recollections of youth may seem trivial in themselves, but since any entity can only be a sum of its component parts, these fragments do have a significance. Thus, while being a Sunday School teacher was of little consequence in itself, it led to a major milestone in my life – I joined the Church Dramatic Society: a shy, clumsy, nervous, withdrawn boy, convinced that I was ugly and useless to man and beast, yet desperately anxious to express myself.

So when the Society put on Ian Hay's old comedy, *Tilly of Bloomsbury*, there was young Frank Howard, pathetically eager to take part in it and do well. And because the producer, Winifred Young, took pity on this stammering youth, she searched for a part for me – and came up with Tilly's father. I read the part in an incoherent gabble, flushing in a manner that would make a beetroot look positively anaemic, knocking over the props in my clumsiness – and embarrassing everyone in my anxiety to please.

Mrs Young, despite being an amateur, proved to be my Professor Higgins. When she asked: "Will you let me help you?" I stuttered an eager "Yes".

"Then come round to my house for two hours every Tuesday and Thursday evening, and I'll see what I can do."

I owe as much to Winifred Young as to anyone else in my career. Who knows: without her there might not have been any career, merely bitter frustration. As it was she gave me a sort of speech therapy, taking me through my role until – irrespective of my behaviour off-stage – I spoke my part slowly and clearly and without stumbling or stammering. She taught me how to "ee-nun-cee-ate", to be calm, to concentrate on the performance – and to forget myself as a self-pitying nonentity.

I did exactly as Mrs Young told me – and was the hit of the night. (Even the local paper was to single me out.)

What followed may sound like a cliché from a bad Hollywood B-picture, but it is none the less absolute fact . . . One of the people backstage said: "You should be an actor," and for some reason that has since been a source of utter bafflement to me, his words – whether sincere, just polite, or merely jocular – acted as a sudden and instant catalyst on all my vague hopes and half-dreams, fusing them into an absolute certitude of determination.

Why it should have happened like that, backstage at the church hall, I do not know, but with astonishing clarity I thought: "He's right. That's it. That's what I *am* going to be: a professional actor. Now, at last, I *know* . . ."

It was an unlikely proposition: an excruciatingly shy, stammering and introspective youth joining what in many ways is the most brash and extrovert of professions, but from that night on I never deviated from a sense of destiny almost manic in its obsessive intensity.

I retained this sense of destiny for a long time – or, to put it another way, I lived in cloud-cuckoo land much longer than is normal.

TWO Disaster in Gower Street

My determination to become an actor inspired me to join the school's Dramatic Society. The talent of the other embryo thespians must have been pretty poor, for I was soon recognised as the school's best performer, was nicknamed "The Actor", became extremely popular – and adored every minute of it! At last I came to lose some of my sense of inferiority. In fact, as far as acting was concerned, I began to get positively big-headed . . . until my delusions of grandeur led me to write a play for the school concert.

Items for this event were intended to last ten minutes: mine, *Lord Halliday's Birthday Party*, lasted an hour. I forget the plot, except that it involved divorce and murder and was probably lifted from a film I'd seen. Although certainly harmless by today's standards, the headmaster read the script, said it was far too outrageous and bold to be performed by small boys, and added that he was appalled that a fifteen year old could be so depraved as to write such filth. (He wasn't too keen on the length, either.) His dressing-down may have been somewhat pompous and disproportionate, but it had the therapeutic effect of shrinking my head back to its normal size – although, looking back, I reckon that even if the play was tripe, I must have been an enterprising lad to have attempted an hour-long drama. As for the depravity of my mind, little did he know its snow-white innocence. I was naïve to the point of absurdity, and if there was anything improper in my script as judged by the standards of the day, then I was far too artless to realise it was there.

My next move was to enrol for acting lessons at evening classes run by what was then the London County Council. One of the teachers was the actress Mary Hope, and she – bless her – thought I had talent and so made me join the LCC Dramatic Society. Then she learned that there was a scholarship going for RADA (the Royal Academy of Dramatic Art) which I could take when I was sixteen, and for which she would coach me if I was interested. *Was I interested?* Choked with emotion, I managed to stammer that it was the most exciting prospect imaginable.

So there I was, appearing in plays at school, plays for the Church Dramatic Society, plays for the LCC Dramatic Society – and was now to start studying for RADA. On top of this I had also formed my own concert party with my sister Betty: we put on shows with the help of protesting local talent in aid of charity. Needless to say my orthodox studies suffered badly.

When I told my mother about the RADA scholarship, I think she was disappointed that I wasn't going to enter the Church, after all; but since her primary concern was for my happiness, she gave me all the support she could.

Children are inclined to take a tremendous amount for granted, and for my part I never fully appreciated the sacrifices my parents made on my behalf. I knew that we were hard-up, of course – I was aware of being a scholarship boy among fee-paying lads from relatively wealthy homes – but I never grasped the degree of the hardship involved in keeping me at Shooter's Hill: a hardship that would be aggravated by winning a scholarship to RADA.

By now, my father had been invalided out of the Army. They found he had a hole in one lung, but denied that it was a result of his Army service. Since he'd been passed A-1 when he joined, how else could he have damaged his lung if not through the rigours of an Army career which had included the ordeals of the Great War? But decisions were even more autocratic in those days than they are now, and so he was awarded a minimal pension. He found a job as a clerk, and since those were the days of the Depression, when work was at a premium, an employer could quite happily pay less wages to a man who wasn't as fit as his fellows. Only recently an aunt told me how she used to urge him to go to the doctor, but he always refused: he was terrified of being laid off work, in which case his wife and family would suffer.

So my father worked on, unable to earn more than a little money, and my brother and sister had to leave school at the then minimum age of fourteen (Sidney to go to the GPO, Betty into an office), while my mother also had to go out to work to help pay the bills and keep me at school. She was a sort of housekeeper to a wealthy family in the area: certainly scrubbing and polishing, but because of a happy relationship with them was much more than a char. (This is not a statement of snobbery, but fact.) However, work she did – and work hard – and it was not until later that my unquestioning acceptance of the situation dissolved into a realisation that much of it was on my behalf.

For my RADA exam I, too, worked hard in my fashion; harder than I'd worked for anything in my life. The set pieces were an extract from some contemporary (and now long forgotten) play, and two popular Shakespeare soliloquies.

The great day arrived, cold and grey. A tall, incredibly thin, gauche boy – possessed of near-idiot shyness away from surroundings that were not familiar – I put on my best suit, and clutching a packet of cheese sandwiches for lunch, caught the train from Eltham to Holborn Viaduct. Trepidations on the train journey were bad enough: by the time I'd walked from Holborn to the RADA building in Gower Street I was a near-wreck.

Grasping my packet of sandwiches, almost as though I had to cling to *something*, I shuffled into the seemingly vast room where the other male candidates were awaiting auditions – and for the first time in my life encountered what might be called the actor "type": rather posturing and willowy youths who today would be called camp, but pre-war were referred to as the Matinée Idol type. All had great presence (if little future) and compared with them I was a scruffy yokel. They looked at this sweating oaf, smiled, sneered – and one or two actually laughed. Added to my existing state of nerves, it was all I needed . . .

I went in for my audition, absently clutching my sandwiches – and my left knee started to tremble. As the examiners stared, fascinated, at this agitated limb, I tried to brace it to stop the quivering, but couldn't. The right leg was fine – but the left one was now positively oscillating. I put my right hand (with sandwiches) on the knee, but all that happened was that knee, hand and sandwiches effected a surreally rhythmic communication of shaking. I thought: *If I hit the bloody knee, will it stop?* It didn't: it succeeded only in bursting the paper bag, scattering crumbling cheese sandwiches over the floor.

"Yes . . . Well . . . Um . . . To-to-to . . . er be . . . or not-not-not to . . . um . . . Yes, well . . . To be . . . Well, that's the question, isn't it? . . ." This sort of thing, accompanied by shakes and blushes, may have been a hoot at a seaside concert party, but for RADA? I should have thrown up my hands and run for my life, but beneath the panic lay that hard subsoil of determination, and so I stumbled and stammered and squeaked and shook my way through all of the three set pieces.

That Francis Alick Howard was not really suitable RADA material was the quickest decision any examining body has ever made.

My journey home was an anguish of desolation and shame. I'd let everyone down: my mother, my headmaster, my schoolmates, Mary Hope – and myself. I was a complete and utter failure. When the train arrived at Eltham I didn't go home, but to the Nine Fields where my bitterness and frustration, my grief and self-pity, exploded into howling agony. Never before or since have I wept as I did on that day . . .

And then, as though the Nine Fields were a resting-place on some road to a personal Damascus, I suddenly sat upright, knuckled away the tears and thought: "You're a fool. A fool. . . . You must have courage. Courage. The way you're behaving is absolutely gutless. . . . Look, you believe in God, don't you? And you know that God seems to have given you talent. You *feel* that to be true. . . . Now God is logical. He must be, otherwise life is stupid. Pointless. Without meaning. . . . OK, perhaps RADA and straight acting aren't for you. What then is the alternative? . . ."

I sat trance-like for some minutes until the glimmering of an answer formed in my mind: "Comedy? Is that the alternative? If you're not meant to be a great Shakespearean, are you meant to be a comedian? Is that it? . . . Why not try and see?"

And so ambition was channelled towards a fresh objective. But as I left the Nine Fields I resolved that while comedy might be my new, long-term, goal, I would not return to Shooter's Hill. I'd betrayed the faith they'd had in me there: the Actor was now the Flop. No, I couldn't go back. Instead, while awaiting some sort of show-business break, I'd find a job. First, however, I had to face my mother . . .

I need not have worried: as always she was sympathetic and comforting.

A postscript to that traumatic day:

One of the examiners at RADA was that great actress, Helen Haye, and years later I was asked to appear at a Gallery First Nighters' tribute dinner to her. During my speech I referred to the disastrous audition in Gower Street, and said to her with mock-severity: "You prevented me from becoming a famous actor. I had to become a comic, instead." To which she replied, matter-of-factly: "And a bloody good job, too. I was absolutely right."

Anyway, after desperate searching, I found a job as a pound-a-week filing clerk with an export/import firm in Tooley Street, in London's dockland. For this generous salary I worked from nine to seven, Monday to Friday, and from nine to one p.m. on Saturday, with Christmas and Boxing Days the only paid holidays. (When my father died of a heart attack it was with grudging reluctance that I was given the day off for the funeral.)

As the humiliation of the RADA débâcle became misted over by time, I again began to take an active part in theatricals: concert parties, the Church Dramatic Society, local pageants – I even regained enough confidence to join the Shooter's Hill Old Boys Dramatic Society. My energy and enthusiasm returned and I was happy again.

It's curious, but although I was resolved to become a pro, once I became one I think that in many ways I was less happy than in those amateur days. This is not altogether the paradox it might appear: as an amateur I performed for fun; as a professional I *had* to do it, and so the stress was enormous. Further: an amateur wants to give a good performance, but has no responsibility towards the audience's pocket – it's the charity they are supporting, not the artist's bank balance, so a bad performance by an amateur may damage his ego, but there's no personal fear of not giving value for money. Nor, of course, does a bad performance threaten an amateur's livelihood. No, the pressures just aren't there.

But if I was happy being back in show-business, I detested my job. It wasn't just the hours and poor pay, but the very nature of the work. It not only bored me, but I was absolutely useless at it. At school I'd been good at maths and Latin, but these qualifications proved to be of little help when it came to filing an invoice or a shipping order. I have always been ridiculously impractical (even now I'm known to sit for hours in the dark, helpless, because I cannot repair a fuse), and my situation was in no way improved by my boss. If ever there was a victim in search of a sadist, it was me – and I found him in Henry A. Lane. War wounds had left him with a limp, a tin plate in his head, an eye patch – and a bitter malevolence. Who better to vent his frustration and hatred on than me?

If a cup of tea stood ready to be spilled in his lap then I, in my clumsiness, spilled it. If a bottle of ink waited to be knocked over, I knocked it. He truly despised me and terrorised me, and the more sadistic his behaviour, the more of a gibbering idiot I became.

As for my colleagues, they were convinced that I was mad. For there I sat studying a file – muttering to myself and making wild facial expressions. The explanation was simple: inside the covers of the file was a script or play part that I was learning. And as far as I was concerned, living as I did only for the theatre, I simply had to do this studying in office hours: my nights and week-ends were almost completely occupied with rehearsals and performances. My fanaticism caused me not even to attempt to try to make a go of my job in Tooley Street, but it did cause me to take on far too many commitments outside, and I was always desperately tired and run-down. I was a boily boy in those days.

My departure from Tooley Street was inevitable, and was accelerated by the discovery that my prowess as a filing clerk had led to a consignment for America ending up in China, while other goods had never left the docks, and a folder of vital documents sent to Russia proved to contain an unsolicited, and somewhat dubious, bonus: the programme for a revue called *Frank Howard's Gertchers Concert Party*. Henry A. Lane's joy in firing me was doubtless tempered by the sadness of losing the perfect whipping-boy.

And so – the dole! God knows there were enough people unemployed in those days, mostly through no fault of their own, but there was still a sense of shame at having to queue every week for what seemed to be the soup-kitchen charity of a state handout. Yet even worse than this was the desolate feeling of being unwanted.

Luckily I was unemployed for only a fortnight: the people for whom my mother worked owned a part of the United Friendly Insurance Company, and they found me a job as a clerk in the firm's head office in Southwark Bridge Road. Not only was the pay better (thirty shillings a week), but the entire atmosphere was much happier, and the hours were easier: ten to six, with half-day working only on alternate Saturdays.

My immediate boss was a spinster of about forty, and I think she fancied me. I liked her, too, but only in the nicest possible sense, for I was still an astonishingly innocent youth. But, believe it or not, I was also very charming and well-mannered (qualities long since lost), and my smile was quite angelic, as distinct from today's leering lechery. And so, since I was still incompetent, but didn't want the sack again, I played up to her like mad, and she mistook stammering gaucheness for gentlemanly reticence.

Poor dear!

I was still working every night, trying as far as possible to concentrate on comedy parts. I also formed *Frank Howard's Knockout Concert Party*. Note that it was not just *The Knockout Concert Party*: talent may have been slow in developing, but the ego was in full flight again. Each concert we put on contained twenty-two items, and would you believe that I was in twenty-one? The twenty-second was given over to a girl singer, and I've often wondered why I never made it a duet.

I was responsible for the written material, but since there's a limit to anyone's inventiveness, much had to be improvised as we went along. I'd think of a tag-line for a sketch and say to the others: "Now you, Betty, will go on the stage and say something. Anything. Then I'll say something. Then Charlie here will say something. We'll make it up as we go along – always remembering that we're aiming for the tag-line. . . . Which *I* will deliver!"

When you think of it, this was what Method acting was to be all about: yet I was doing it before the war – a sort of early Marlon Brando with Music Hall jokes. Again, the famous American team of Mike Nichol and Elaine May were also to evolve this technique: take a subject and improvise a complete situation around it. So in his amateur way Frank Howard was something of a pioneer, although inspired not by genius but necessity.

We put on our charity shows at scout halls and church

halls and old folks' homes, knocking together primitive bits and pieces of props and costumes, and I would travel to these dates by tram or on foot, often walking eight miles each way (I had little option on half-a-crown-a-week pocket-money). I did have star-status travel once, when the rich man in the concert party gave me a lift in his tiny old Ford. I thought the car very grand, and he thought himself very grand: he earned £5 a week, thus establishing that he was a member of the middle class. Another trip by private transport was when a girlfriend's brother took me on the back of his motorcycle to join the annual Sunday School outing at Herne Bay. That ride was memorable because it gave me pneumonia.

Mind you, I was always in a state of debility because of my over-exertions. My mother was worried, of course, but understood that there was some mad compulsion – only she, being so religious, regarded it as a "Calling". And although, deep down, she wished I'd been "Called" to some more conventional cause, she had an unswerving faith in the inevitability of my success. What did disturb her, though, was that I decided to change my name to Ronnie Ordex. That's right: Ronnie Ordex – a name I assumed (for a mercifully short period) because it seemed to have irresistible star quality . . . God preserve us from the follies of our youth!

One more memory from that concert party period: my double-act with a lad called Philip Mackie, he in evening dress, me a natural scruff – like the old duo of Clapham and Dwyer – with Philip acting as my feed. We weren't a bad act, but when the war came we had to go our different ways, and I didn't see him again until fairly recently. If the name rings a bell it's because since then, he has become a very successful playwright both for stage and television.

Now in those days "Friday Night Is Talent Night" was one of the popular features of the local Music Halls. And a regular feature of "Talent Night" was Frank Howard . . .

I started off with a comic monologue. That didn't do well, so the next Friday I went to a different theatre and tried impressions. Without a shred of originality, I did the people everyone else was doing – Noël Coward, Gary Cooper, Charles Laughton, James Cagney, and so on. Why I thought I could do impressions I don't know, because I couldn't. But I did them. When they failed, I switched to a comedy song dressed as a small boy . . . another disaster. I'm pretty sure that I attempted everything, apart from acts that demanded any degree of physical dexterity, such as conjuring, juggling, the trapeze and the high wire. My greatest fiasco was at the Lewisham Hippodrome during a week when Jack Payne and his Band topped the bill, and the supporting acts included comedians Derek Roy and Jimmy James.

Nervous, as always, I was going to try my hand at telling a few jokes and singing a couple of songs. I went on stage – and found myself in the centre of the most enormous and powerful spotlight I had yet encountered. Its blinding intensity was so painful that I screwed-up my eyes in an attempt to blot it out. When this proved to be unsuccessful, I started sidling about the stage to get away from its glare, but there was no escape. Finally I faced the audience and began to do my stuff, but that damn spotlight was so disconcerting my thoughts became progressively more dominated by it until I could no longer concentrate on my act. Finally I completely forgot my lines and dried-up – and stood there gaping and shaking and squinting, my mouth working but with no words emerging.

The audience began to laugh, but it was the most dreaded of all laughter for a performer – derision. And the more they fell about, the worse I became. The orchestra leader hissed from the pit: "Do something, or get off!" I stumbled off – in tears.

It's mad to think that that disaster was caused by the sort of spotlight I was later so anxious to hog as my very own!

It was so frustrating: there I was, often successful as an amateur – comedy, straight acting, pantomime, writing – but I couldn't make that vital leap to the professional side of the business.

As you are aware by now, much of the trouble lay within myself, of course: the nerves and shyness that destroyed me every time I went through the stage door of a "real" theatre. Yet I kept on trying, because the utter conviction that I did have talent was stronger than the flaws of personality that crucified me when it came to an actual performance. And so, although failure led to black depression and heartache, I'd bounce back after a few days determined to have another go. Nobody could say that I wasn't trying: *very* trying to those who didn't share my ideals and my dreams of stardom, which didn't involve fantasies of riches: merely success for its own sake. (I found out the hard way that fame in itself doesn't pay the rent, and it was only when my career collapsed that I swore that in the remote event of a comeback I'd be practical about the financial side of the business.)

In an effort to conquer my timorous lack of self-confidence in public, I began to go to dances, and I wasn't a bad dancer, either. I'd take girls from the concert parties (Joyce and Betty and Dulcie, where are you now?), and I was considered a refined lad because of the courtly manners I copied from Leslie Howard in some film or other: bowing, kissing their hands when I said goodnight, doffing my hat. . . . And my popularity was enhanced because I was a clean-living Sunday School teacher who didn't smoke or drink or try to take liberties. (Thinking about it now, I suppose I must really have been an abominable prig – and stupid with it!) However, when I went to a dance on my own I'd walk around the outside of the hall for at least half an hour before working-up the courage to go in!

And so to 1939. War was declared, and I promptly volunteered – for ENSA. They gave me an audition at the Theatre Royal, Drury Lane, and needless to say I failed that one, too. Without being defensive about it, I'd point out that my attempt to join ENSA wasn't in order to dodge the column, but to try to be of service at something I thought I was good at: entertaining.

But ENSA didn't want me, so I stayed at my job, and in

another effort to overcome my nerves had a go at a solo act away from the concert parties. I did it at various fire stations, dressed as a fireman and telling fireman-orientated jokes and singing comic songs. I didn't do too badly, either, in terms of getting through a performance all on my own, and the firemen seemed to like it well enough (probably, on reflection, because they were desperate for any sort of entertainment in those early, uncertain days of the war!).

Then, in February 1940, I passed my first audition. Despite vague hopes that I'd be rejected on the grounds of insanity, the Army signed me up for what is known as a run-of-the-show contract.

As a contract it was a powerful pointer to the future, had I been able to read the signs: the management could retain my services for as long as they wished, but I wasn't allowed to quit; I had to perform wherever they, in their absolute discretion, decided; they determined how much money I would receive, and where I'd appear in the billing; while any breach of the management's multifarious rules involved heavy penalties. (I had no say in the choice of my costumes, either!)

THREE The Defence of Southend

My spirits reflected the weather – grey and glum – on the morning I reported to Shoeburyness Barracks, clutching a bundle of personal possessions, and the obligatory brown paper, string and gummed label so that my civilian clothes could be posted home. Those of us at Shoeburyness that day were the stereotyped regional, social and emotional cross-section that makes up any military draft; and although in terms of emotion some were wary and others stoic, some were filled with bravado and others were scared – none was as stammeringly terrified as F. Howard, who once again found himself a stranger in a strange land.

The Sergeant Major roared the inevitable cliché about never having seen such an 'orrible shower, for some reason singled me out for an extra, personal, blast – and I made a clumsy riposte. It wasn't anything as clever as wit – merely a nervous reflex. The look on the Sergeant Major's face not only told me that I wasn't going over big, but also taught me a basic commandment of Army life: only superior officers are permitted to be funny on the parade-ground.

By definition, Army training is tough, especially in war-time, and our discomforts weren't helped by the severity of that 1939/40 winter. There was, however, one discomfort from which the War Office was determined to save us – unrequited lust, and this they did by the traditional method of putting bromide in our tea. (Or maybe it was the soup: they both tasted much the same.) And lust would have been unrequited: there was no leave during those days of initial training, and while most of the ATS girls at Shoeburyness were spoken for by the officers, the only other birds around were the Thames estuary seagulls.

For me, the worst agonies of those early Army days were suffered on the barrack square. Being so clumsy and uncoordinated, marching and counter-marching, forming fours and wheeling to the left or right in column of route turned me into a one-man disaster area whose ineptitude could transform an entire parade into a lunatic shambles. As for shouldering, sloping or presenting arms, or stripping-down my rifle – my antics would have been considered too outrageous for even the most primitive and undemanding farce on children's TV. Some protective angel must have saved me from spending my entire Army career in the glass-house, for it was generally supposed that nobody could be so useless by nature: I had to be a truculent rebel. Sergeant Major Tonks couldn't quite make up his mind, however, and nicknamed me the Unknown Quantity.

Anyway, I somehow got through my basic training and was transferred to another part of the barracks where they proposed to make me a gunner in the Royal Artillery. I'd still been dreaming of show-business, of course, but the passion and the fire had been damped down by the practicalities of circumstance. Then they burned hot again – in that part of the barracks to which I was transferred was situated the YMCA, and Sunday concerts were staged there by garrison personnel. Yet I didn't rush to join in: my surroundings were still sufficiently strange to cause me to lack the necessary confidence.

Two memorable leaves . . .

During one I went to the Saville Theatre to see the show, *Up And Doing*, which starred Leslie Henson, Binnie Hale, Stanley Holloway and Cyril Richard. During the performance an air-raid warning sounded, and those of us in the gallery and circle were asked to go to the stalls for greater safety. We shuffled down, to stand and squat as best we could in the gangways. The show went on, but when it was over we were asked not to leave the theatre: although no bombs were falling it was considered wiser to stay under cover until the all-clear sounded.

The cast continued to entertain us, and although all were splendid pros, the point came when even they began to flag. So they asked for volunteers to go on stage and "do something". I thought I'd give them my send-up version of the song "Three Little Fishes" (a number that was to become something of a favourite when it was part of my act after the war). I said to myself: "At least you'll have what might be your one and only opportunity to appear on a West End stage" – but every time I started to get up, shyness forced me back into my seat. I bobbed up and down like a jack-in-the-box *for five hours* – until the all-clear sounded at three a.m!

The second leave is memorable for precisely the same reason, only this time it was a visit to the old Holborn Empire where Max Miller and Vera Lynn were appearing in *Apple Sauce*. (Max's stooge, incidentally, was a beautiful twenty-year-old called Jean Carr, later to become famous as actress Jean Kent.) Again the air-raid siren sounded, again we were asked to go down to the stalls, again the point came when the call came for volunteers – and again I vacillated until the all-clear went in the early hours.

Then there were no more leaves. The British Expeditionary Force was retreating towards Dunkirk, and we were all confined to barracks to combat the German invasion which it was generally assumed would follow the fall of France.

So, apart from serving us tea (or maybe soup) that was almost neat liquid bromide, there was a sudden need for garrison-produced entertainment. When the call went out: "Can anybody do anything?" I now felt sufficiently confident, settled enough in my surroundings, to volunteer to perform a patter act the following Sunday. It went down very well: in fact it was successful. I became a Sunday regular at the YMCA. (There's an odd sidelight to the first of those concerts: when the sergeant-compère introduced me, he did so as "Gunner Frankie Howard of B Battery". Now this was the first time that anyone had ever called me Frankie. At home, in concert parties – when I wasn't using some preposterous stage name – it was always Frank. And that in itself was a diminutive, since I was christened Francis. I didn't like Frankie a bit; it seemed positively babyish. But it caught on in the barracks – and finally stuck. A pity, really: Francis is much more elegant. More *me*, don't you think? . . . Oh well, please yourself!)

Now it occurred to some military genius that if there really was going to be a German invasion there wasn't much point having all the available soldiery cooped-up in Shoeburyness Barracks: there was the entire Thames estuary in need of defence. Troops would have to be deployed along its considerable north bank – and round the corner up the Essex coast, too. This totalled a somewhat large area, but the Shoeburyness garrison was relatively small – so, logically, the available manpower would have to be used with extreme economy.

The defence of Southend-on-Sea and its 200,000 inhabitants was entrusted to Gunner F. Howard and one other.

On our first night we were told to make sandbags and take up position behind them: a formidable initiative test in itself since Southend, for all its popularity as a seaside resort for Londoners, has a beach made up almost entirely of shingle. But we created a few lumpy sandbags on the foreshore, lay spreadeagled behind them, and with our rifles pointing through the barbed-wire towards the Kent coast on the other side of the estuary, were ready to Defend Our Cherished Heritage Against The Hun.

The two of us. On either side the damp, grey emptiness seemed to stretch to eternity. God alone knows what would have happened if the German High Command had indeed chosen that stretch of beach below the Palace Hotel as the focal point of an invasion, defended as it was by two raw recruits with Short Lee-Enfields and ten rounds of ammunition between them! Fortunately, all that attacked was cramp. My mate was also assailed by boredom, but the hours passed easily enough for me: I worked out scripts and devised concert party sketches.

Then the British military genius once more asserted itself: what if the invasion wasn't by sea up the Thames estuary? Suppose the Germans were caddish enough to land by parachute, disguised as nuns? What then?

Farewell Southend, your inhabitants now exposed and unprotected – and hello Wakering, the little Essex village to which a positively vast force of eight was sent to share a tent and scan the skies for parachutists caddishly disguised as nuns. We patrolled round the clock in watches of two at a time, and my partner was a young Welsh boy who was absolutely terrified by it all. When we were on guard during the hours of darkness he'd stay in the trench that had been dug, while I marched up and down the road scanning the night sky. I came to be regarded as extremely brave (or dim).

Now it may have a comic quality at this stage of the game, but in 1940 the threat of invasion was indeed real – yet there was Gunner Howard spurning the trench and patrolling the roads with his rifle cocked, ready – nay eager – to Fight For Those Things We Hold Dear.

The truth was somewhat different . . .

Put it down to that bump on the head, but I enjoyed patrolling: it provided a sort of privacy in which to work out concert party sketches and jokes for my patter act. I was fearless only by default: I was never *aware* of danger. It simply didn't occur to me, I was so wrapped-up in my own egotistic dream world. As I plodded up and down, doing my mental script writing and Walter Mitty-ing a touch of the Charles B. Cochran's, I'd hear a panicky: "Where are you, Frankie?" and I'd snap back: "I'm here, you idiot. Everything's all right. So shut up!" – and my annoyance at having my thoughts and fantasies interrupted were interpreted as a Bulldog Drummond contempt of danger!

There was a large farmhouse nearby, and one day the

farmer came to me and said: "We're so grateful to you." When I asked why, he replied: "Because we can hear your boots marching up and down and it gives us a sense of security in case there *is* an invasion." And I thought: *Poor soul – if only you knew the truth you'd take to the hills.*

Apart from anything else, none of us had been told what to do if the Germans did in fact land at Wakering dressed as nuns. There had been ponderous jokes on the lines of, "Do whatever you like, Frankie, as long as you don't get into the habit . . . Get it, Frankie: nuns . . . habit?" – but when it came down to the basics no one told me whether to say: "Evening all; I am Gunner Howard and I place the hundred thousand of you under arrest for invading us caddishly dressed as nuns," or whether it was supposed that a rifle shot would echo across to Shoeburyness and so bring the cavalry to our rescue.

Thank God neither alternative was put to the test, and when the fears of invasion receded we were recalled to barracks. In many ways I was sorry to leave Wakering: it was a pretty village, the summer had been hot and dry, and I'd always loved the countryside. Life under canvas in the cornfields, away from barrack square regimentation and assault courses, had been something of a Boy Scout camp. . . . On the other hand, return to Shoeburyness meant a return to concert parties.

Although I was far (very far!) from being Entertainments Officer, I virtually took over those Sunday occasions at the YMCA. I had enthusiasm and an experience of amateur entertainment – which led to colossal arrogance: for me the smell of greasepaint had the same effect as a whiff of cocaine on a junkie. This resulted in some tricky moments. I'd have truculent arguments about programmes with the actual Entertainments Officer of the day (appointed because *someone* had to do the job, and whose experience of show-business was probably a gift for post-dinner renditions of the National Anthem on comb and paper), and I would also be bossy with the officer-performers, impatiently brusque when they got their lines wrong, since in the context of shows I treated them as bad performers and not as men with pips on their shoulders. I had yet to learn – *have* yet to learn! – the virtues of what passes for tact in show-business: that when it comes to manipulating people it's often better to take the long way round. Nor could I employ that gushing and ubiquitous show-business address: "Darling", even if we were in camp (if you'll pardon the expression!).

Of necessity, the pattern of these concerts was different from those I'd put on pre-war. In Tooley Street and at the insurance office I could spend my days learning scripts and devising sketches: in the Army there were now duties that positively had to be performed, and many needed all-out concentration, particularly for a military nincompoop like myself. This meant that I had little time to write and devise material. Then again, because of duty rosters, it was seldom possible to get all the cast together at one time for rehearsals. Taken together, these factors meant that we put on more of a Music Hall bill of individual acts than an orthodox concert party – with Gunner Howard appearing four or five times, and also topping the bill (who else?). Fortunately there was a great deal of supporting talent around the place: soldier and ATS singers, musicians, conjurors, jugglers and dancers (luckily few comedians!).

There were some sketches, of course, but they often had to be improvised towards a pre-selected punch line as we went along, as in the old days, for most of the scripts that I did have time to evolve – during such mind-empty periods as guard duty and route marches – I needed for my solo appearances. And it is interesting how the very dearth of proper rehearsals forced me to develop more and more as a solo performer, and made me begin to develop what people came to regard as an original and characteristic style. I stress the word "style" because no comic is original in terms of basic material: there are a limited number of joke situations, so only the technique of their construction and delivery can change. In my case an individual style was created and governed by two circumstances that were not of my making, but which I gradually welded together and exploited: my nervous stammer and a paucity of material. I used one to strengthen the other.

No artist (and I use the word in its most modest sense) can explain technique in half a dozen words of over-simplification: it's an evolutionary process that develops and matures over the years, and (as in any other profession) contains ingredients that virtually defy definition or analysis: qualities such as charisma and intuition and talent. (Are you still with me? . . . No? . . . I'm not sure I am, either! So you'll gather that if entire books have been written on the Anatomy of Laughter, a new one is unlikely to come from the chewed pencil of yours truly.)

All I can tell you about style is that in my case the basis was this: I'd think up a simple joke that involved some misadventure, or steal someone else's gag (the times I could have been arrested for theft!) and would tell it by capitalising on my nervous stammer. You know the sort of thing: "Ah yes . . . Well . . . No *lis-sen*! . . . You see . . . There I was, and this woman . . ." And I would make the story wander down a dozen by-ways before coming to the punch line. Sometimes, with an old gag, I'd change the punch line too, and turn a joke inside-out as it were. So my shyness and lack of material caused me to create an act that was, in effect, a one-man situational comedy. It may have been born of circumstances, but it is possible that I stumbled into a little originality at that particular time.

There were other helpful factors: my face, which had now acquired some comic fluidity of expression; a wide voice range; and (most important, perhaps) a technique I evolved for not putting over my act *to* an audience, but *with* an audience. They were a vital part of the act. In other words I told these stories of misadventure in the form of a cosy "just between you and me" gossip, as though leaning over an invisible garden fence or chatting to cronies in the local pub. And just as Mrs Jones can evoke laughter and sympathy by telling her neighbours about her troubles, so I found I could create laughter and sympathy by making the audience share the preposterousness of the improbable (but not impossible) situations in which I put myself as the innocent and misunderstood victim of *Them* (i.e. authority).

As I say, an entire book could be devoted to the subject: let it suffice to say that what technique I acquired was to take me years of work and experience to develop and, of course, was later helped by superb scriptwriters – but my act as you know it today was born of natural shortcomings and weaned on necessity during those days at Shoeburyness.

I did have one enormous bonus during those garrison concert parties: my sister Betty. Partly as a result of my bullying, partly because she wanted to help me, she'd come by train from London every Sunday morning to take part in the shows: sing, do a double-act with me, and be my stooge in a patter routine. Her appearances were devised, rehearsed and performed all in one day. (I billed her, for some reason, as Bettina Heyward.) She, too, could have made it as a pro – she had a fine voice – but her energies were always to be channelled towards furthering my career. At Shoeburyness I made her sing the most extraordinarily eccentric repertoire: there'd be nothing unusual in her following "A Nightingale Sang in Berkely Square" with "Christopher Robin Is Saying His Prayers"! She even sang songs for which I composed music and lyrics, and was to use professionally after the war. Not that I could write music: I'd hum a tune and get one of the barracks' musicians to notate it. These compositions weren't chart-toppers by any means (in fact they are well forgotten by now) but they were modestly popular in their day.

I remember going into drag for one concert, dressed as an ATS girl. This wasn't the modern transvestite concept of looking glamorously feminine – my version was the traditional pantomime travesty of femininity. Absurdly large balloons, not a padded bra, served as breasts, while my make-up was a grotesque mouth lipsticked to cover half my lower face, and my wig was made of straw. I sang a comic song in the role of an old ATS scrubber. Nothing dirty, however – I was too innocent for such material, as you shall see.

Anyway, in the middle of this song an alert sounded. The audience stampeded for the exit, and I rushed back-stage. I had time to change into my own uniform, but not to remove my make-up. So there I was on parade with rifle and pack – and this face!

A young subaltern came to inspect the ranks. He arrived at where I was standing . . . Moved on . . . Stopped . . . Shook his head as though not believing what he had seen – and turned. I tried to stand rigidly to attention, but body and rifle trembled.

The officer stared at me, but I kept my eyes focused on the far side of the parade-ground. After some hours of silence on both sides (or was it seconds?) the officer permitted himself a discreet question mark of a cough.

"C-concert party, sir," I explained, my eyes still fixed straight ahead. "The alert went in the m-middle of the c-concert party." The situation was in no way helped by panic strangling my voice into a squeaky falsetto.

"Concert party . . . Er yes . . . Mmmm . . . Concert party . . . Jolly good . . ." He moved along the line, but from the corner of my eye I could see him turn his head, turn it away again, shake it – slowly this time, as though debating whether the sight he had just seen was a matter for the Military Police or the Medical Officer.

They were happy days in their fashion – then, inevitably, it was my turn to be due for a posting. Now I was still a church-going lad, and when the padre, Reverend Mackenzie, heard I was to go, he said that I ought to stay where I was.

"Why not remain here in Administration and keep on doing your shows?" he asked. "It would be foolish of them to post you. You might be of more value here . . ." Then came the crunch: "By remaining here you won't exactly *impede* the war effort, will you?"

Again I don't want to appear defensive, but I did suffer a dreadful agony of indecision. On the one hand I felt I should go with my mates – after all I was in the Army, there was a war on, and duties had to be performed; on the other hand I could see the sense in staying and doing something for which the padre thought I was better suited. It was not an easy decision to make, but in the end I persuaded myself: "You're never likely to become much of a combat soldier, and certainly no threat to Montgomery as a super-strategist, but if you stay you might at least be of some use organising entertainments. It's something you know, something you can do." And so I agreed to allow the padre to use his influence to get me transferred to the Administration establishment in the Quartermaster's office – although for months afterwards half of me suffered outsize pangs of conscience for not having left with the others.

A further insight into the bizarre thinking of the military top brass: they promoted me to bombardier.

I now became even more involved in garrison entertainments, and, knowing how unhappy I was with the overall attitude towards this aspect of barracks' life, Reverend Mackenzie arranged for me to write a letter to the General Commanding at Shoeburyness in which I outlined my thoughts about what was wrong, and the changes that should be made.

It proved to be an absolute stinker of a letter! It is doubtful whether any bombardier before or since has written such a letter to a general. In no uncertain terms I said that it was outrageous that officers should dictate to the men the way they should entertain and be entertained. . . . That there was too much censorship. . . . Too much patronising paternalism by the entertainments officer. . . . That an entertainments committee should be set up on which the men should be represented – instead of this vital matter being left in the hands of an Entertainments Officer completely lacking in any semblance of qualifications for the job. The letter went on and on, florid with such adjectives as disgraceful, stupid, appalling, ridiculous . . .

This wasn't Bombardier Howard being deliberately rude and aggressively tough – just plain naïve. Had I been more discreet in my wording, and wrapped the modified result in such phrases as "It seems to me, sir" and "May I respectfully suggest, sir" it might have been all right – but I was far too ignorant for such circumspect subtleties.

The result: I was thrown in the guardhouse and charged with gross insubordination. There was even talk of hardening the charge into one of revolutionary activities. Suddenly I was a Communist agitator!

Praise be to the padre. He intervened on my behalf and explained to the General that the wording of my letter may have been clumsy, but it wasn't intended to be impertinent. "You asked him to write – and he did. The tone may not be Sandhurst, but he was merely being honest." For a while the situation was what is known in military circles as "sticky" – but I got away with it, and did in fact achieve a measure of what today is referred to as "workers' participation" in that an entertainments committee was established.

Another bad moment:

Sometimes, apart from taking a joke, turning it inside out and developing it into an entire act, I'd tell one straight – as a joke in its own right. And since I was short of material I'd use jokes that people gave me. One such came from a garrison officer who was always telling me tired old gags which I'd hitherto ignored. He told this one with great relish and when it was over burst into waves of booming laughter. I managed a weak titter: since I couldn't understand it I could hardly find it funny. But I decided to include it – I thought it politic to use one of his jokes, and in any case just one joke in an entire concert was neither here nor there.

I told it – but no laughter. Instead, gasps of astonishment from the men present, and squawks of shocked embarrassment from the women. I frowned: had I fluffed it? No, I hadn't. Indeed, I was all too word-perfect – and was nearly on another charge, this time for using obscene language. It transpired that the joke involved the mention of the slang names for various anatomical appendages and their uses, and although I wouldn't dare to tell such a story today, I told it with great aplomb at that concert party – because I was still so incredibly innocent I simply didn't understand it!

I know it sounds absurd: a man in his twenties, and in the Army to boot, ignorant of even the basic facts of life – but it's absolutely true. I lived in such an extraordinary private dream world for so much of the time that even the most explicit barrack-room discussions didn't register. I wasn't even curious, and until sexual awakening came with actual experience – and that was a year or so off – I still had the idea that babies came, via God, from the navel.

Even as a child I'd been too wrapped up in my own fantasies for curiosity – and remember, too, that I was a God-fearing lad (and doubtless an excruciating bore). Yet I liked girls, although my attitude towards them was governed by my religiousness and the glossily romantic images projected by the pre-war cinema. In any case I was obsessed with the conviction that I was ugly (I must have been stark, raving mad!), and even as an adult my stage make-up was devised to turn this supposed ugliness into comic grotesquerie.

As for swearing – I didn't. Once, when I was about five, I repeated a four-letter word I heard the greengrocer use, without having the faintest idea of what it meant. My mother got into such a fury, and gave me such a whack, that I've never again used the word – even to this day. It may sound like a touch of the holier-than-thous, but it is simply the traumatic effect of that youthful chastisement.

Back to Shoeburyness . . .

Jokes that involved taking the mickey out of commissioned and non-commissioned officers always went down well, and I worked out one routine centred around the padre: some daft situation in which he bought a horse in order to visit his parishioners, and the misadventures that resulted. Now he had to attempt to get on the beast's back, and so I used the phrase "mounted his steed" – and the way I said "mounted" was considered to be absolutely disgusting. I suddenly found I'd acquired a reputation for being positively controversial and *risqué*, because of the manner in which I put over salacious material with an air of apparent innocence. Nobody realised that I was *genuinely* innocent. . . . Such is the way reputations are made!

Success with the concert parties revived my interest in "Talent Nights", and one was held at the Palace Theatre at neighbouring Westcliff-on-Sea. I was pretty relaxed and confident, since most of the audience were wearing familiar khaki. I started my act with the words: "Good evening, ladies and gentlemen. I'm now going to sing a little song, 'She Sits Among The Cabbages And Peas' " – and the manager's voice hissed from the wings: "*Get off!*"

I looked at him and said: "Eh?", the audience laughed, thinking it was part of the routine – but down came the curtain.

Before I could ask for an explanation, I got one from the manager: "Filth! Filth! Utter filth! Get out of my theatre!"

I left, broken-hearted and completely baffled.

And when you consider what some comics get away with today . . . (present company excepted, of course).

Duties in the Quartermaster's office included such basic clerical tasks as the making out of requisition forms. Experience said that such jobs, entrusted to F. Howard, must have guaranteed him a Court Martial within the week. But this was not Tooley Street, watched over by a sharp-eyed sadist: it was the Army. Add the vast amount of paperwork demanded by such an organisation to a ponderously slow and red-tape ridden system of buck-passing protocol, and it can be seen that my ineptitude was absorbed without notice into the gigantic no-man's-land of the bureaucratic machine. Before (if) any clumsy mistake could be traced back to me – the failure of blankets to be ordered for shivering recruits, the non-despatch of a top priority signal requesting that the ammunition we'd received be exchanged for some of the right calibre to fit our guns – the war would long be over.

Perhaps it was because I was so admirably suited to the job that they decided to move me. "Bombardier Howard!" barked Sergeant Major Tolworth.

"Sar'nt Major!" I replied, dreading that he was going to "request" that he be permitted to sing (for the eighth time) "The Road to Mandalay" at Sunday's concert.

"You're being posted, Bombardier."

"P-posted, Sergeant Major? Me, Sergeant Major?"

"Not too far away, Bombardier. You'll still sleep in the barracks. Still run your little minstrel shows. . . . And stand to atten-*shun* when I talk to you!" (I stood to atten-*shun*.) "I've got a really cosy little number for you. Oh yes. Very cosy. Over at Foulness Island. They're starting an Experimental Station there, Bombardier, and you'll be one of their strength – God help 'em. Very hush-hush. Full of prestige. Oh yes, bags of bull. You'll even get XP stamped on your Identity Card."

"Experimental Station, Sergeant Major?" The place had an ominous sound. "What am I to do?"

He winked and tapped a forefinger against the side of a Guinness-marinated nostril. "Very hush-hush." After a quick look over his shoulder: "But I can tell you this much: secret weapons."

"Eh?"

"Secret weapons, Bombardier. There's a war on, you know. And we've got to win it. So we need secret weapons: new bombs and explosives. Poison gases. Germ warfare. . . . You're going to be a right little old hero, Bombardier. Oh yes."

"H-hero, Sergeant Major?" I squeaked. "What do I have to do?"

"Well it's no use using these secret weapons unless we know they work, is it? So we need guinea pigs. You're a volunteer to test them on, you 'orrible little man!"

He stalked off, smiling broadly at his joke – but it took me an hour or so to convince myself that he *was* joking: you could never be sure with Sergeant Major Tolworth.

In the event, duties at the Experimental Station didn't cause some monstrous mutation, and if anyone had to requisition *Plague, Eight Capsules, Experimental Station for the use of*, it wasn't me. My duties were quite ordinary, left me with plenty of time for entertainment, and at one YMCA occasion I was asked if I'd like to join a concert party – the Co-Odments – that toured the Southend area in an old van, putting on shows for the troops. It played in church halls, at remote anti-aircraft sites, and even rather grandly on the bandstand at the top of the cliffs near the war memorial. I was delighted to be asked, and roped in some of the other lads, too.

A member of the concert party was a Mrs Vera Roper, and she played the piano for me when I did my songs. One evening I asked her something, but she was preoccupied and didn't hear me. I repeated the question, but again she didn't hear. I muttered: "That's all I need – a deaf accompanist," and that night I pondered and developed the comic possibilities of such a daft situation. And so, with "Madame Vere-Roper, known to me as Ada", I devised the act which seemed to tickle the public fancy, and so I still use it (although the scripts do get updated!).

Over the years I've had about eight different "deaf" pianists, including Blanche Moore ("Madame Blanchie Moore") who was also in that Southend concert party, playing the piano for her two dancing daughters – but the deaf pianist routine ("Poor dear; she's past it. . . . Now don't laugh: don't make mock of the afflicted") had its origins that wartime evening at Southend because Vera Roper was pondering how many meat coupons she had left in her ration-book.

And in some ways it was accurate to say "poor dear": carried away with over-enthusiasm I'd bully Vera (and Blanche) into doing more concerts than they intended, with a resultant neglect of their domestic obligations. Vera's husband, a policeman, was particularly upset: he thought she was putting me before him, and I nearly caused a divorce.

One song I wrote at this time was called Miss Twillow, Miss True and Miss Twit, and was performed by myself and two other lads dressed as ATS girls. (In case you haven't guessed, I was Miss Twit.) It was wrapped up in a comic sketch, and went in part:

Here we come, here we come,
The girls of the ATS –
Miss Twillow, Miss True and Miss Twit.
(Repeat.)
The huge amount of work we do,
You know, you'll never *guess.*
But in Army life we fit . . .
To bend we never ought,
Because our skirts are short.
But they really do reveal
That we've got sex appeal.
And if you want a date,
Enquire at the gate
For Miss Twillow, Miss True and Miss Twit . . .

(What did you expect: Shakespeare?)

When we performed this number in barracks, it was OK: we could borrow suitable ATS uniforms. The same was true when we were officially allowed out to join the touring concert party. But my passion to entertain was such that despite my still-potent terror of authority, and the two stripes on my sleeve, I'd go to concerts even when officially confined to barracks – persuading the other lads to come with me. With no passes, we'd slide off through a hole in the hedge, clutching our rifles and gas masks and a kit-bag filled with bits and pieces of props – but three vital items were lacking: ATS uniforms.

There was only one thing for it: we'd roam the streets picking-up victimesses* who'd fall for the sleazy line "We're doing a concert tonight – want to see the show?" We had to choose them carefully, to make certain their uniforms would more-or-less fit: I was six feet and thin as a rake; one of my chums was almost as tall, but fat; the other was virtually a midget (the disparate shapes and sizes being

* No such word? There is now!

part of the visual joke). Believe it or not, it always worked. Always. Somehow or other we'd find suitable birds and con them into coming to the concert.

During the interval we'd invite the poor creatures back-stage for a drink (lemonade!) and charm the clothes off them – literally. With much bowing and smiling and hand-kissing, I'd ask: "May we borrow your uniforms for the next act, please?" – and it never failed. Never. The unfortunate girls would strip to their khaki-issue bloomers and shiver in the toilet while we went on stage.

It's extraordinary when you think of it: there wasn't one occasion when we had to scrap that number because of an absence of ATS uniforms.

It's remarkable, too, that we were never picked up for being absent without leave, or for being in an area that was out of bounds, even though we were on public display at these concerts. We did come close to trouble one night when we were stopped by a Military Police patrol in Southend High Street. Fortunately I had the kit-bag, and we all had our rifles and gas-masks, and the sergeant among us – Harry Harrison of the Pay Corps – had a flash of inspiration. Pointing to me: "Prisoner and escort. We're taking him to the glasshouse at Colchester."

Without pretending that being in the Army was my idea of paradise, I enjoyed my time at Shoeburyness (well, most of it); but in 1942 I was posted to a new Experimental Station at Pen-clawdd on the Gower Coast near Swansea in South Wales.

FOUR Parlez-vous Howard?

In those days Pen-clawdd was a small fishing village, and the Experimental Station a scatter of nissen huts on its outskirts, so there was little scope for concert parties; although I joined the local amateur dramatic society to keep my hand in, as it were. Then I heard of an Army concert party that had been formed to go the rounds of the fighting areas: "Stars in Battledress". Four times I applied, via my C.O., to join the cast. Four times I was auditioned. Four times (in case you haven't guessed) I was turned down. The first audition was typical of them all: me at one end of a vast mess hall, the interviewing officer (a pre-war part-time conjuror) at the other end. Now that might have been fine for a singer, violinist or someone who twists and tears copies of the *News of the World* into rows of chorus girls, but by now a proper audience was essential to my act; was an integral, participating and responsive part of it: I couldn't perform to a bored and remote audience of just one! Add this circumstance to my natural nervousness, and it can be seen that I died a death, and that this gentleman, detailed to ferret out talent, didn't think I was worth the ferreting.

Gradually the months passed, and awareness grew among us that the Allies were about to invade Europe. Again I went to the C.O., this time to say that since "Stars in

Battledress" didn't want me (for the fourth time), could I please do *something* positive for the war effort: even if it was my destiny only to get my name in the papers as one of yesterday's casualties? Anything was better than dying of creeping rust caught from the nissen huts. The C.O. told me not to worry: orders had arrived that very day which included my posting to Plymouth, "For the big show – and I don't mean telling jokes, what?"

So to Devon, where I found myself on a Commando course. Me – Francis – up and down rope ladders and over assault courses! It's true that I was fit – but I was no Tarzan! Nevertheless the military genius asserted itself yet again: decided I'd done "jolly well", promoted me to Sergeant, and sent me (poor, uncoordinated me) on a driving course. After a few rudimentary lessons they put me behind the wheel of what seemed to be the world's largest lorry packed with the entire British Army . . . and which I predictably drove straight into a hedge. It was on the cards that I'd be on a charge again, this time for sabotage, or being in the pay of the enemy; but since none of my passengers suffered more than mild concussion or shock, it was solemnly ruled that driving might not be what I was best suited for, after all.

D-day was now only a formality of when and where, and I didn't have to be a military genius to realise that something was in the wind when I was given an unexpected twenty-four hour pass to visit my mother. She (like so many women) had struggled on bravely and alone during the war years, enduring the bombing, coping with rationing, and surviving on a minimal income since my brother was in the RAF, and my sister now in the ATS. Anyway, the twenty-four hours over (and it was far less than twenty-four hours, of course, when you allow for the eccentricities of wartime travel), I made my way back to Paddington station – and was caught in the most dreadful thunderstorm.

A certain amount of the moisture turned into steam in the railway carriage on the journey to Tilbury, but I was still sticky damp on arrival – and had no time to change before being sent aboard a merchantman taking troops across the Channel for the invasion.

Result number one: flu.

Being in the Royal Artillery, they put me in charge of a Bren gun on a conning tower hastily soldered to this sad, old vessel. And with the sort of madness of fate that has always been my destiny in one form or another, when we arrived off France the sea was so rough the DUKW landing-craft couldn't come alongside to take off the troops.

Result number two: seasickness.

The only port operating in the storm was Mulberry Harbour, and that was so crowded they couldn't accommodate us. So for eleven days (that's right: *eleven days*) this creaking tub pitched and tossed, rolled and yawed – while Sergeant Howard lay coiled up on the floor of the conning tower dying of flu and seasickness: a horrific combination, I promise you. God alone knows what I'd have done if German bombers had attacked.

So to result number three: malnutrition.

For by the time the sea did calm down, Sergeant Howard had mastered the movements of ocean and stomach – and was extremely hungry. But since no one had allowed for eleven days at sea, there was no food left but ship's biscuits – and I was close to starvation. When they got us off I was so thin that only the sergeant's stripes on my arm distinguished me from the barrel of the Bren gun.

When I was fit enough to stand I was posted to Lille in northern France, where an officer came round and asked: "Anyone speak French?"

Diffidently: "We-ll . . . Yes . . . You see, I did go to school. I did learn some French. But it's a bit primitive."

"Uh-huh . . ." Then followed a lengthy gabble in what I assumed to be French, so I said "*Oui*". Another spasm of gibberish, and I said: "*Non*".

"Soo-pah! You're in."

"In? . . . In what?"

"We're a bit short, Sergeant, so you're an interpreter."

I said: "Eh? . . . Yes . . . But well . . . Look . . ."

And he said: "Never mind, old chap; we're a bit short."

Now I know this sounds like something out of one of my acts, but it's absolutely true: I was an interpreter! Worse was to come . . .

Sergeant F. Howard was posted to Brussels, seconded to the Military Government. I asked, with some trepidation: "Who are we governing?" and they said: "The Germans soon, because we're winning the war," and I said: "That's one blessing, anyway."

And I was sent off to a village with a Major who couldn't speak a word of French to discover if there were any expectant mothers there: they'd get priority when food was distributed. "It's jolly simple," said the Major. "All you have to do is tell them we want to know of any women who are pregnant."

I went to rehearse . . .

I didn't know the French for pregnant, but I reckoned I could manage with: "We'd like to know if any woman is going to have a baby."

So I worked out: "We is: *nous* . . . We would like is: *nous voulons* . . . To know is: *savoir* . . . If is: *si* . . . Any woman . . . I don't know about 'any', but woman is: *une femme* . . . Is going is: *allons* . . . To have is: *avoir*, and a child is: *enfant* . . . So there we are: *Nous voulons savoir si une femme allons avoir un enfant*."

After some practice, I decided to chance my arm and walk around the village asking this, adding a few *oo-la-lahs* and a touch of the hooded-eyed, purse-lipped Charles Boyer's to give it an authentic Gallic *flay-veur*.

The first woman I tried it on looked at me blankly; the second bleakly. The third frowned and sidled away. The fourth screamed and fled – to return with an enormous brute of a man with vast biceps that seemed to positively throb. Encouraged by his presence, other men and women arrived – and the fact that many were carrying cudgels, pitchforks and shotguns I put down to their patriotic fervour: they were ready to fight to the death should the Germans counter-attack.

The man with the muscles machine-gunned a burst of French at me. I attempted what was meant to be a non-commital shrug, then repeated my carefully-rehearsed statement in French.

A murmur, a muttering, a gesticulation with cudgels, pitchforks and shotguns – and a slow, shuffling advance. It dawned on my tiny mind that I wasn't going down all that well, so I took a step backwards. . . . They took two steps forwards. . . . Even a mathematical novice will realise that in this backwards–forwards proportion it wasn't long before Mr Universe (Belgian branch) was breathing garlic up my nostrils.

I cocked my rifle – then realised I'd left it back at the hotel.

With a shrill howl I skidded round on my heel – and fled.

It transpired that something had gone a trifle wrong in the translation: instead of saying that we wanted to know whether any woman was having a baby, I'd asked if any woman wanted to have a baby!

The Major and I hastened from the village – and got lost in a sudden fog. I can only assume that the Germans were after Sergeant Frank Howard R.A., because they used the cover of the fog to make a push. The point came, as we drove aimlessly around the countryside, when even my pidgin French among the peasantry established that we were now behind the enemy lines.

What, I sometimes wonder, would have been the fate of the British theatre if we hadn't found our way to safety?

With little help from me, the Germans capitulated, and I was sent to Holland where the Dutch were said to be surviving on tulip bulbs. I headed the first convoy to arrive in The Hague – by accident (naturally!).

It was simply that as the convoy of vehicles was about to set off I was told to get into one. It seemed logical to get into the one in front – and the others lost themselves *en route* to The Hague. So there I was, in a chauffeur-driven staff car, and with no signs of rank on my odds-and-end of a uniform, mobbed by the frenzied Dutch! God alone knows who they thought I was, and to this day they probably don't know that the gallant gentleman who liberated them was Sergeant F. Howard. But I can tell you one thing: the people of The Hague were the most appreciative audience I've ever had! I was cheered, carried shoulder-high, made to sign autographs . . . and since by now I'd learned the facts of life, I can assure you that all the girls in Holland aren't interested only in Edam cheese.

I was never told whether Montgomery was jealous of me, whether Churchill decided to exploit my success as Liberator Extraordinary, or whether it was assumed that my demoralising presence would utterly destroy any vestige of German resistance – all I know is that with an Army captain I was sent to Stade, near Hamburg, as the Military Government. That's right: the Military Government. Just the two of us. (Shades of Southend!) The result? The poor Captain had a nervous breakdown, and despite my lack of manual dexterity I managed to type and send a signal that said, in effect: "Help!"

In typical fashion, the Army did indeed send reinforcements: two hundred of them. There were now more governors than governed!

I let them get on with it, and being assured now of a large audience started to organise a concert party. When someone told me that up the road they were shooting location scenes for a film, *The Captive Heart*, I scrounged a lift to see if I could persuade Michael Redgrave and Jack Warner to appear. But by the time I got there Jack had gone home and Michael Redgrave told me with much regret that he couldn't do anything on his own. So I did the concert almost as a one-man show – and it went down well.

Then another familiar situation: General Horrocks issued the order "No fraternisation", which meant bromide in the tea again (or was it the soup?) followed by the call: "Can anyone do anything to entertain?"

The C.O., reckoning I wasn't the most outstanding success in military government, sent for me and almost begged me to go to Nienburg for an audition. I said dolefully: "With my record I'll be back tomorrow." And with his hands pressed together in an attitude of prayer, the C.O. replied: "Maybe you'll be lucky this time."

I was. For once an audition went well. The Major in command was Richard Stone (now a distinguished agent); with him a Captain Ian Carmichael (yes, the same one). They put me in charge of a concert party touring north-west Germany – but my glory was short-lived: three months later, after six years in the Army, I was demobbed. So back to Eltham with a chalk-stripe demob suit and pork-pie hat, a gratuity of something less than £100, and a kindly reference from Richard Stone detailing and praising the concert party work I'd done for him.

What now? One argument was that I should return to the insurance company and so have some basic income while I tried to make it as a professional entertainer. But I thought back over the years and said: No. If I do that I'll never get away again. It's now or never. I've had so many ups and downs, I've got to concentrate on an all-out effort to become a pro. No more compromise: this is it, make or break. If I succeed, fine. If I don't, I'll somehow force myself to abandon dreams of show-business. Then – but only then – will I consider the insurance office. First I must have a go.

I went to agent after agent: gauche, beanpole-thin in my ill-fitting demob suit, and with no ability to sell myself – a shuffling, awkward yokel, petrified with fear. Sometimes my nerves were in such a state I'd send in Vera Roper or Blanche Moore to do the selling: tell the agent about the clever young man waiting outside. And once inside an office I'd crumble into even smaller pieces when confronted by some man who appeared as an almost Godlike figure with finger-snapping powers of life and death. (Invariably they were smoking enormous, somehow menacing, cigars – and to this day there's a residual touch of nerves when I'm in the presence of cigar smokers.)

And agents were indeed extremely powerful men. The Music Hall in that post-war, pre-television period was enjoying a huge boom. Every city, town and suburb boasted at least one Empire or Palace or Hippodrome or other theatre, and the agents had a great deal of say in terms of who appeared in them.

But even when I did get interviews, and even if the agent concerned was sympathetically understanding about my new-boy nervousness, the chat boiled down to one stock question: "Where can I see you perform?"

And I had one stock answer: "You can't. I'm not working."

"But I can't hire you until I see your act."

"But I can't do my act until I'm hired."

"But I can't get you work until I see you perform."

It was a mulberry bush which you could go round and round until you spun off into a strait-jacket.

It has a comic quality now, but at the time I was almost suicidally depressed. There I was, convinced I had talent, and wanting only an opportunity to demonstrate the fact. . . . But how?

Then I heard that they were auditioning at Butlin's Holiday Camp at Filey, Yorkshire. I counted the money that remained of my gratuity, shrugged, and bought a railway ticket. I did two shows up there, for which I received a total of three guineas, and I didn't think I went all that badly. But in the second show I'd included a joke about a woman who went into a shop to buy a bra . . .

"How much is that, please?" . . . "Five and eleven, missus" . . . "Five and eleven? *Five and eleven!* I'll see 'em swing first!"

Not very funny? Well don't blame me: blame Arthur Askey – it was him I stole it from. Anyway, maybe it was the way I told it, but what was good enough for Arthur Askey was too much of a good thing for me: Billy Butlin's Man in Filey denounced me for my disgusting filth!

Years later, when as a gesture of friendship, he appeared with me on a radio show, Billy said that his Man in Filey had perhaps made a mistake in turning me down. (I wasn't too keen on the way he said "perhaps" – but he's a nice chap for all that.)

So back to the rounds of the agents, growing progressively more dejected as one joyless day followed another, until I arrived on my list at Harry Lowe. I told him, without exaggerating, that I was desperate, but his answer was the inevitable: "Get yourself on somewhere and I'll come and see you." I hit a new low of misery as I caught the train home to Eltham visualising a future that offered nothing but an eternity of frustration and boredom behind a desk in an insurance office.

My mother, in an attempt to cheer me up, said: "Let's go to the Lewisham Hippodrome." I was in no mood for it, but we went. I was too overwhelmed with self-pity to remember anything about the show, except that it starred Vera Lynn, but I vividly recall the interval when the advertising slides came up on the safety curtain, and my mother said: "You know I sometimes get feelings . . ." I nodded, aware that at times she was remarkably psychic. "Well," she went on, "I'll tell you this: within two years you'll be topping the bill in this theatre."

My laugh was a great cynical hoot. "Top the bill? Don't be silly! I'm not even inside a stage door, far less *bottom* of the bill!"

A couple of days later, walking down Piccadilly, I passed the Stage Door Canteen, a sort of posh Naafi with a concert hall attached. They ran variety shows, and pros – very big names of occasion – topped the bill (for no fee), while the supporting acts were men and women in the services. I looked, regretted I wasn't still in the Army – and desperation led to inspiration . . .

Next morning I put on my old uniform – something quite illegal since I'd been demobbed for too long to have the right to wear it – and went back to Piccadilly, clutching the now somewhat dog-eared reference from Richard Stone. I saw the lady secretary, controlled a mad impulse to assume an heroic limp but mustered all my olde-worlde (i.e. corny) bowing and hand-kissing gallantry, added soulful hints that I'd learned the technique during my years in the French Resistance with Charles Boyer – and swept the poor dear off her feet.

Result: she gave me a date at the Canteen for the following week – and I rushed to a telephone to tell Harry Lowe. My luck had certainly changed: he said he'd come along.

Gloom was replaced now by nervous impatience, but when I went on at the Canteen the familiar sight of uniforms helped me to relax, and determination inspired the performance of my life.

There was only one snag: Harry Lowe didn't bother to come.

A curious numbness now, as though I was beyond feeling. I had no money and no hope: I was utterly demoralised.

Then, a few days later, while still in this state of indescribable melancholy, a letter arrived from the Stage Door Canteen. They were short of artists for the following Friday, so could I help out? I didn't see any point, but my mother urged me to go.

"Why not?" she argued. "What can you lose?" I went, but in my own mind I'd accepted defeat: this was to be a valedictory performance before abandoning all hopes of a show-business career.

Fate . . . God . . . Luck . . . Coincidence – call it what you will. But in the Stage Door Canteen building that night, although not in the audience, was a man who heard some laughter and looked into the theatre to see what it was all about. He stayed to see the rest of my act, and when I finished came back-stage and asked: "Who represents you?"

Me hollowly: "Nobody."

"I'm with the Jack Payne office. Would you like us to represent you?"

I thought it was some kind of a sick joke, for Payne was now no longer a bandleader, but a powerful agent and impresario. When it filtered through that the man was utterly serious I gaped, stammered, flushed beetroot red and groped for a chair. "Yes . . . Well . . . Of course . . ."

"You'll have to see Frank Barnard. He'll want to see your act."

"Of course . . . Yes . . . Um . . . Yes . . ." An apologetic shrug. "Who's he?"

"*Who's he?!* Jack's general manager. Didn't you know?"

"Yes," I lied. "But I get people mixed up. I was thinking of the Barnard Brothers," I babbled on. "A great act . . . Yes . . . Well . . . Er, where will he see me?"

"In his office."

"Sure, but where will he see me perform?"

"I just said: in his office."

How's that for a twist? I'd been traipsing around the offices of agents who'd wanted to see me perform on stage – which had been impossible – but this one wanted me to do something equally impossible: do my act in his office! "*His office!*" I shrilled. "I c-can't perform in an office! I need an audience."

"Look, sonny, he's got a lot of people to see. He's casting for a show with Dorothy Summers [of *ITMA* fame] to go to the troops in Germany. Are you interested, or aren't you?"

"You bet I am!"

"Then you perform in his office."

Perform in his office – shades of those disastrous Army auditions. But as my mother might have said: what could I lose?

Now if you are a pro you have your band parts: the music which accompanies your act. Me, I couldn't afford such elaborate aids – I'd grab the nearest pianist and ask: "Do you know 'Three Little Fishes'?" (or whatever song I was sending up). For this occasion I asked Vera Roper to come along, but when I turned up at Barnard's office, she didn't. (It transpired that she was suddenly taken ill, and since neither of us were on the telephone there was no way of contacting me.) The point of the story is that the first question put to me by Barnard (another intimidating cigar smoker, incidentally) was: "Got your band parts?"

When I said with some diffidence that I only had a friend who played the piano but who hadn't arrived, and asked if there was anyone around who could play "Three Little Fishes", he went berserk. Seldom have I heard such a screaming tirade. I was unprofessional, unfit to entertain a gallery queue in Widnes, should never have had the impertinence to take up his time, had no right to call myself an entertainer if I didn't have band parts. . . . He went on and on, whipping himself into a frenzy of near-apoplexy – while I sat literally shivering with terror.

He screamed himself into exhaustion with a final: "Wait outside."

I waited for four solid hours: time enough for my heart to stop pounding my ribs, my flushed face to return to its normal pallor, and for terror to reduce itself via trepidation to ordinary nervousness. . . . Time enough, too, for *me* to grow annoyed. I thought: *Who the hell does he think he is? I'm a human being, and I'm entitled to be treated like one. What right has he got to push me around?* . . . Anger grew to black, bubbling rage, and when an underling came to tell me: "Mr Barnard will see you now," the worm not only turned, but grew teeth.

With cliché-laden outrage, but hardly a stammer, I snarled: "I wouldn't go near that man for all the tea in China. I've never been so insulted in all my life, and I'm not so desperate that I'll go on my hands and knees to that ignorant pig. I'd rather not be in show-business at all – and that's that."

Now this may not seem much of an outburst to you, but coming from me it was pretty powerful stuff.

The underling made soothing noises and patted my shoulder. "Calm down. Swallow your pride. You may never get this sort of chance again."

"But how *can* I go into that man's office?" I howled. "How *can* I go to a man who plainly hates the sight of me – and make him laugh? Look: he doesn't like me, and I detest him. With the mood I'm in I haven't got a chance in hell."

"Have a go," said the underling.

Something seemed to snap inside me, and seething with fury I crashed my way into Barnard's office. I fixed him with a baleful glare and said with all the sarcasm I could muster: "I am now going to make you laugh, you clot. You're going to fall about with laughter, you idiot. Because I'm a very funny man, you oaf." And do you know – he *did* start falling about! For my part, as though some safety-valve had opened, I poured out all the bitter frustration of the years – and the more I insulted him, the more he shrieked with hysterical laughter.

I couldn't have been very good at insulting people, because by the time I'd emptied myself of emotion, Frank Barnard was still rolling in his chair, laughing his head off. Wiping his eyes, he said: "That's a great act. Great. It's a hoot. . . . Can you do any more?"

There I was, having purged myself, as it were, of life's accumulated miseries in an explosion of concentrated vituperation – and he thought it a hoot of a comic performance! And then asked if I could do any more!

Exhausted of rage, possessed instead of a strange confidence, I did do my proper act, and Barnard was so delighted with it that he even found (irrespective of band parts) a pianist to play "Three Little Fishes" for me. When it was all over he said that it was the best cold audition he'd ever seen in his life.

The best cold audition he'd ever seen in his life – just because I'd given up hope, lost my temper, and simply didn't care any more.

So Frank Barnard hired me (later we became very good friends and he helped me all he could) and said he wanted Jack Payne to see me. Not in an office this time, but included in a concert for the troops at Arborfield in Berkshire. To Hell with modesty – I stole the show, and instead of sending me with the relatively small party to Germany, Jack put me into a Revue he was staging in the UK: "For The Fun Of It". Top of the bill were Donald Peers, Nosmo King, Jean Adrienne and Eddie Leslie. I was to share bottom of the bill in a feature called "They're Out" – a sort of "Opportunity Knocks" for ex-servicemen and women.

And that's how I finally became a professional.

With my mother. I'm facing a camera for the first time . . . and not looking very happy about it!

With Sidney and Betty.
That's me at the back –
amateur actor and would-be
saint!

Large photo: "There are those among us tonight . . ." During a *Variety Bandbox* broadcast.

Inset right: Bombardier Howard – intrepid defender of Southend-on-Sea.

Inset left: My first fan photo – I didn't look like a root vegetable then, did I?

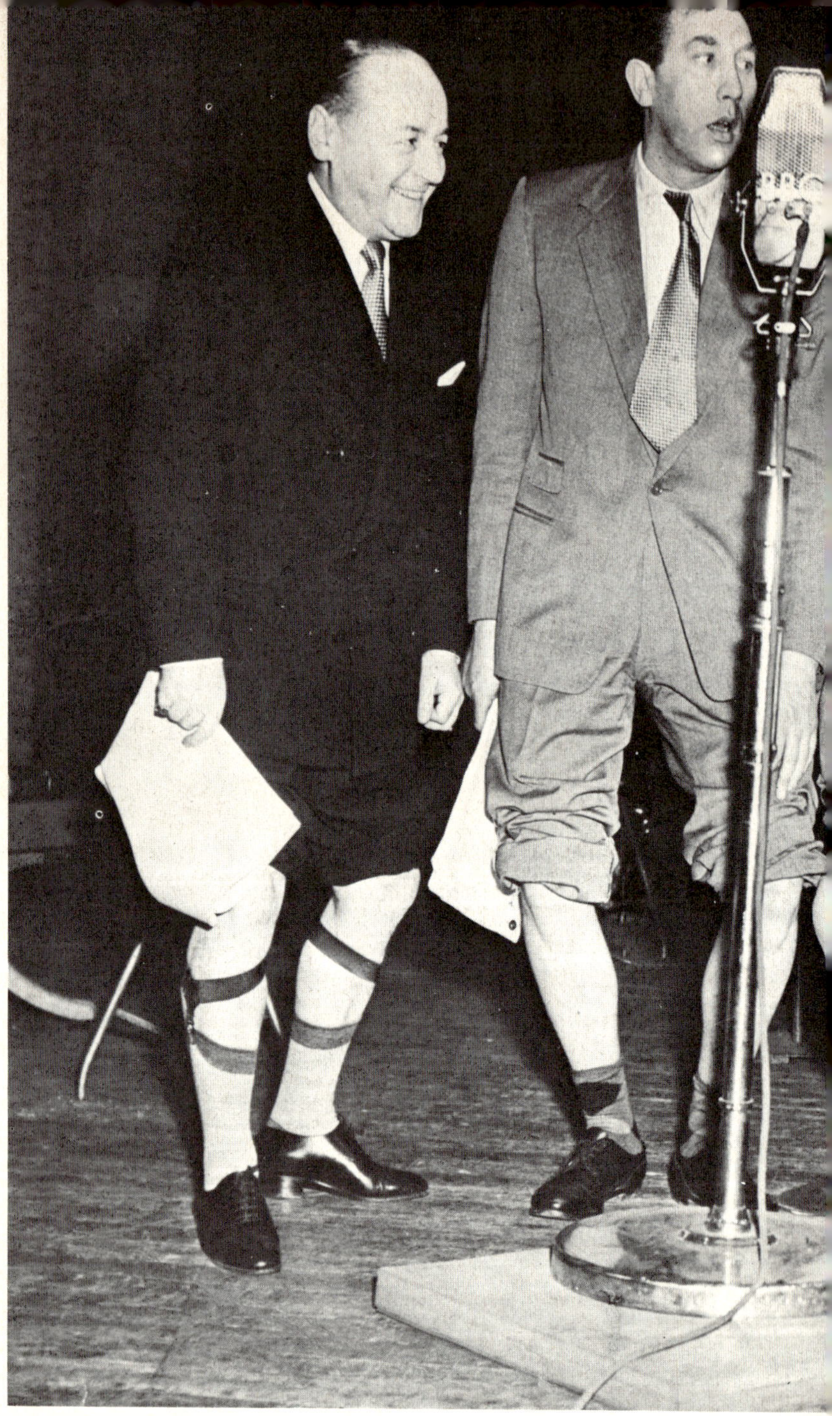

Leg show on *Variety Bandbox* with (*left to right*) Billy Ternent, Jimmie James and Billy Butlin.

With one of my "deaf"
pianists – the splendid
"Dame" Blanchie Moore.

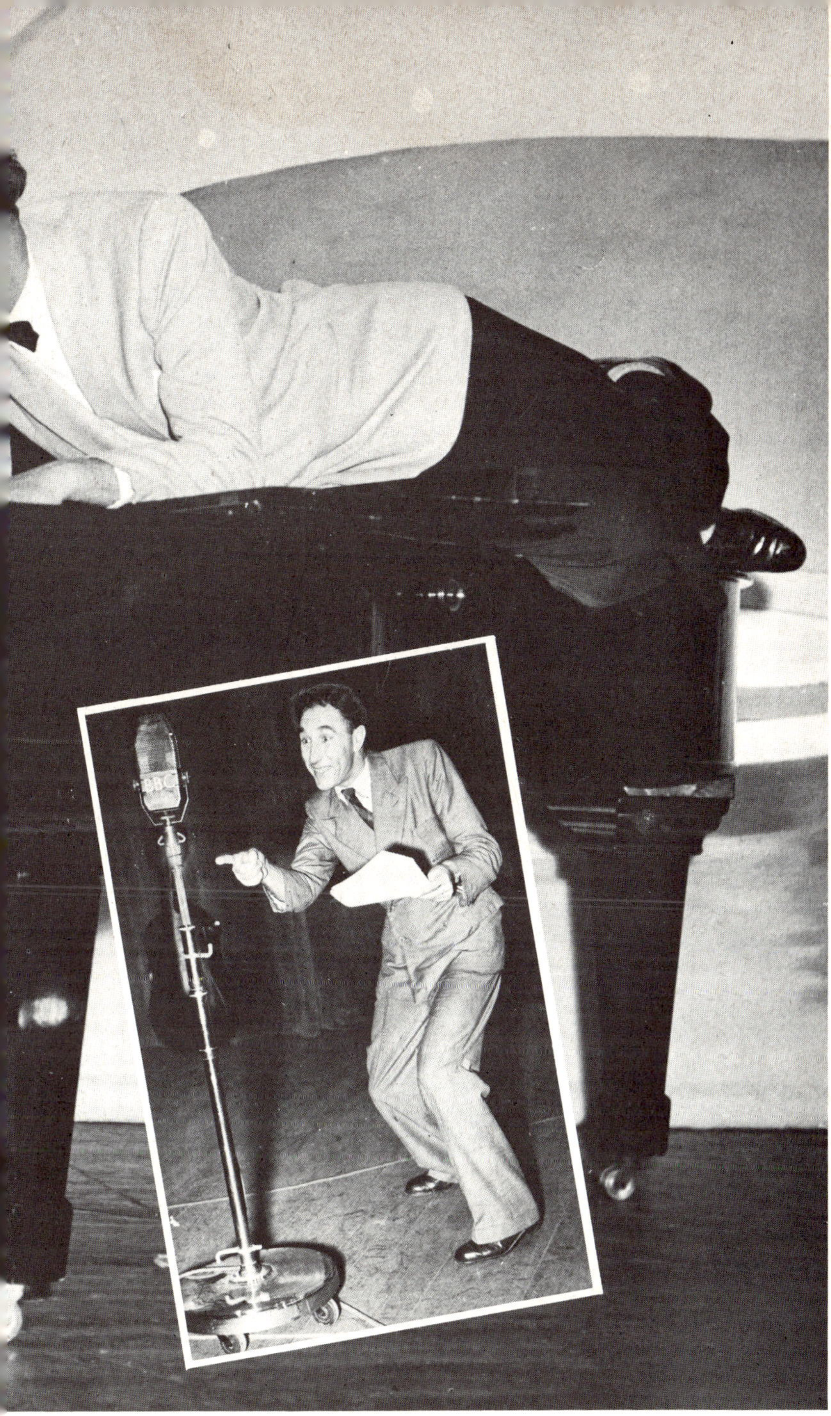

Another shot of me during
a *Variety Bandbox*
broadcast.

1950 at the London Palladium in *Out Of This World* – Gracie Fields pays a backstage visit.

FIVE Ladies and Gentle-*men*

We opened at the Sheffield Empire in summer, 1946, and by now I'd decided to change my name. I wanted people whom I'd entertained during the war to know that I was around, but it seemed to me that there were too many Howards: among them Trevor, Sidney and Arthur. So how to stay Howard, yet alter it? I hit on the idea of a change of spelling: Howerd – which, I argued, would have the added advantage of making people look twice because they assumed it to be a misprint.

I needn't have bothered.

Apart from changing my name, I also had to have what's called "bill matter": on bills Max Miller wasn't just Max Miller, he was the Cheeky Chappy; Donald Peers was Radio's Cavalier of Song; Vera Lynn was the Forces' Sweetheart – and so on. By the same token Frankie Howerd was the Borderline Case. . . . Or was meant to be, for when I arrived in Sheffield I looked at the advertising bills, and all I could see was "They're Out". My name just didn't appear (and I'd spent a small fortune having photographs printed for my adoring fans).

Then I did see it: at the bottom of the bill in the same-size type as that of the printer. The only person aware that Frankie Howerd, the Borderline Case, was appearing in the show had to be a *real* borderline case – someone who wandered the streets of Sheffield examining show bills with a magnifying glass. I was heartbroken.

The other two acts in "They're Out" were a young impressionist, Max Bygraves, and a girl contortionist, Pam Denton (who finally got unknotted and left show-business). Max and I shared the same dressing room and digs, and became great chums. He was a tremendous morale-booster, being quite the opposite to me in temperament: extremely confident and outgoing, while I was in a continual state of introspective nerves. He couldn't understand my trepidations – and in all truth I couldn't understand his confidence!

Again there's no point in false modesty: the press said that we three newcomers were the hit of the show. I was tremendously bucked, of course; my first professional date – and I seemed to be successful. (I don't think it made me – or Max and Pam – very popular with the stars, because the press were to say the same wherever we played, but at the time we were so pleased with ourselves we didn't think of any dissent we might be causing.)

The second week of the tour was played at Nottingham, and despite the enthusiastic reception my act had received at Sheffield, Frank Barnard wanted me to change its pattern. At Sheffield I'd gone on for nine minutes in the first half, my material including "Three Little Fishes" and a comic monologue. (I know that a total of nine minutes doesn't sound much, but in those days of Music Hall there were always at least nine acts on the bill, and even someone like Donald Peers, the star of the show, only did eighteen or twenty minutes. You had to be really something to warrant half an hour. Today's club entertainment – the follow-on of the Music Halls – is vastly different, of course: supporting acts are expected to do three-quarters of a hour, and the star at least an hour.)

Anyway, Barnard wanted me to change my act – cut out the monologue and do more patter. This upset me, not only because of the apparent success I'd had in Sheffield, but also because I felt I'd worked out the best way to project myself. Seeing my depression, Max Bygraves (without my knowledge) marched in to see the management and asked: "Why don't you stop bullying him? You can see the boy's a nervous wreck, so why don't you leave him alone until he gets settled?" It had no effect – I still had to alter the act – but I've always been grateful to Max for speaking up for me, and I've always admired his guts: after all, like me he'd been in the business just a week, yet there he was arguing the toss with the management and risked being tossed out of the show on his ear.

Another enormous help to me was my sister, Betty. Out of the ATS now and working in an office, she always managed to come up on opening nights, no matter where we were playing, paying her own expenses (I was earning only £13 10*s*. a week) to act as my unofficial manager.

One Music Hall technique I had to learn was to perform to three layers of people at once: stalls, circle and gallery. I had to please them all – especially the gallery, which was where the whistling and cheering (or boos and catcalls) came from. Thus I learned the meaning of the phrase "Playing to the gallery". So Betty would move around the theatre to make certain people could see and hear me; make sure I was projecting my voice and facial expressions – especially those made by my eyes. A man with a masterly ability for making his eyes an integral part of his act was Max Miller, and from watching him I'd learned the secret of putting lots of blue on the lids to help the eyes sparkle. Otherwise I used virtually no make-up.

Costume was no great problem. There were those who had their gimmicks of dress, varying in degree from Max Miller's outrageously-coloured plus-fours, dressing-gown and diamonds to Tommy Trinder's trilby hat – otherwise evening dress was fairly standard. But I wore an ordinary, far from immaculate, brown lounge suit, since for my act it was vital to attempt to give the impression that I wasn't one of the cast, but had just wandered in from the street – as though into a pub, or just home from work. And I'd emphasise the calculated amateurishness of my presence and dress with a reference to the rest of the acts on the bill: "I'm not with this lot . . . Ooh no, I'm on me own!"

Why a brown suit? Because I thought it was a colour that didn't intrude. It's warm and neutral and man-in-the-street anonymous. If people *did* notice my suit or tie I thought it would mean that they were not concentrating on my face. When playing coastal resorts I'd even wear shorts. (I don't know why I say "even", because those of you that watched *Up Pompeii!* know that I'm blessed with rather gorgeous legs!) The point is that I dressed the way I did to suit a particular image, just as Chaplin, Liberace, Norman Wisdom and Max Wall dress to suit theirs.

Nor did I make a formally stylised entrance, but went straight up to the footlights and began: "I just met this woman . . . No, don't laugh. *Liss-en!* . . . There was this woman . . ." as one would indeed do in a pub or on arriving home.

One provincial critic on the tour attacked me for being unprofessional: "This man wears no make-up, doesn't dress, doesn't even take a bow at the end."

I was a bit upset by this, for I'd thought in my innocence that I was being clever. As I explained in a letter to the gentleman: "When I made my professional début I had little money and so I had to be tight with the pennies when I had a new suit made for the occasion. In return the tailor was tight with the material – and this communicated itself to the back seam of my trousers. So I started to take a bow – but had to stop half-way when I became aware of bursting stitches. The audience seemed to think my look of bewildered horror somewhat droll – so I've tried to cash in on it ever since by deliberately not taking a bow, but looking bewildered as though by the fact that people think me funny."

His reply was short and sharp: "You certainly bewildered *me*, and I thought you were singularly unfunny."

"Ah well," I remarked to myself, "you can't win 'em all." I have made that remark to myself with great regularity ever since.

Even to this day I fight against evening dress. I can't bear it, although there are formal dinners and prestige occasions when it would be discourteous to wear that old brown suit.

But the real secret of whatever success I had was my delivery. In those days comics were very precise: they were word perfect, as though reading their jokes from a script, and to fluff a line was something of a major disaster. My nervous, stammering, jabbering delivery was a bit different. Then apparently, it had never been heard of before. Yet it worked, because the ordinary chap whom I was portraying *is* imprecise. You've only to listen to the answer when a TV interviewer asks what someone thinks of the Government: "Well . . . You know . . . Yes . . . Well, the Government . . . Who is it now? . . . I mean, well you know . . . The Government . . . Yes, well . . . What more can I say? . . ." People in real life don't talk precisely as though from scripts, and neither did I attempt to on stage. My act sounded almost like a stream of consciousness, which is why I often didn't finish sentences. "Of course, mind you . . ." trailed away into silence – as again happens in real life.

Frankie Howerd: the Kitchen Sink Comic!

As I've said earlier, circumstances had shaped my act into a one-man situational comedy, and although informal dress such as open-necked shirts and jeans are common enough today on TV, I was considered quite bold to combine casualness of dress, material and delivery. But I just had to do my act that way – and, thank Heavens, it worked!

Anyway, I'd been in the profession for no more than six weeks when Jack Payne's office contacted me to say that Joy Russell-Smith, producer of *Variety Bandbox*, was auditioning for a new, regular act to take part in the show, and that they'd fixed up for me to go along. Now this was the most astonishing compliment that could have been paid me, for in those days radio was supreme, unchallenged by TV, and one of its most popular variety programmes was *Variety Bandbox* on Sundays. Pros with years in the business were delighted to be asked to go on the show, so for a novice even to be considered for an audition for a regular appearance (albeit bottom of the bill) was quite something.

The show's resident star was comedian Derek Roy, but he appeared only once a fortnight, guest stars topping the bill on the Sundays in between. It was a wild dream, but somebody could be impossibly lucky and work his way up the bill to fill that alternate top spot on a permanent basis . . .

I got an act together – material I used in the show, new gags I evolved, others I "borrowed" and messed about with – and went to London. It was, as ever, a grey and glum and spirit-reducing day, and as they showed me to the audition studio I was in a desperate state of nerves, the small measure of self-confidence I'd acquired on tour evaporating at every step. Then they opened the door of the studio – and I gave a squeal of horror. For it was just an empty room (save for a mike in one corner) with its walls soundproofed with what appeared to be sandbags, like a wartime bunker, except for a glass inset behind which was the control room. But I had to stand with my back to this, so that I couldn't see a living soul – not even a lone, cigar-smoking agent! I'd always felt my act depended upon a live, responsive, audience – so how in God's name was I supposed to have a comic gossip (accompanied by funny facial gestures) with a wall of sandbags?

I was about to protest, but thought: who on earth am I to argue with one of the BBC's most powerful producers? I sensed that the audition was going to be a failure, but told myself that for the future it was wiser not to make an enemy of Joy Russell-Smith, and via her the entire BBC. So I shrugged, convinced that the audition was doomed in advance – but did it, shaking like a leaf and stammering as badly as ever I'd done. I managed to get through it, and when it was over I reckoned that if an artist's act is reflected by the measure of the audience's applause, the muteness of those sandbags was a fair summing-up of an abysmal performance.

The door of the studio opened . . . I braced myself . . . Joy Russell-Smith came in – laughing.

The *ooh . . . ah . . . ooh* of nervousness had again proved to be an enormous asset, for Joy Russell-Smith gushed: "A completely new art form," and I replied with an archness I was far from feeling: "It's nothing, really."

I was asked to go back for what's called a "seeded audition" – a live audience of other artists who were also auditioning for shows. I was more comfortable and natural on a proper stage with an audience (although there was still sufficient tension to give me a bad migraine), and I went home slightly more hopeful than on previous occasions.

Since I wasn't on the telephone, the news came by telegram: *YOU HAVE BEEN CHOSEN*. My immediate reaction? No, not to rush out for a bottle of champagne: I was so overcome with emotion I had to rush to the bathroom.

On December 3rd I was at the old Camberwell Palace from which *Variety Bandbox* was broadcast, on probation at three guineas a show. I began: "Ladies and Gentle-*men* . . . No . . . Now listen . . . No, don't laugh" – but, thank Heaven, quite a lot of listeners did laugh.

Before I learnt of the favourable reaction, I reckoned that I'd been far too twitchy to be good, and it must be remembered, too, that in those days shows went out live, so there was no opportunity to revise or edit. Timing was to the second – so what was done was done. The first kindly reassurance came from Jessie Matthews who was top of the bill that week, and who bothered to seek me out to say: "I think you've got a great future." A superb gesture from the star of the show to the lad at the bottom of the bill.

So there I was, after no time at all in the business, a success on radio. Naturally I was very excited. But it held enormous new problems. In Music Hall you could use much the same script for the duration of a tour – it appeared new to each town played. But on radio the total audience heard it all at once, so I needed a fresh script for each broadcast. Since I was far from being able to afford a scriptwriter, I bought joke books and cannibalised their contents, and had to make one joke go a long, long way. But since my technique (for want of a better word) was in the telling, and not in a quick-fire succession of wisecracks, I could make three jokes last an entire act. (I had to!) And Max Bygraves, although not doing quite as well as me at that time, was extremely generous in supplying me with much-needed jokes. (I remember getting a touch of the intuitions on one occasion and saying to him: "You're going to be a big name one day, but it won't be as an impressionist but as a singer." And while he certainly became a fine comedian, it was indeed his singing that led to his great success. So if the worst comes to the worst [as it undoubtedly will!] I can always earn a few bob as Gypsy Frank on Southend Pier.)

During those early *Variety Bandbox* days I was approached by the Jack Payne organisation and asked to sign a contract whereby they'd handle my Personal Management. The existing contract was for "the run of the show" – when "For The Fun Of It" came to an end, so did the contract. The new offer was this:

A contract to handle all my affairs, renewable every six months for a total of five years. But the option was on Jack's side only: if I continued to be successful he could renew it; if I flopped he didn't have to bother. Me? I had no say in the matter. Nor was he merely to take the usual ten per cent of my earnings. He'd pay me a fee of £25 a week (rising by £5 every six months if the option was taken up) and he'd also pocket fifty per cent of my earnings. So if he got me a booking at £100 a week I'd get £62 10*s*., and he'd get £37 10*s*. And, of course, he'd also have the profits of the show if it was one that he staged.

More important than money, if I continued to be a success I was tied up for five years, compelled to do as I was told. Instinct told me not to sign, but I was an innocent in the business, and was finally talked into it by people who pointed out that if I continued to do well I'd have behind me a powerful man whose name carried considerable weight in show-business; while, if I failed, no agent would be of any use to me, anyway. So I signed, and although Jack was rather inclined to boast over the years about what he'd done for me, he always omitted to add that if he'd had more faith in me he wouldn't have included that one-sided option clause.

We never really got on. At this stage there was no specific cause for animosity: it was a matter of personality. He was a dynamic, outgoing, veteran; I was a shy and introspective newcomer. Our attitudes and temperaments, our standards of values and methods of reasoning were diametric opposites. It wasn't a case of right or wrong: simply a complete inability to communicate. (Nor were matters helped by the tale-bearing and petty mischief-making of certain other people on his books.) Later he was to do things with my career to which I objected, but I'd signed that contract . . .

There were never great slanging matches – perhaps it would have been better if there had been. Instead I grew progressively more dejected about things. In the end it did boil over into a distasteful High Court action.

Anyway, back to Easter, 1947. By now *Variety Bandbox* had moved to the People's Palace in the Mile End Road, and "For The Fun Of It" was playing Peterborough, Northants. I remember that Easter well, for it brought a message from Jack Payne telling me that the BBC had carried out one of their polls among a cross-section of listeners, and while Derek Roy was liked by more than seventy per cent, my figure had dived down to the thirties. If it didn't improve I'd be off *Variety Bandbox*. The reason? Jack Payne blamed the scripts.

So I have every reason to remember Easter, 1947. The news would have shaken even the most hearty extrovert: I nearly collapsed on the spot. Miserable beyond words, I walked the streets in an utter daze. Then, as my brain cleared, I began to wonder what I should do. I knew that I wasn't the world's greatest scriptwriter, but I didn't think my material was all that bad. It may have been part of the problem, but I was convinced that it didn't hold the complete answer. So what other factors were there?... Only me.

Was it my technique? Was my delivery bad? Were my gestures and facial expressions wrong? . . . I froze, and uttered some shrill sound, much to the consternation of passers-by . . . *That's it!* . . . It was ridiculous that neither the BBC nor the Jack Payne organisation had spotted it, and I was singularly stupid not to have been aware of it much earlier on: *I'd been giving stage, not radio, performances.* It was as simple as that. Listeners weren't able to see my expressions and gestures, and were baffled when the live audience laughed for no apparent reason – bafflement giving way to annoyance at the frustration of not knowing what was going on.

Diagnosing the cause, I effected a cure: starting with my next broadcast I didn't stand back and project myself to the audience, but addressed myself to the microphone – and as a result "Thing" from the BBC told me I was in favour again. (This didn't mean ignoring the live audience – indeed, I'd have been lost without it. What it did mean was yet another new technique: transferring from *visual* to *vocal* clowning. I didn't find it all that easy. In fact it was extremely difficult . . . *just to learn to stand still* was like being back on the parade-ground – complete with attendant apprehensions!)

I did the summer season in 1947 at Clacton, taking an early train to London for Sunday rehearsals and the broadcast. Radio scripts are read out over the air, but I was so idiotically conscientious I knew mine almost by heart, for I never rehearsed my lines less than seventy times. (How I admired artists who could instantly read "on script" with little rehearsal or none at all.) And since the stage of the People's Palace was always crowded with other artists and technicians, and because the dressing rooms were also packed, I did these rehearsals in the cemetery behind the theatre. I must have presented quite a sight: this tall and gangling young man wandering among the tombstones, reading from pages of foolscap and making wild gesticulations as he went . . .

One of the gimmicks I evolved which I thought might be good for radio was to mispronounce certain words in a special way. Thus "Ladies and gentlemen" became "Ladies and gentle-*men*", while "ludicrous" became "ludi-*crouse*" and so on. Equally, I wasn't just "amazed" at the situations in which I found myself, I was "a-*mazed*!". This became a popular catchphrase, as did "Not on your Nellie!" and "What a funny woman!" and (of my supposedly deaf pianist): "Poor soul – she's past it." There were many more, non particularly droll when written down, since these verbal punctuation marks are comical (if at all) only in their delivery. But I think it's fair to say that while other shows used catchphrases almost as characters (like *ITMA*'s "Don't forget the diver", and "Can I do you now, sir?") I was a character who used catchphrases.

One of them has passed into immortality (and how much further than that do you want to pass?). It came about when I introduced into *Variety Bandbox* those appallingly badly sung mock operas, starring the show's bandleader Billy Ternent (tenor), Madame Vere-Roper (soprano) and Frankie Howerd (bass – "the lowest of the low"). Vera, while singing (if that's what you can call it) would pause for breath before a high C, and as she mustered herself for this musical Everest, I'd mutter: "And the best of luck!" Later it became: "And the best of British luck!"

The phrase is so common now that I frequently surprise people when I tell them that it was my catchphrase way back on *Variety Bandbox*.

Censorship was very tough in those days, which was not a bad thing in my view, since it meant that an artist had to be subtle and clever rather than take the easy way out: dirt. Despite arguments to the contrary (and without setting myself up as some greasepaint saint), I've used mildly bawdy material, in the same spirit as the old Music Hall and the belly-laugh, seaside postcard, but I've always been sensitive about causing offence (although you can't please everyone!). Even today, in shows like *Up Pompeii!*, I cut material from the script if, in my mind, it goes too far.

Mind you, some of radio's censorship at the time does seem odd in terms of contemporary standards: the total ban on words like damn, God and bloody, for instance. Blimey was all right – but Gor blimey was out. And when I did a sketch playing a psychiatrist – I had to be called a "professor"! To use "flipping" as an adjective was OK, however – it wasn't reckoned to have any innuendo; but no branded products could be mentioned, nor any physical deformities: the deaf were "hard of hearing", people who stuttered had "an impediment of speech" – and so forth. There was no mention of royalty or public figures – what came to be known as satire was still many years away. Equally, no knickers or bellies, although, if you were very daring, you could say: "There was a young girl called Nelly, who had a great pimple on her . . . um . . . chest." It was pretty strong stuff, and whether or not you got away with it depended upon who you were.

To say "I'm going to do you" was considered very naughty, yet I got away with the catchphrase: "There are those among us tonight whom I shall do-o-o-o." And there was another that I'd use with Billy Ternent. He'd say something like: "I've just been orchestrated," and I'd reply: "Dirty old devil!" Or he'd say: "I'm ossified," and again I'd come back with "Dirty old devil!" Not madly funny written down: it was how it was said that gave it any comic impact. But to say "Dirty old devil" at all (especially with my voice) brought letters of protest for both my daring and obscenity.

How standards have changed – for good or bad is a matter of opinion.

The events that followed my return to favour on *Variety Bandbox* astounded me. (I may say, brethren, that never was my ass so stounded.) First, I was promoted to three spots on the bill instead of one, and my fee upped to £20. This wasn't much, even for those days, but radio was never a great payer. The compensation, as with TV today, was that radio success had an enormous publicity value. So much so that when I finished at Clacton I was astonished to find myself touring the variety circuit again – this time *top* of the bill!

When Jack Payne called it "one of the great romances of show-business" I blushed – and I don't blush easily when this suffusion of blood is inspired by praise! Jokes aside, I really was very touched when he added that he'd never seen anyone shoot to the top of show-business so quickly. Radio was to be thanked, of course. In my view, better artists than me spent a lifetime struggling to get as far as closing the first half of a show, yet I was top of the bill at £85 a week. After such a short time as a pro I was as bemused as my fellow performers must have been!

But when, during that second tour, we played Lewisham Hippodrome, my mother was in the happy position of being able to say: "I told you so."

This is the point when, according to the cliché of show-business legend, a Rolls-Royce and swimming pool and caviar face packs should have entered my life. But they didn't, and for two good reasons. First, I just wasn't interested in a flashy life style. I didn't drink or smoke, wasn't fussy about clothes, and had no need for a mansion within a first-tee drive of Windsor Castle. Which was as well because, secondly, despite the fame I didn't have all that much money once I'd allowed for Jack Payne, the Inland Revenue, basic expenses and domestic obligations.

I was interested only in performing. What little fame I had acquired had come astonishingly – improbably – quickly, and I was extremely aware that it could vanish with even greater rapidity. So I spent my free time sweating to improve my technique and my scripts, with radio the great anxiety. For on tour, with one act (i.e. one script), I could be relatively relaxed once I'd got over the terror of opening night: but on radio the material was always new, and so every broadcast was an opening night. I worked so hard on my material, and was so bedevilled by nervous insecurity, that after every *Variety Bandbox* I'd go home with a dreadful migraine.

Having got to the top of the bill, I sweated desperately

to survive. I had no interest in money (at that time!) – only to be the Mr Universe of Comics. (Nay, of Show-Business!) That, after all, had been my compulsive ambition: I was an Artist (the capital A is deliberate), and above such petty considerations as financial reward. Do I feel the same today? (Pause for hollow laughter.)

So on tour I always stayed at the same three guineas-a-week digs in Leeds, Birmingham, Manchester or wherever it was. And since the rest of the cast did the same, it strengthened the family atmosphere that much of the old Music Hall contained. It would be sentimental to the point of absurdity to pretend that we were one, big, happy family for twenty-four hours of the day, but it's certainly true that most of us shared a kind of chummy companionship that is often lacking in the business today. We'd do our two nightly shows, go back to our digs for supper, then listen to the radio, go for a walk, play cards, read, or just talk, and next morning open our mail over a communal breakfast.

One of the great problems was the comic who always had to tell jokes (at least I wasn't guilty of this – I've never made a witty remark in my life); even worse was the *would-be* comic: the man with a dog act whose jokes were old even when Rin-Tin-Tin was the runt of the litter. For the rest, it was much like any other form of boarding-house life. Many readers will be aware of the man or woman with the Boarding House Reach – the elasticated arm that could stretch the entire length of a table to grasp the last slice of toast, while at night there were the inevitable nocturnal punctuation marks: the snores, the occasional creaks and squeals, and the twanging of bedsprings. (At least I hope they were bedsprings and not corsets!)

But while there were amatory adventures, they were rare. Despite the popular image, the chorus girls, for instance, were (unfortunately!) very moral. Similarly, although there were those who went boozing, drink (reflecting a general pattern) was less of a problem than it is today – perhaps small theatrical salaries had something to do with it.

In the afternoons there was maybe a cinema – then to the first house. The only real concession about stardom was that I had my own dressing room. It was as tatty as the rest – and they *were* tatty, I can tell you – but it had "Number One" on the door.

It's different today. When I play the clubs I'm not on until midnight, don't have to arrive until 11.30, and seldom see anyone else. . . . It's a change that isn't necessarily for the best (except for those for whom a little of me goes a long way!).

So I lived simply, and was, as ever, a compulsive worrier – not now about making it, but keeping it!

My sister Betty still came on opening nights (she does to this day) to advise and guide. She and my brother continued to live in Eltham with my mother (who had now moved into a nicer house in the town). If I say that my mother still worked, it isn't in the earlier meaning of the word. The people for whom she'd been housekeeper were now family friends; but my mother being an active, independent and essentially religious person, occupied herself with what for a better term could be described as "good works". She was a "good-doer" rather than a "do-gooder" (if you know what I mean). In other words she helped people – but quietly and unassumingly.

The one difference in my life was that I took a flat in London. Although, like most pros, I travelled between dates by train, when I did get to London – if only for *Variety Bandbox* before rushing off to another week's touring – it just wasn't practical to travel to Eltham in the early hours of the morning before rushing off again. (Remember, too, that I was now a big boy: romance with the ladies involved something more than lemonade and gallant hand-kissing outside the church hall!)

The flat was in Holland Villas Road, not far from Shepherd's Bush, and I lived there for eleven years. The house was eventually owned by Ben Warris, but at the time he occupied the basement flat and I had the top flat. I'd put it around that he was in my basement, while he'd say that I was in his attic. . . . He proved to be a great landlord – when I'd pop down to borrow a bowl of sugar, he'd raise no more than a questioning eyebrow when I ended up with sugar bowl, Nescafé, biscuits – and a loaf of bread for tomorrow's breakfast.

The one luxury was to employ a driver and car. Touring could be very tiring, and a sleep at the back of a car meant that I didn't have to madden other second-class passengers with my dreadful snoring.

Anyway, at Christmas, 1947, I opened at the Lyceum, Sheffield, as Simple Simon in *Jack and the Beanstalk*. While I was there I had a letter from a lad who was earning £3 10*s*. a week in repertory at Winchester, and wanted to do better. He said that by coincidence he'd followed me into various Army concert parties where he'd done my sort of act (which I found most disturbing!), but added that because of this he reckoned he could write for me. The letter was signed "Eric Sykes".

SIX A Right Royal Flop

Eric Sykes came to Sheffield to see me in my dressing room, and told me that although he was a straight actor (his Titus Andronicus must have been a sight to behold!) he wanted to write for me. He added that he'd also worked out a comedy routine for himself as a character called Wag who had flat feet, and demonstrated a sample of this as well as reading some of the scripts he'd devised for me. Also in the dressing room at the time was a girl in the show with whom I was friendly. Too friendly: she was a positive female Svengali when it came to influencing me. But when she put it around that she was writing my scripts – that was too much: she had to go! Anyway, she pronounced that although Eric might become a comedian one day, for the time being he'd do better to stick to his scriptwriting. For it was plain that he had enormous talent in this field, and I was sufficiently impressed to offer him a job on the spot.

He proved to be a marvellous writer for me because of his great inventive genius for the near-fantastic. There was, for instance, the classic script which had me as a messenger boy told to take two elephants to Crewe. Again it may be one of those things that are not all that comic in cold print, the laughs being in the telling – how I secured these beasts together with string, but one got away, so I tied the other to a chocolate machine, and the runaway was found in a cinema ("in the best seats – cheeky devil!"), and as I was trying to prise it loose a woman behind me said: "Would you mind taking your hat off?" . . . And so on. It was fantasy, yet in a way kept this side of utter absurdity: it was something that just might possibly have happened. And it was perfect for radio since it left so much to the listeners' imagination. They did the visualising and so, in a way, were part of the act.

Other crazy situations had me on a train journey (but I found there was no engine driver aboard) . . . I got a job as a lion tamer . . . I was in the Rocky Mountains . . . In the jungle – there were dozens of them, all surrealistic, all superbly written, and all perfect for my technique at the time.

But since Eric wanted to perform himself, I arranged for him to do a BBC audition with a "feed" I sometimes used, Miss Sunny Rogers. The BBC said they'd employ him to "warm-up" the *Variety Bandbox* studio audience before the show actually started: get them in a happy, relaxed mood. But it didn't go well, and Eric resigned himself to writing but not performing for the time being.

I worked every week of the year in 1948. My career apparently just couldn't go wrong. I was one of *the* names on radio, and so was also one of the biggest draws in the theatre, for radio fame in those days was like TV or pop success today. There was an added dimension: radio was non-visual and the public were curious to know what I looked like. (And it was worth the journey – for I was still a very beautiful sight to behold!) Box-office figures showed that I was one of the "in" performers of 1948. I know this may sound conceited, but it's no more than a statement of recorded fact (apart, perhaps, from the bit about my good looks which forever have been a matter of some controversy!).

During 1948 Jack Payne "sub-let" me (as he was entitled to do under our contract) to a man who was presenting a revue called *Ta-Ra-Ra-Boom-De-Ay*. It did enormous business, and we broke box-office records wherever we played. But the irony was that the man presenting the show put on a second edition the following year: *Ta-Ra-Ra-Booms-Again* – but was certain that other acts were the draw, not me. He thought I was too young and inexperienced to be the star attraction. So he poured all his money into this second show, dropped me – and I'm not mentioning the names of those other acts because *Ta-Ra-Ra-Booms-Again* did no business. And the reason I'm not mentioning the name of the show's impresario is because the next time I saw him – years later – he was a doorman at the BBC. His misjudgement had cost him every penny he had. I'm not gloating: it's too sad for that. No, the other acts certainly had as much talent as Frankie Howerd – if not more – it was simply that at the time I was the big draw, but this man just didn't realise the fact. His misjudgement may have been odd (as mine was to be), but he didn't *seem* unhappy at the BBC. Maybe life had been kind to him in other ways.

However, at the end of a super 1948 I did *Jack and the Beanstalk* again, then had a summer season at Blackpool. At another theatre at the town Julie Andrews was playing. She was about twelve years old at the time, and her parents (Ted and Barbara Andrews) were doing a spot in my show. I remember how she'd come to watch me with her brother, Christopher, and twenty years later in Hollywood she still remembered my rendering (or should it be rending?) of "Three Little Fishes".

There were, as ever, many stars at Blackpool, but I saw little of them. I didn't even stay in the town, but rented a small house at Cleveleys. This wasn't aloofness on my part: for one thing I still wasn't interested in the bright lights when off-stage; secondly I was usually tired after appearing twice-nightly plus matinées; thirdly I was rather occupied with a gorgeous girl who was also in a show in the town. In fact I was so smitten I nearly married her.

The first time I'd been seriously involved with a girl was back in Wales when we were both at the Experimental Station. She lived in the area with her father, but I got posted, and when I contacted her again I learned that she'd married someone else. So that was that!

The next girl who might have had the joy of becoming Mrs Howard I'd met in Germany. There was supposed to be no fraternisation, but I fraternised as though there was no tomorrow, the situation made easier by the fact that this fräulein was connected with my concert party. We communicated in pidgin French and what might be termed Body Braille, and I was so besotted that when I was demobbed I thought of re-enlisting (I must have been out of my tiny mind!) in order to be sent back to Germany. But when I was advised that re-enlistment might mean a posting to Japan, not Germany, I thought better of it. As it transpired, I did go back to Germany for a charity show for the troops towards the end of 1947, and discovered that she'd found someone else. It's the story of my life – for the girl I was so close to in Blackpool married a well-known writer instead. Then, again, years later there was a famous actress with whom I was very much in love – but she, too, ended up marrying someone else.

Since I presume that these women are still happily married, I won't name them: why embarrass them with reminders of romances now dead and beyond recall?

But, thank heavens, I've never been lacking. Putting it politely, I never went short of it . . . then! (These days I read books about it – illustrated if possible!)

Anyway, the professional highlight of 1949, as distinct from the romantic, came when I was invited to do a Christmas show at Buckingham Palace, it being suggested that I was asked because King George the Sixth and Queen Elizabeth both enjoyed *Variety Bandbox*. The Master of Ceremonies was ventriloquist, Peter Brough, and the other acts were impressionist Florence Desmond, and Jimmy Edwards, RAF pilot, academic, comedian and tippler. He opened the show, then came Florence Desmond, then me.

I was driven to the Palace by someone from Jack Payne's office, and trust it to happen to me – once through the main gates we lost our way. We drove round and round, into all manner of forbidden areas, causing absolute chaos among the security people, the Guardsmen and the corgis. Finally, all in a tiz, we found our way to the ballroom.

I was petrified – understandably so on this occasion. I remember ordering a large port and brandy for my nerves, and hid this huge strengthener behind my make-up mirror. . . . And I also remember that when I reached for it the contents had disappeared. Someone must have been an alcohol drinker (and I'm not even going to suggest Jimmy Edwards since the royalties from this book are hardly likely to cover even a tiny libel action). However, as I've said, I wasn't much of a drinker, but this was for courage – and all I had was an empty glass.

Florence Desmond came off in tears, convinced she'd been awful (in fact she was marvellous), but the communicative effect was such that I nearly *went on* in tears, convinced I was *going to be* awful! The King and Queen sat at the front with Princess Margaret, and I assume the rest of the audience on those little gilt chairs were Palace staff.

Madame Vere-Roper was there to play the piano for me (even more badly than the act demanded, despite the special quality of the audience), and so with her accompaniment I did my bit.

Now my act was, as always, an intimate gossip with the audience – even if the audience did happen to be the King and Queen of England and not Joe Bloggs and his wife. This made it very tricky – it's a bit terrifying to talk to the King and Queen in terms of: "No listen missus! No . . . No, don't laugh moosh! . . . There are those among us today whom I shall do-o-o" et cetera, but if I *didn't* say such things then I wasn't doing my act. It was very fraught. I'd thought about it earlier, of course; but it's one thing to rehearse an act, quite another to do it with the Royal Family actually sitting there.

After my twenty minutes I came off in a muck sweat. Had I been funny? Had I gone too far? Should I have devised something different for Buckingham Palace? The act seemed to have gone down well, but did the laughter have a somewhat hollow ring about it? . . . I was overcome now, not only by nerves, but by fear that I'd been an impertinent idiot. I had visions of the Tower (and I don't mean Blackpool's).

The first person to whom Peter Brough presented me was Princess Margaret who told me – thank God! – that she'd had to stuff a handkerchief into her mouth to stop herself laughing too loudly. This helped to calm me a bit. . . . Then came the Queen, and as I began to bow she said how thrilled *she* was to meet *me*! To coin a phrase, my flabber was never so ghasted – and I thought that had I met her before the show I'd certainly not have been so twitchy.

It's an old joke to say that the trouble about being invited by the Royal Family is that you can never invite them back – but the Queen Mother (Queen Elizabeth as she then was) seemed the sort of person I felt I could have invited back. . . . Well, *almost*! I mean, I'd have had to rush home and tidy up a bit. . . . But she was homely and chatty, without a trace of snobbishness or of being patronising, and as we talked, and knowing that she was a Scot, I told her of an experience I'd had in Glasgow while touring in *Ta-Ra-Ra-Boom-De-Ay* . . .

Now the Glasgow Empire had a terrible name in those days as far as English comedians were concerned: indeed it was known as the graveyard of the English comic. In fact it had an undeserved reputation – except occasionally for the second house on Saturday night when much of the audience came in straight from the pubs. I was warned about this, yet wasn't too nervous because I'd had a great week, and just didn't see why the second house on Saturday should be any different from what had gone before.

Nor did it go badly – until I came to a joke (which I'd told without trouble all week) based upon the fact that I am half-Scottish, and which was meant to be a send-up of myself for being half-English. They took it completely the wrong way, and it served as the needed catalyst: suddenly the theatre exploded into a madness of boos, jeers, catcalls and a slow handclap. Absolute pandemonium: the audience dissolved into a shrieking, raving mob. At first I was baffled, then humiliated – then terrified. Instinct told me to pack it in – but this was a revue, the girls used my spot to change for their next appearance, so if I left the stage there would have been an appalling gap. In any case I was a pro who'd been paid to do my stuff. . . . So I did it.

Doggedly I finished my act, even to the closing song, took a bow – and then came back for my encore! Nobody could hear a word because of the savage screaming, but I was determined to do it, and I did it – even if I then rushed from the stage in a state of near-hysterics. Eric Sykes was to say in a rash moment that carrying on my act the way I did was the bravest thing he'd ever seen in the theatre. Looking back I suppose I was brave. . . . Would I do it today? You must be joking! Brave or foolhardy, I didn't think about it either way at the time – everything resolved itself into a gut feeling that I had to finish what I'd been paid to do . . . which was why I even went on to take a bow in the finale – and which provoked a renewed frenzy of booing. Looking back, it amazes me that bottles weren't thrown, or the stage stormed by the mob. But even without physical violence, a theatre filled with people screaming hatred at you is a horrific experience. I'd never had a reception like it before, nor – thank Heavens – since. (Pause, while I touch every piece of wood in sight!)

There was a gang of yobbos waiting at the stage door, so I had to stay in the theatre until they dispersed. I then caught the train to London for the next day's *Variety Bandbox*, shaking, quite literally, during the entire journey south . . .

This was the story I began to tell Queen Elizabeth, and after a while I realised something we've all suffered: I was going on for far too long. Apart from the fact that I must have been boring her stiff, she had other people to talk to, but how on earth do you bring such a story to an abrupt end a quarter of the way through? I stammered and gulped and gurgled towards a stumbling halt – then the King came up and Queen Elizabeth said: "You really must listen to this." So I had to start from the beginning again and this time continue to the bitter end! If they were bored to distraction by the time I finished, Royal training prevented them from giving any sign of the fact – but my burning memory of that Palace occasion remains the embarrassment I felt at having reached the point of no return of what seemed to me to be the world's longest and most tedious anecdote, with the King and Queen of England as my audience. . . . They really did show the most amazing tolerance.

I did the summer of 1950 at Great Yarmouth, and by now was also doing a large number of charity shows – orphanages, hospitals, theatres of war, old folks' homes, and so on. (Yet, ironically, there were those who wondered if I did any at all. The explanation is simple: I was brought up to believe that one should do good works privately – not cash in on other people's sufferings. Then, one day, I was sent to do a show at a home for the disabled – and was livid to find a photographer waiting. I complained bitterly about turning the event into a public relations exercise – and was amazed to be given a severe dressing-down from the people in charge. For what I'd failed to realise was that the disabled people with whom I was to be photographed got enormous pleasure from having their pictures taken with a "star"; that the publicity was of enormous value to the charity concerned, since it drew the public's attention to its needs – and so *I* was being selfish for not wanting any pictures taken!)

Anyway . . .

There was still *Variety Bandbox* in 1950, of course, in which I topped the bill on alternate Sundays with Derek Roy, and the film companies wanted us to plug the stars of their productions. (Now the target is usually the chat shows.) So in the spots where I played "Professor" Howerd, I had no shortage of top guest artists who came to my "consulting room" for "advice" – among them Margaret Lockwood, Dirk Bogarde, Richard Burton, Robert Newton, Tony

Hancock, Richard Attenborough – it's a long list. Memories of them are naturally fragmented by now, but there was one thing upon which I always insisted: that the scripts shared the jokes fifty-fifty. I was meticulous about this – these stars weren't to be just stooges, left with egg on their faces, but had to be an integral part of the comedy routine. (It was the same attitude that the great Morecambe and Wise were to use years later on TV.)

There were also three guests whom everyone reckoned it would be impossible to get. One was Billy Butlin, the holiday camp tycoon (maybe he came because he felt contrite about having turned me down at Filey); another was Val Parnell, boss of the London Palladium and the Moss Empires circuit, and so the most powerful figure in the theatre at that time. He was a tough man, and a strict disciplinarian, but he agreed to come on the show – although he assured me that he'd never do it for anyone else. (This was probably untrue – but I was touched just the same.) That a man of his reputation and stature should appear in a comedy sketch on *Variety Bandbox* was not only a feather in my cap, but a truly moving gesture of friendship – although, I hasten to add, it didn't prevent him from being tough in business matters! (Mind you, I had to resist the enormous temptation on *Variety Bandbox* of telling him that while he could complain of comics ruining *his* shows, this time he was in danger of ruining *mine*, for as a performer he was an utter amateur!)

One of the most memorable – and difficult – of all my guests was the third of the unexpected ones: the late Gilbert Harding. He drank too much and was fantastically rude – yet despite these drawbacks (or maybe because of them) he had an enormous following. He was intelligent, complex, acerbic, and one of the true eccentrics of his time.

When he was asked if he'd appear on *Variety Bandbox*, he read Eric Sykes' script, then came to my flat to discuss it with us. I was in such awe of the man that as I heard him climb the stairs I was shaking like a leaf and wondering whether I ought to call him "Sir". In the event he arrived reeling drunk and started off by saying that the script was rubbish and that I was clearly a neurotic. He really lambasted me and then Eric – who sat there quivering.

I had a bar in the flat for guests, and Harding helped himself – liberally and often. The point came when he asked: "Where's the bathroom?"

I pointed. "At the top of the stairs on the next landing."

He never made it – as was testified by the trickle of liquid that appeared under the sitting-room door.

He telephoned next day, overwhelming me with apologies, and pathetically contrite. Yes, he'd love to appear on the show, he was sorry if he'd been rude, he thought Eric and I were splendid people – and so on and so forth.

On the night he was as good as gold, even with lines like: (shyly) "Now, Mr Harding——"

Graciously: "Don't be formal, dear boy. Don't call me Mr Harding."

Confidently: "All right . . . Now look, Gillie——"

Irately: "Don't you Gillie me!"

But Gillie he remained on my shows (of which he was kindly to do many on radio and TV).

We became chums after that first, disastrous, encounter, and I came to see him as a sad, basically very unhappy man – lonely, confused, and really very kind and soft under the abrasive public veneer . . .

So 1950 proved to be another lucky year for me, but it had what might be termed a double climax. First, I did a season at the London Palladium in a revue called *Out Of This World* with Binnie Hale and Nat Jackley – and it was another crazy show-business fairy tale: although the show marked my first West End appearance as a pro, I was top of the bill. (And, praise be, a success: the critics were very kind and we played to full houses.)

On the day we opened, October 17th, I went to Leicester Square to look at the huge posters advertising the show, and as I gazed at them I was emotional almost to the point of tears, for my thoughts suddenly took me back through the weight of days to my early struggles, and I realised that despite my success on radio and in the provinces, it was this that I'd really dreamed of . . .

I stood looking at my name for so long I was nearly arrested for loitering with intent!

The second great event of the year – or was meant to be! – was the Royal Variety Show: an overwhelming honour, for in those days it was rare indeed for a comparative newcomer to be included among the pick of the talent.

It was, as I recall, the twenty-first anniversary of the Show and there was a formidable "senior" cast that included Max Miller, Jack Benny, Gracie Fields, Tommy Trinder, Billy Cotton and his Band, and the Crazy Gang.

To celebrate this special occasion there was also a lunch for the cast and the Press at the old Café de Paris. A very swank affair – and I was scared to death, for despite the fact that I was a so-called "star", I just wasn't used to these posh events. I sat at a table with Dick Richards, then show-business writer for the old *Sunday Pictorial*, and as I dropped knives and forks all over the floor, he said: "Calm down. You look as though you think you're about to be assassinated at any minute. Relax."

"I'm sorry," I muttered from under the table where I was frantically groping for spilled cutlery.

The Royal Variety Show was put together in two days: commitments made it impossible to gather international artists together for a longer period of time. So we rehearsed all Sunday through to five a.m. on Monday morning – then did the show on the Monday evening. The scene during rehearsals was therefore chaotic, and to add to the pandemonium, Press reporters and photographers were present in strength.

I thought it wouldn't be a bad idea to have my picture taken, but I reckoned that it needed some stunt if it was to be chosen for publication from among the hundreds that were being shot. Finally I hit on the ruse of doing the one thing nobody else was doing – nothing! I went and sat at the back of stalls, put my feet on top of the seat in front, pushed my hat down over my face (but not too far down!) and pretended to be so relaxed and unworried that I was having a quiet doze.

I sat . . . and I sat . . . and I sat. . . . But after twenty minutes no one had spotted me. I felt I'd be there all night (if I survived the cramp that was setting in), then attempted to attract attention with loud snoring noises. That did it: the cameramen came bounding up the gangway and my picture was to make several of the papers. As the photographers clicked away I felt very pleased with myself – but when it came to the show my self-satisfaction quickly evaporated.

I was to appear towards the end of the first half, and this was *usually* (and I emphasise "usually" with good cause) quite a help, for the Royal Variety Show was one of the few events at which artists positively clamoured to get on early. There were sound reasons for this:

In the first half the audience was fresher, of course. Which meant they were more receptive and responsive. The show tended to be very long, was packed with talent, and by the time you're into the second half the customers are inevitably wilting – and the performers can sense it.

More important than this is the matter of nerves. The Royal Variety Show was like a thousand auditions and first nights rolled into one, so that even tough old campaigners wanted to get their acts over and done with rather than wait and wait and wait. Many famous artists, through the sheer build-up of nerves caused by waiting, have died on their feet when they've come on at the end of the more prestigious second half. I even saw it happen to Danny Kaye.

The reasons for the nerves? Well, the Royal Show was *the* variety event of the year. It contained (in theory, anyway) the pick of the world's talent, and so was tremendously competitive; while in the audience were the Press and powerful and highly critical agents, managers and impresarios – all vitally important and influential. Particularly the Press. It really did matter who they decided won or lost on that night of the year, for in those pre-TV days the public judged only by what they read.

Another factor that contributed to nervousness was the split-second precision required in the timing of the show. No one was allotted a great deal of time: some as little as five minutes, while I had only nine. The top of the bill performers didn't have much more. For all of us it was dreadfully difficult to put ourselves over within such strict limits – especially when the real stars of the night were the Royal Family, and you had to fight snob sections of the audience whose eyes were riveted on the Royal Box (the Royal Family being far less exposed to the public in those pre-television days), and who laughed only when the Royals did.

A classic example of what happens when you mess up a Royal Variety Show occurred the very year I made my first appearance on it. This was the famous occasion when Max Miller went over his time. Val Parnell uttered warning hisses from the wings. Max, referring to the foreign acts that were to follow him, was reported to have hissed back: "I'm British!" Parnell was livid – and Max overran by eight minutes: the equivalent of an hour in an ordinary show. The result? Parnell (I was told) cancelled a big revue at the Prince of Wales in which Max was to have starred, and years were to pass before he again gave him work. So for good or bad, you could not underestimate the importance of the Royal Variety Show in those days.

However, I arrived back at the Palladium that Monday, a fixed grin on my face for the crowds lining the way to the stage door – and went on to close the first half . . .

I've mentioned that to appear in the first half was *usually* a blessing. I'll now explain the "usually" – on this occasion the preceding act was the Billy Cotton Band.

Billy's music was loud, brash, boisterous and brilliant, and his act ended with the band throwing balls of cotton-wool into the Royal Box while they played and sang "Oh, What A Lovely Bunch of Coconuts". Great stuff, but it was the sort of spectacular that traditionally closed the first half – it was murder for a fairly gentle solo patter act to follow. I had the impact of a drizzle following a typhoon.

I'd realised this at rehearsals, of course – but what could I do? Refuse to appear – and so cut my professional throat? No: what I did was to perform my act – a gibbering idiot of an artist to whose natural nerves were added the stress of it being a Royal Variety Show and the certain knowledge that following Billy Cotton and his Band was living dangerously to the point of absurdity.

Nor was I wrong. There were a few titters – and that was all.

I was devastated with shame. I thought: "My greatest chance ever, and I've blown it" . . . I was so upset I put on my hat and mac and fled the theatre. I calculated the time of the finale and mooched round the streets of Soho; mercifully unrecognised, my mind a blank wasteland of pain: the same ache of undefinable agony I'd known after the disaster at RADA and those dreadful rounds of agents which culminated in the non-appearance of Harry Lowe at the Stage Door Canteen.

I arrived back at the Palladium in time to change into evening dress for the finale. Next came the formal presentation to the Royal Family, and when the show was over there was a party for the cast. But I felt too humiliated to attend.

Looking back, I realise that I'd over-reacted to the point of ridiculousness: if splendid and experienced pros had died at the Royal Variety Show, why not yours truly? And with the benefit of hindsight I can say that compared with some shows I was to do, that Royal Performance was a triumph!

Fortunately the Press was discreetly silent – Max Miller stole the headlines. But when I next saw Val Parnell I told him how ashamed I was about my abysmal performance, and how I felt that I'd let everyone down – the situation made worse by the fact that I was starring at the Palladium at the time.

He replied: "Don't worry. It wasn't as bad as you thought.

These things happen. Do you suppose I don't realise how difficult it was for you to follow Billy Cotton? Anyway, the King said to me afterwards that he thought you've got a very nice personality."

This cheered me, but it took a long time for the wounds to fully heal.

SEVEN A Different Court Appearance

By the end of 1950 I'd been with *Variety Bandbox* for about four years, and after such a period the inbuilt problems of success were beginning to show – both myself and the format were now over-familiar, ideas were running short and were in danger of becoming repetitive, and I thought I was perilously close to staleness and of becoming a bit of a yawn to the public. The situation was not reflected in the listening figures – yet – but I was anxious to avoid another gloomy call from the Jack Payne office. A further, important, consideration: after four years I was keen to extend myself a bit.

So early in 1951 I took a gamble: I quit *Variety Bandbox* and negotiated a new series with the BBC – *Fine Goings On*. It was written by Eric Sykes and featured the very talented Hattie Jacques . . . yet turned out to be no kind of a success.

Now it's easy for an artist to blame an ambiguous *Them* – I must take my fair share of responsibility. But (and there's always a but, isn't there?) in my defence I'd say that the theatre from which we broadcast – the Paris in Lower Regent Street – was much too small for my technique at that time. It had been converted from a tiny cinema, and I still needed a large, music-hall type auditorium in which to project myself, even for radio, and I found the Paris claustrophobic and inhibiting. . . . And maybe the format of the show wasn't right.

One thing was certain: my morale zoomed down. (The emotional Kamikaze of show-business, that's me!) Here was an entire half-hour built around me, but it just didn't work. Did this mean, as one critic wrote, that I was OK for scattered spots in a show like *Variety Bandbox*, but wasn't able to hold my own programme together? And having cut myself off from *Variety Bandbox*, what did the future now hold for me?

If radio popularity in those days was reflected in Music Hall popularity, by the same token a decline in radio popularity was equally reflective. So to add to my depression I found that although I was still topping the bill in Music Hall, I was less of a draw than I had been.

Thank God my reaction was positive: I went for a walk. A long walk. One of my very long walks around the back streets of Kensington. And as I walked I pondered. (Well, there isn't much else to do when you walk *but* ponder, is there?) I thought that if a tiredness is setting in, and if this means the danger of skidding on my backside down to the bottom of the heap, how can I apply the brakes? I felt in a pretty desperate situation . . . I walked and thought, walked and thought – and the problem led to a further question: what has been lucky for me in the past? To this there *was* an answer: I'd had great success in Army concert parties, and it was, of course, via a Services' audience at the Stage Door Canteen that I'd had my big break.

And so I asked myself: Why not take a small unit and record a series of shows with the troops? For in those days we did still have troops around the globe, and with the help of the BBC and the War Office (as it then was) I worked out an itinerary that would include Tripoli and Benghazi, Egypt, Jordan, Cyprus and Malta. In the party were singer Marcia Owen, pianist Blanchie Moore, and Eric Sykes to write the scripts. The title of the series: *Frankie Howerd Goes East.*

Hindsight makes me realise the lunatic risk I was taking, for what I had in mind was to go back to the pattern of those wartime Army concert parties – to get servicemen to read scripts for the first time in their lives – and what was all very well for an amateur do at the Shoeburyness YMCA could spell instant disaster for the professionalism of BBC broadcasts (a disaster I could ill afford). But although I've only gambled once in my life with money (more later), I've gambled with my career as though there was no tomorrow (and there were to be times when it would indeed seem that there wasn't one!), so off we set on one of those slow, pre-jet planes, for the blazing heat of Cyprus . . .

There the pattern was established for our subsequent stops. On the first day we looked around and talked around in search of topical situations, and Eric Sykes sweated blood writing the script. On the second day we picked the cast on a typical Army "You . . . you . . . and you" basis. On the third day we recorded. Now these lads were complete and utter amateurs who'd never read a script before in their lives – and while, as I've said, such a style had been great fun for the soldiery of Essex, it was another matter to offer it to the listening millions on BBC. But we'd committed ourselves, and so the tour went its way.

Apart from the recordings we did concerts for the troops in camps and airfields, and on the decks of warships – wherever the lads were to be found. This part of the tour was successful enough – even if I did get a draining attack of dysentery after eating an ice-cream in Port Said. Fortunately I was still basically very fit, and had to miss only one show, but since this was a bit of a disappointment for the RAF boys concerned, I did an impromptu turn in their canteen – standing on a table and, quite literally, with people holding my legs to prevent me from falling over. I hadn't realised dysentery was so enervating, and the hangover of weakness remained with me for the rest of the tour.

That was one personal problem, but what really worried me was the quality of the material in the can.

Of course, the lads were amateurs (although many of them were very good indeed). Of course, the shows were hurriedly put together. Of course, the scripts, written against time, were hardly award winners. And (of course!) the Press were quick to recognise these defects. But the listening public took to the series, combining as it did a version of a "Talent Night" with a sentimental reminder of the lads defending King and Country. And Marcia and I were there to give the series a measure of professional backbone. So on that occasion my gamble paid off, and I was back in favour (with the added satisfaction of having given a worthwhile tour for the Forces).

The next memorable date (to me, if not the viewers!) was January 11th, 1952, when I made my TV début: *The Howerd Crowd with The Beverley Sisters.* The Press, I recall, were generous, but all I remember of Eric Sykes' script was that it contained a sketch poking fun at the trendy TV cooks of the day – some madness involving the making of Tittlepong Tarts and Bees' Knees Puddings in which (needless to say) everything went wrong. I remember, too, that TV make-up was then fairly primitive, so that I also resembled a grey boiled pudding of a gastronomic disaster.

I was certainly nervous about going on TV for the first time, yet not as worried as I might have been – for in those days variety came from "real" theatres, and so the atmosphere was familiar.

Or so it seemed . . .

In truth, my performance was not as good as it might have been, for I didn't have the technique for projecting myself in this new medium. Nor am I making excuses for myself when I refer to the relatively amateur methods of producing and photographing variety shows in those days – a matter of sticking cameras in front of and around the stage and hoping for the best.

It's easy to shudder about it now, of course, but one must take into consideration that I'm talking of nearly a quarter of a century ago when the medium was still in its technological adolescence. And, of course, my nerves were shockingly emphasised by the TV cameras.

So perhaps I wasn't right for TV in those days, or maybe TV wasn't right for me.

One show I did was televised from the People's Palace, an enormous theatre that held about two thousand people. This was a superb theatre when I did *Variety Bandbox* from it. But for TV, not only were the cameras set up yards in front of me – bad enough – but they were so placed that I couldn't see the audience, and they couldn't see me! So there were no intimate camera close-ups for the benefit of the viewers, and I certainly couldn't entertain the invisible audience in the theatre. Believe me, to go on stage with a huge audience sitting out front, and hardly get a titter all night because they couldn't see me, was absolute murder. It was the worst of both worlds, and it was to prove difficult to work out a compromise . . .

The Americans solved the problem very simply: they didn't bother with studio audiences and just dubbed-in the laughter. Shows were scripted to contain "Laugh" at various points, and when they got to the word, performers would stop talking for a few seconds as though pausing while the audience roared its head off, the shrieks having been dubbed in.

I couldn't work that way. Personally I prefer a live audience in the studio. It helps my timing (to use the word loosely) to have a human response to my act – people to whom I can address my asides (to say nothing of my affronts). And I feel that for the viewer the laughter of a studio audience has a tremendously infectious quality if it's not overdone. (Mine seldom is!)

What would the "Last Night" at the Proms be like without the promenaders in the Albert Hall? And without the 90,000 fans at Wembley, the greatest-ever Cup Final could be played – but few viewers would think so. The same is true of the Gillette Cup Final at Lords. The best efforts of the sound-effects department would be patently spurious. *Atmosphere* can be contagious. (So is measles.)

The situation is vastly different now, of course. Modern studios are built with the audience very much in mind: they sit above the cameras and look over them, so they can see the artist without hindrance; while today's cameras allow the performer to establish an intimate contact with the viewers through zoomed-in close-ups.

One of the stories about British TV is that during live shows studio managers appear at the side of the stage bearing signs that say "Applause" or "Clap". In my experience, such signs are an absolute myth. No one has ever announced me with a printed notice demanding "Clap" or "Laugh". There are times I wish they did!

Back to 1952 when Francis was asked to entertain the troops in Korea.

In those days it took five days to get there by the BBC Argonaut – via Malta, Athens, Cairo, Hong Kong and Bangkok. I arrived in Hong Kong with singer Eve Boswell on a Sunday, and found two shows scheduled for Monday – nobody having allowed for travel fatigue. It was a bit cheeky, for journeying like that does take it out of you – especially when (*a*) you've got to appear bright and jolly for the performance, and (*b*) Francis was again smitten with the galloping trots.

Anyway, there's no point in heroics: I did fourteen concerts in the week in Hong Kong, and went on to Korea where the lads were a damned sight more heroic than I could ever be.

We did a number of two-hour shows in the natural amphitheatre of the rocky Korean valleys with the troops on the hillsides around us. The nights were bitterly cold as we curled up in our sleeping-bags close to the front line, our lullaby the sounds of war. But discomfort is relative and life has bitter ironies . . .

I'd played variety at the Swindon Empire that year, and one night I was told that the King's Regiment was moving from the town to go East. Would I say goodbye to them? At eleven o'clock, the Empire show over, I went to their canteen for a chat. Their transport didn't turn up, so I was there jabbering away for three hours! By which time they were delighted to go to Korea! . . . You'll have guessed the point of the story: I ran into the regiment two months later in Korea, talking to them in dug-outs and listening-posts, and, most movingly of all, in the hospitals where lads I recognised from Swindon were now recovering from all manner of ghastly wounds. In view of this it seems impertinent to talk of my own minor discomforts, so let me confine myself to one memory . . .

Rain. . . . Duckboards across the mud. . . . The distant *ker-rump* of artillery. . . . A lorry arrives with the concert party who are tired, filthy – and in my case, terrified! . . . And minutes later, after an instant change in a tent, and with Wellies hidden under a full-length sequined gown, Eve Boswell brings a moment of glamour to a mad and ugly world . . .

So there had been a continued upsurge of good fortune for me in 1952. It continued with a TV show, *Frankie Howerd's Korean Concert Party*, from the Nuffield Centre (a replacement for the old Stage Door Canteen), and the year reached its climax with pantomime at the Palladium: *Dick Whittington*. I played Idle Jack (who else?) with Jerry Desmonde as my feed – the Squire. Also in the cast were Richard (Mr Pastry) Hearn, Sonny Hale and Vanessa Lee (of Ivor Novello musicals fame) as principal boy. It was a Val Parnell production, mounted with a spectacular lavishness that costs would make virtually impossible today, alas.

There's a distinct and logical division in panto audiences: at matinées you get the children, while in the evenings you can sometimes have the house almost entirely made up of adults. So I'd play the matinées in a style deliberately calculated for the kids: I made it far more visual by cutting out some of the jokes and clowning instead. In the evenings, for the adults, the emphasis changed: I'd play it rather tongue in cheek, sending the show up a bit – and since we opened with an evening performance and a typical first-night audience, I played my part this way.

The result? The following morning I had an almost unanimously hostile Press. Everyone in the show was very good – except me. The reason? I was far too sophisticated for children and clearly unsuited to pantomime! Predictably, the reviews played havoc with my morale, for I could hardly telephone all the critics to explain my matinée/evening performance tactics. Then, in the afternoon, the adrenalin pumped again when I read a terrific review in the *Evening Standard*, in which Kenneth Tynan absolutely raved about me. What gave it an added fillip was the fact that Tynan was considered to be *the* tough critic of his day. But me he praised, and his review was almost compensation for the others.

In the event, the pantomime was a great success and ran until Easter.

I've mentioned earlier that my relations with Jack Payne were never all they could have been, and the situation finally boiled over into the High Court in March 1953. Just to remind you of the background, my contract, signed in 1947, said that Jack Payne paid me a small basic, if gradually increasing wage, and then took fifty per cent of my earnings, and that the six-monthly option on contract renewal was essentially one-sided . . . in his favour.

This situation went its unhappy way until 1950 when I was at the Palladium in *Out Of This World*, and received a tip that while I was being paid £600 a week (of which Jack got £300, less my basic salary), he'd made a separate contract with Val Parnell whereby he got an extra £300 for himself. In other words, by my reasoning, my salary was really £900 a week, of which Jack Payne got best part of £600! (These figures may seem high, but even in those days many top stars were earning £4,000 a week.)

Now if this was true, Jack was in breach of contract, and so I demanded to see (as was my right) every contract Jack had signed on my behalf. Sure enough, the deal with Parnell was there – but Jack argued that the £300 was not extra salary, but compensation for "sub-letting" me and so not being able to use me in his own shows.

My advisers didn't see it that way, and early in 1951 told the Jack Payne office that in their opinion Payne had broken his contract with me. It was now null and void, I had no further obligations to them and so I wanted to go my own way. Jack replied that he had not broken the contract, and that I was now breaking it. Impasse – to which there was only one, messy, solution: to take the matter to the High Court and let the Law decide. I hated the thought of legal proceedings, but in my innocence I relied on my advisers. So we sued, Jack counter-sued, and while I was primarily concerned with establishing my legal position, by the time the case opened on March 15th, 1953, I was up to my eyes in "sue-age".

The judge was Mr Justice Hilbery, and my counsel was Gilbert Beyfus, QC – a huge, florid, theatrically larger than life bear of a man. He said to me before the case: "The man's obviously a crook."

I replied that he wasn't. "I don't think it for a second," I assured Beyfus. "He believes in his own mind that what he did was absolutely correct. He may have faults, he may be guilty of misjudgement – but that's all. He's no crook."

"He's a crook," said Beyfus flatly, "and when I get him in that witness-box I'll tear him to shreds."

"But he's not a crook," I protested.

"Whose side are you on?" Beyfus demanded.

So we went to Court – and I loathed every minute of it.

A basic disadvantage from which we suffered was that Mr Justice Hilbery obviously knew Jack Payne. (I was later told that they were golfing chums.) Indeed he referred to him all through as Mr Payne, while I was "Mr . . . er . . . the Plaintiff". I don't think I was honoured with a "Mr Howerd" during the entire proceedings.

When it was our turn, Beyfus said: "Payne was so greedy that when booking Howerd's services by ordinary, formal agreement, he made a secret agreement with the management. He received very large sums for himself. When Howerd became suspicious, Payne tried to conceal these agreements by lies. Payne's share of Howerd's £600 a week at the London Palladium was to be £250–£300. But Payne made a secret agreement giving himself a further £300 . . ."

Strong stuff, but it was at about this point that Hilbery

interrupted to say: "Look, I'm quite convinced that Mr Payne is honest. I do not intend to have his honesty impugned . . ." In this particular case I believed the judge to be absolutely right – but Beyfus was furious.

When it came to Hilbery's summing-up, it seemed to be all in favour of Jack Payne, and I thought: "Hello, we've had it" . . . Then came the words: "Of course, I must take the Plaintiff's point of view into account" and he went on to talk about points of law. It was then that Beyfus tapped my foot with his: the Old Fox knew that we'd won, after all.

I was awarded a total of £5,216 and Jack's counter-claim was dismissed. Outside the Court we went through the formality of shaking hands for the benefit of the Press, and I said (and this was not a formality, but was absolutely sincere): "I'm sorry it had to come to this."

"I'll appeal," Jack replied.

The appeal was heard on October 15th, but by now I was so fed up with the entire, squalid business I told my lawyers to ask for an adjournment and come to some settlement. After all, I'd wanted only to establish that I was legally entitled to claim breach of a contract that had now expired anyway! As for the damages, I didn't particularly want that sort of money.

When Jack was finally convinced that I'd personally never questioned his honesty, only his judgement, he reckoned his honour was saved and agreed to an out-of-court settlement that involved no more than legal costs. So that was that.

We never met or spoke again – Jack could not forgive me for that court action. Later he had financial troubles which he blamed on me – although, for the life of me, I don't see how I could have been responsible, since after our dust-up he went on to earn a lot of money on television. Thinking back, I've often regretted not having got together with him again, just to say "Hello", but I was too embarrassed. A pity . . .

One irony: during the period between suing Jack Payne

and the actual court case, I did a summer season at Brighton which Jack Payne presented. I consulted my solicitors, who said: "On no account must you take any money from him – although you must honour your Brighton contract." So Jack got three months work out of me, free of charge!

Having severed my connection with Jack Payne I'd thrown in my lot with a consortium of scriptwriters working from a small office in Shepherd's Bush: Ray Galton and Alan Simpson and Eric Sykes. Eric was a free-lance by now, and had written the very popular radio series, *Educating Archie*, for Peter Brough, and which really made Tony Hancock and Max Bygraves. The office secretary at the time was the young Beryl Vertue, of whom more later. (This will keep one reader in suspense, for she's bound to have got herself a free copy!)

In 1953 Galton and Simpson wrote a radio series for me, *The Frankie Howerd Show*, which included comedienne Gladys Morgan, singer Joan Regan, Billy Ternent and his Orchestra and various guest stars. It was very well received, as was my TV show in May of that year called (appropriately) *Nuts In May*. Why be modest? The *Daily Express* called it "a triumph". (No, I wasn't their critic at the time!)

And 1953 wasn't over yet: in that year I made my first film, *The Runaway Bus*, with Margaret Rutherford and Petula Clark.

The basic idea was simple enough: a comedy in which I was the driver of a London Airport bus whose passengers included a much-wanted villain. Val Guest thought it up, wrote it (with gaps for my dialogue which I provided myself), and also produced and directed it. Oh yes, Val had plenty of talent – all he lacked was money. There was just a ludicrous £45,000 in the kitty. But Val was no slouch: he overcame this financial absurdity by setting the entire film around the bus being lost in a fog!

In this way he needed virtually no scenery – little more than a mock-up of a bus and a fog machine. I think we spent only half a day on location – even the fields were studio backcloths, their patent phoniness wreathed in fog.

Yet it worked in its daft fashion (although, come to think of it, he could have done it for even less money if he'd set it in a Ford Popular during a power cut).

Then, on the last day of shooting, Val came to me, his eyes misted (or should it be fogged?) with sadness: in those days a film had to run for seventy-five minutes to be a "feature" – i.e. to qualify for a West End showing – and he'd discovered that *The Runaway Bus* ran for only seventy-two.

"So what shall we do?" he asked. "Apart from anything else I've only got the studio for another half-hour."

I thought carefully, and came up with: "Another three minutes of fog."

"Don't be a (censored) fool – and now we've only got another twenty eight and a half minutes."

This time I thought even more carefully, for the situation was really far from funny. "There's a telephone box among the studio props, isn't there?"

Val, suspiciously: "So?"

Frankie, airily: "So if you get the telephone box I'll write a three-minute monologue as though, somewhere in the film, I'm telephoning my old granny. Just give me a pencil and some paper."

Val, incredulous: "But you'll never learn it in time."

Frankie (smugly), "I don't have to. I've read from scripts before, you know. Frankie *has* appeared on radio. Just put the script on a music-stand out of view of the cameras. All the audience will see is me on the phone."

Val had no option: there were only twenty-three minutes left by now!

So I scribbled a script and read it from the music-stand through a window of the telephone booth. "Hello . . . How are you? . . . *Never!* . . . Have you seen the doctor? . . . The dirty old devil! . . ." And so on.

The Runaway Bus did win a West End showing. It opened the following year at the Dominion, Tottenham Court Road, got a good Press, and earned a lot of money. From time to time it still emerges from the fog to be shown on TV.

When I see it I become extremely depressed: not only because I wasn't all that good as an actor, but I look in the mirror and sigh for what the ravages of time have done for my youth and beauty!

As I've said, my co-star in the film was Margaret Rutherford: a wonderful person, and I adored her. Among other things, she did an enormous amount of social work, which the public knew little about – such as her interest in the rehabilitation of boys from approved schools, frequently taking them out and about, to help give them some positive interest and purpose in life.

The great paradox about Margaret Rutherford was that while she was an incomparable comic actress, many of those who knew her said that she had absolutely no sense of humour. None! And I must confess that I found myself agreeing with them.

Her great, unfulfilled, ambition had been to be able to play Shakespeare's Cleopatra – her favourite theatrical role – but she ended up a superb performer of comedy roles. Not a comedienne, because she never deliberately played for laughs, but as a serious actress interpreting and portraying eccentricities of character. For if she had no sense of humour, she did have a great sense of audience – she knew how to project a role.

Fame came to her via the London stage in 1941 as the dotty medium, Madame Acarti, in Noël Coward's *Blithe Spirit*, a role she repeated on film and in which there was never anyone to touch her. She told me how she'd chosen her wardrobe for the part, but Noël Coward didn't like it – he insisted on clothes that were more bizarre. She said that after that she lost all interest in the role because it turned her into a caricature. . . . Yet it was Madame Acarti that made her name!

She was never really aware of her popularity, especially in comedy, and would have been much happier doing poetry readings. She yearned for dramatic parts in films and plays, and this deep and bitter sense of frustration must have been responsible, in part at least, for the mental illness that burdened her life, manifesting itself in quite appalling bouts of depression. It was a psychiatric problem she suffered for most of her adult years. It was very sad.

I did a number of charity shows for the Forces at the Nuffield Centre, inviting other artists to help me, and I once asked Margaret to come.

"Oh no," she replied, "I couldn't. For one thing these youngsters wouldn't want me there; an old woman like me." She was quite sincere.

"You're absolutely wrong," I said. "They'll adore you."

"But I wouldn't know what to do."

"All you have to do is go on and introduce the acts. Just to see you will give them a great thrill."

Doubtfully: "I don't see it, but if you say so . . ."

She came to the Nuffield Centre as compère. There was no script, so she did it in her own way: seriously, flowery, full of long and poetic words – and the audience shrieked. Margaret was being absolutely serious, but the audience thought it absolutely marvellous. What an ovation they gave her! She came off, moved almost to tears.

"I . . . I had no idea," she gulped, "that they'd be interested in me. That they'd even know me. Such dear, dear boys . . ." She just didn't realise the impact her films had made on mass audiences. We were to make many appearances together and she was a joy to work with.

Years later she had the added disability of an arthritic hip, and did no work for a long, long time. Then a television producer offered her the part of Miss Havisham in a BBC serial of *Great Expectations*: a role she could have played entirely seated.

"No, I'll never be able to work again," she said morosely, but those of us close to Margaret assured her that this was nonsense: here was a part ideally suited to her physical predicament.

Finally she agreed to do it, but after she'd studied the script she broke down and sobbed: "I can't remember the lines."

She never performed again.

She died after a series of strokes in May 1972, when in her eighties. I went to see her – a pathetic and shrunken figure tucked in a bed in a small ward, her devoted husband, Stringer Davis, sitting by her side as she lay like a curled-up baby. Her eyes seemed to show that she recognised me, but she was past speech, so Stringer and I sat and held her hands and talked while she listened.

Now so-called "fame" is all very nice, but there are people who expect me to be on stage all the time, and recognition can have its drawbacks, especially for a supposed comic. It happened when I was sitting there by Margaret Rutherford's death bed. . . . Suddenly a hospital sister rushed in, gushed over me, brought in kitchen staff and nurses to meet me, then said: "The ladies in the next ward know you're here, so they've dolled themselves up and *can't wait* to meet you. And there are others in the recreation room, so do please hurry."

All I wanted to do was sit quietly holding Margaret Rutherford's hand – but I was dragged off to make personal appearances all over the hospital.

There are times when stardom has its difficulties.

EIGHT Frankie Howerd, Ac-tor

Back to 1953, which still wasn't over from a professional point of view: in September I opened at the Prince of Wales with Winifred Atwell in the spectacular Bernard Delfont revue, *Pardon My French*. (My "feeds" were Sunny Rogers and Lee Young.) The first night was an ordeal – not only because it *was* a first night with its inbuilt nervous tension, nor because of the fact that being a Folies Bergère-style show the stage was littered with topless showgirls: I'd got accustomed to them during rehearsals (more or less!).

What really devastated me was that just before the opening I agreed with some bright spark's suggestion that I should make my entrance by parachute! Had this been attempted at rehearsals I'd have soon chickened out, for as I've said, even mounting the bathroom scales gives me the vapours – yet here I was, conned into climbing to the flies at the top of the theatre like some demented trapeze artist. . . . And I sat there for at least five terrifying minutes before being lowered on wires to the stage. I didn't even descend gracefully: I swung from side to side like a petrified spider, with the supporting harness about to give me a sex change I was far from wanting. I was not only in agony when I landed, but reeled around completely dizzy – which the audience thought marvellously funny. One up for the bright spark who conceived the idea – except that after the show I told the management that I was doing a revue, not

Peter Pan, and that in future I was going to walk on like an accident-prone mortal.

The show itself was a winner. It ran for over a year and there was never an empty seat in the house.

Despite a popular misconception that I started my career at the old Windmill Theatre, this was my first experience at working with nudes, and for some numbers they lined the back of the stage while I did my stuff in front of them. They provided me with many tittersome moments.

For instance, in those days there was none of your *Oh Calcutta!* larking about – nudes, far from moving, had to stand statue-still. This included their mouths, so they developed an almost professionally ventriloquial technique for making comments about certain members of the audience – for the very presence of these ladies, no matter how classically statuesque, attracted a few of the dirty mac trade. So I'd hear their frozen-lipped asides: "Get that one there! Him in the third row, second from the right". . . . Not spoken in any sense of outrage, but gently mocking the situation. (I would hasten to add that these private pleasure-seekers didn't make up the bulk of the audience: Winifred Atwell and I were hardly shabby mac bait, gorgeous though we were!)

Then there was the show on New Year's Eve when, by tradition, the stars linked hands with the audience in the front row and sang Old Lang Syne. Suddenly the audience's good humour erupted into wild laughter. I didn't understand what was happening, but it transpired that the nudes at the back of the stage who weren't supposed to move even their lips, had had a few seasonal gins – so they'd also linked hands, and their breasts were thumping up and down to the music! OK, so it's tame stuff compared with today – but in 1953 it could have had us all arrested.

Pardon My French was my first show for Bernard Delfont. He has as much authority and knowledge of the theatre as Val Parnell ever had, but was diametrically opposite in personality: Parnell the tough, square-jawed, no-nonsense Sergeant Major; Delfont the polite, quiet, self-effacing diplomat – but no softie for all that, take my word on it!

While at the Prince of Wales I had trouble with a stiff neck, and a masseur came to visit me at the theatre. He told me he had a friend who was anxious to get into show-business as a scriptwriter, and could he bring him along to meet me? When he added that the friend worked in an insurance office, he had my instant sympathy. "Bring him along," I said. And that's how I met Johnny Speight and bought from him (for no great sum, as Johnny will be quick to tell you) the first gag he ever sold professionally. I still remember it: "I'm livid – they're pulling down my house to build a slum!"

I did another Royal Variety Show that year: a potted musical sketch with Jack Buchanan and Joan Sims, called "The Shopgirl Princess".

So 1953 had been tremendous for me, but to demonstrate how much I am a yo-yo jerked by a manic hand at the end of the umbilical cord of Fate . . .

March 1954. Sunday night was *the* big night on TV. And an enormous attraction was *What's My Line?* starring Isobel Barnett, Barbara Kelly, David Nixon and Gilbert Harding, with Eamonn Andrews in the chair. It was top-ten popular, particularly with such gimmicks as Kelly's huge ear-rings and Harding's booze-encouraged outbursts. But one Sunday Gillie couldn't appear, and I was invited to replace him. The programme had such an audience that it was an enormous honour to be asked – so I went. The publicity I received by replacing Harding was extra-ordinary – but read on . . .

I was absolutely appalling in the show!

The point of the programme was that the panel asked questions in order to identify a person's profession – but I sat there, lunatic with fear, frozen like a rabbit caught in the headlights of a car, my mind an utter blank, incapable of asking even the time of day. Barbara Kelly sat next to me, and felt so sorry for me that she passed me bits of paper on which she'd scribbled questions for me to ask. I was so paralysed I couldn't even read them!

I was a spectacular flop, so much so that the telephone lines to the BBC were jammed with complaints. The Press was scathing – and rightly so.

Some time later there was a charity show which Noël Coward organised at the Palladium for the Actors' Orphanage: "Night of a Thousand Stars". The cast included Laurence Olivier, Danny Kaye, Burt Lancaster, Kirk Douglas, Margaret Rutherford and me. We did a sketch as two women aboard a cross-Channel steamer, and Margaret had something to say about getting away from all the things that were wrong with England. To which I replied: "Yes, including *What's My Line?*" – and it brought the house down. It just shows the enormity of my failure.

Indeed, a full year later at Bournemouth a friend of mine heard some gentleman mention my name and add: "I'll never forgive his disgraceful conduct." As my friend strained his ears for some juicy tit-bit of gossip, the man went on: "The exhibition he made of himself on *What's My Line?*" (Cries of "Hear, hear".) It was generally agreed that I'd let down the entire nation: compared with Frankie Howerd – Fuchs, Philby, Pontecorvo, Blake, Burgess and Maclean were incidental and fleeting trivialities.

So what had gone wrong? Answer: I may have been a bit of an expert by now at reading, rehearsing and memorising scripts, I may have been able to write a few comic lines, but when it came to spontaneous, ad-libbing chat, I just hadn't got it. Instead, I went to pieces with nerves. My stammering, stumbling impediment came back – and I was lost.

There are great ad-lib comics. Tommy Trinder is probably the finest in my experience, closely followed by Ted Ray and Arthur Askey. Veterans all – but still the sort of people who are marvellously funny on today's chat shows. In my own defence, I remember talking to Pete Murray of radio's *Open House*, and he told me how the most unlikely people get tied up with nerves on the programme – particularly actors and actresses who are superb at playing parts, but became quite tongue-tied when appearing in public as *themselves*. As for me, I *can* converse, but only at my own pace. I talk on and on to obtain an approximation of what I mean. As for being an ad-lib wit. . . . Never!

What doesn't help matters is that I'm a very good listener. . . . Well, I used to be! When people came to interview me I was often so fascinated with *their* jobs I'd interview them! So much so that they'd end up telling me all their troubles, as though I was some Father Confessor. You'd be amazed at the number of journalists I could expose, had I the mind to (which I haven't).

So despite the effect of spontaneity that I strove for in my patter act, actual spontaneity was quite another matter. And just as there were those things I certainly couldn't do, so as a corollary there were those things that nerves and lack of confidence told me I didn't dare attempt – yet I was to find that I had to. West End cabaret, for instance. I felt that this sort of posh entertainment was far too sophisticated and intimate for a Music Hall comic like me. I reckoned that it needed a specialist artist – someone (in those days) like Beatrice Lillie, Jack Buchanan, Hutch or Marlene Dietrich. Which is not to say that these people couldn't appear on a larger stage: it meant only that I thought that I couldn't appear on a small one in front of a highly blasé audience.

A propos Marlene Dietrich, one vivid memory . . .

When I was at the Prince of Wales she was appearing across the road at the Café de Paris in just the sort of cabaret I've been talking about. Now I was also doing a radio series at this time and one of the banes of my life was the song plugger. Francis bothered by song pluggers? Yes, indeed, for I'd end the show with a vocal burlesque – and the song pluggers nagged at me to do a send-up of one of *their* songs; they said that even a cod version had enormous publicity value: my "singing' it on a successful radio show may not have had the same effect as Tommy Steele putting it over at the Palladium, but it apparently didn't do the number any harm.

One of the song pluggers was Norman Newell who also produced records for Philips, and it was in this latter capacity that he was to do an album of Marlene Dietrich live at the Café de Paris.

When I told Norman that I'd like to meet her, he said: "Why don't you come to the opening night? Pop across when you've finished at the Prince of Wales. Then I'll take you back-stage."

It was a memorable show, and an indication of her professionalism is that she'd spent *three hours* just supervising the lighting. Anyway, when her act was over I went back-stage with Norman, and Marlene – gorgeous and glamorous – said: "Why don't you come to the Dorchester later for a drink?"

I got there, as arranged, at two a.m. The hotel itself overwhelmed me, for I'd never been a Dorchester sort of person, but I made my way to the luxury Oliver Messel suite where Marlene was stretched out in a negligee on a chaise-longue. I stayed for three hours, but those of you with dirty minds will kindly leave the page, for we just talked. . . . Let's be accurate: *she* talked for three hours – entirely about herself! I got in one sentence somewhere during her marathon monologue – then on she went again: witty, amusing, anecdotal, but utterly self-orientated.

I wish I could remember that sentence of mine. It must have been uncharacteristically profound – or was about her! – for the pay-off came the next day when she said to Norman Newell: "That Frankie Howerd – what an intelligent man!"

However . . .

It follows from what I've said so far that I wasn't the world's most natural or enthusiastic public speaker. My first stab at it came when I was at the Prince of Wales and Winifred Atwell and I were guests of honour at a Variety Club lunch. Winifred had raised money for one of the Club's charities by the brave gesture of playing the piano in a lion's cage – with the lion present. For this (and thank God she picked a honky-tonk-loving lion!) she received a Variety Club award, and my task was to reply to the toast "The Guests".

It was disastrous! For I made what I fondly imagined to be an "in depth" speech about show-business. I did mention that I was glad that the award to Winifred wasn't posthumous – and that was as near as I got to being funny. The rest was deep and intellectual (or was meant to be). There was polite applause, then the elderly Jewish comedian, Harry Green, came up to me and said: "Can I give you some advice?"

"Of course."

"Never do that sort of thing again?"

"W-what do you mean?" I asked.

"I've never heard such crap in all my life," Harry replied. "You were asked here to be funny. So as I say: never do that sort of thing again."

I never did . . .

It may sound daft to say that I was overawed by the Dorchester when I went to see Marlene Dietrich, but it's true. I was supposed to be a "name", yet I was still basically a simple soul from Eltham. Perhaps that's why I found it fairly easy to play "Simple Simon" in pantomime.

Sometimes, of course, I'd have to go to big West End restaurants for a meal, but I was (and am) essentially a steak-and-kidney pie man. This wasn't only because I was too ignorant to read a menu: I always have preferred that sort of food.

My life style was comfortable, and I think unostentatious, but even though I liked being at home when I wasn't working, I was far from being a recluse. For instance, although I still didn't drink very much myself (a sherry, or Pimms or a lager suited me well enough), I threw parties for friends and family and other people in the business. (I have a vivid memory of Richard Burton's passion for nuts – the edible variety. He'd sit on the floor of my flat surrounded by what appeared to be mountains of empty shells. My mother sometimes came to these parties, and Richard was very fond of her. Years later, when he was playing Hamlet on Broadway, a friend of mine went to see him and Richard's first question was: "How's Frank's mother?")

Relaxation? Well I was, believe it or not, a fair tennis player. (If I add Wimbledon class, think of Wimbledon Common.) I've always read a lot, particularly historical biography and books about the theatre, and am passionately fond of music. In those days I'd sit for hours playing records: anything from Fats Waller to popular classics. I also walked a great deal, and now had a boxer dog, Red, to keep me company. These walks around the streets and park were sometimes for exercise, sometimes to work out ideas, sometimes to rehearse scripts – for I find it very difficult to learn words while sitting down. Even at home or in a studio I have to pace up and down to do my memorising.

I was (and am) useless around the house. I'm far too maladroit to be trusted with a hammer or screwdriver. As for cooking, I'm a dab hand at instant coffee (although when I make one cup I have to prepare enough for two in order to allow for spillage). I suppose that I could cook an egg – but I'm not sure that I'd eat it!

I don't say this with any pride: I've long felt that all children, male and female, should be taught the basics of cooking in order to be able to tend for themselves in some primitive fashion. But since my mother wouldn't trust me with even a box of matches (and who's to blame her in terms of my clumsiness?), to this day even lighting the gas remains an adventure sufficiently fraught for me to have had the house converted to electricity.

In terms of holidays, it must be remembered that at the time of which I'm writing there were strict controls on the amount of currency one was allowed to take out of the country. There was a period when the limit was £25, and it was during this patch of austerity that I went in search of some sunshine in the South of France with a girl friend. Also with me were my sister Betty and a friend.

We went to Juan les Pins for a week, and somehow survived on our £25 allowances – until the night we went to the casino to see Josephine Baker in cabaret. A marvellous experience – and so was the bill: £11 for four gin and tonics. Gasps all round, but we divvied up – and found we had just £1 left between us: not even enough to get us all to Nice Airport.

We tottered out into the night air (which now had a distinct chill about it) and Betty asked: "What on earth will we do?"

For some reason I've never been able to explain, I suddenly acquired a calm confidence, took from my pocket the francs that represented the remaining pound, said: "Wait here" – and returned to the casino. This time I went to the gambling rooms, showed my passport to procure an entrance card, got chips, walked to the nearest roulette table and plonked down the money on some combination of numbers.

I won precisely £11 on that spin of the wheel, cashed the chips and walked out!

I know this is the sort of incident which, in a novel or TV script, would cause people to shake their heads and say: "That's stretching it a bit," but it's absolutely true.

I remember walking to the foyer, where the others were waiting with faces registering various degrees of horror. . . . I showed them the money. . . . And then I uttered a dreadful scream as the shock of realisation of what I'd done came to me.

I'd never gambled in my life before – yet some mad impulse, almost a psychic possession, had taken hold of me and had led me, trance-like, to perform that utterly uncharacteristic action.

As I say, I'd never gambled before. . . . So make what you will of it. (One thing is certain: this flash in the roulette wheel didn't inspire me to go on to become another Man Who Broke The Bank at Monte Carlo.)

Anyway, 1954 ended with me touring with a version of *Pardon My French*, and Christmas saw us at Nottingham. For one entrance I came down a flight of stairs and walked along a catwalk made up of boxes placed close together – only on one night my foot slipped between two of the boxes and I came a cropper. The audience thought it a hoot. I didn't: I'd broken my ankle and went through the rest of the tour in plaster.

On December 27th, I did a somewhat different sort of show for BBC-TV: with Eleanor Summerfield and Jack Melford I appeared in the old Tom Walls–Ralph Lynn farce *Tons of Money*. It was an experiment on my part and the first public demonstration of stirrings of restlessness: the feeling that had slowly grown over the months that I needed to diversify my talents.

For I'd gradually become aware that although there were still West End revues like *Pardon My French*, their number was not only of necessity limited, but they were facing the growing challenge of the American musical spectacular. The provincial Music Hall was in a state of accelerating decline; my sort of radio show was being replaced by new names and styles (e.g. by comedians like Tony Hancock and The Goons); while the sensations of television were less and less the comics and more and more the pop stars (e.g. Tommy Steele, Cliff Richard and Adam Faith). Certainly I still got TV dates, but I hadn't really mastered how to put myself over – as was demonstrated in June 1955, when I did another *Howerd Crowd* for the BBC which brought no great accolades. (Come to think of it, I hadn't really done all that much TV during my career, partly because there weren't all that many variety shows or revues *to* do.)

But all this was now academic: as I saw it, my sort of patter act was now dated irrespective of the medium for its expression, and there had to be a *different*, more modern, Frankie Howerd. It wasn't a matter of scripts, but direction.

There were, of course, people like Betty with whom I could discuss and argue the situation, but in the end, for good or bad, a man must "dree his own weird" as the Scots put it – must follow his own destiny.

So I gambled on a change of course and turned to comedy acting: to have a go at funny parts in plays instead of patter. Which explains *Tons of Money*. Promisingly enough, it was followed by the enormous success of *Charley's Aunt* which opened in December 1955.

First, however, I made another film, *Jumping For Joy*. This was shot in eight weeks at the White City – a comedy about dog racing and dog doping. It didn't do too badly: but it was no blockbuster.

Charley's Aunt. . . . The H. M. Tennent Organisation put on this stand-by classic at the Globe, with Gerald (Hadleigh) Harper, Richard Waring (now a brilliant writer for TV), and me as Lord Fancourt Balberley. Since there is such a dreadful down period to come, why shouldn't I be big-headed about *Charley's Aunt*? Said the *Observer*: "An historic stroke of miscasting has produced a performance which could (and should) run for several years." Allow me that bit of glory, for *Charley's Aunt* was indeed surprisingly successful.

The only problem was that Richard Waring, a fine actor, had one awful weakness: there were times on stage when he found me so funny (the splendid fellow!) he couldn't stop laughing. I well remember Boxing Night when the theatre was so crowded that even my sister Betty had to sit on a beer crate at the back of the stalls. . . . And was most embarrassed. Not by her splinter-spiked perch: she was too much of an old trouper for that. What threw her was that at the beginning of the show, when I made my first entrance, Waring started to laugh – and from then on, every time I looked at him, he howled. He was unable to control it: his hysterical laughter just exploded.

All very flattering, but most off-putting – and as I've said earlier, laughter is contagious. It spread throughout the theatre, and then back to the stage. . . . I joined in, as did the rest of the cast, and the performance became a complete shambles. Irrespective of lines or acting, everyone was caught in a madness of wild laughter. We just screamed throughout the play – until the last act which we performed back-to-back because nobody dared look at anyone else. It must have been one of the craziest theatrical occasions on record.

When it was over, Betty came back-stage – furious. "How dare you!" she cried. "It was shameful. Utterly unprofessional. How can you treat an audience like that? People who paid good money to see a play?" She was right, of course, as was Billy Chappell, the director, who summoned the entire cast the next day for an eleven a.m. lecture and described our behaviour as "One of the worst exhibitions in the theatre that I've ever seen." But the infection of Richard Waring's cackling laughter was absolutely impossible to inoculate against.

After London, *Charley's Aunt* went on tour, and Waring was agony to play with. I don't know what it was about me that so tickled him, but there were those nights when some nerve-end was agitated, and he'd curl up with mirth. . . . He'd have been a godsend in the audience, but was absolute murder on stage.

To this day there are times when I'm rehearsing, a manic cackle suddenly echoes round the BBC studio – and I know that Richard Waring has wandered in. The hyena still haunts me!

In June 1956 I took a concert party to Cyprus to entertain the troops who were fighting the EOKA terrorists. It was a claustrophobic trip, since we were heavily guarded all the time because of possible booby-traps and gunmen. There was no clear, recognisable distinction between "good" or "bad", of "them" and "us" – *anyone* could be a terrorist, and the most innocent-seeming circumstance could conceal danger. Apart from personal trepidations, they were hardly the most relaxed conditions in which to give concert parties. But the lads seemed to like the shows, and we went on to visit the troops in Jordan.

I came back to do my first ITV show, *Sunday Night At The London Palladium*, but, despite this, I was still convinced that my principal outlets as a comedian – Music Hall and radio – held little future for me: the one dying, the other changing its comic direction. And the success of *Charley's Aunt* seemed to confirm that my destiny now lay in comedy acting. People were later to accuse me of having a Hamlet complex, but this is quite untrue: my ambition was aimed exclusively at becoming established as a *comic* actor.

It seemed realistic at the time although, looking back, the decision contained an element of the self-destructiveness that so many artists have – a condition that is a natural result of the doubts and uncertainties of a profession based upon insecurity.

Perhaps Tony Hancock was a classic example of this self-destructiveness. He also tried to alter direction and, like me, jettisoned the ingredients that had made him so successful: including his writers, format and producer. In my case, however, my judgement may have been outrageously stupid, but at least I was lucky enough to survive, and in the long term I believe I benefited from the experience. Tony, however, disintegrated, the burden of mental instability adding to the pressures of failure. He had many personal, as well as professional, problems (drink among them), frittered away the components of his genius, and committed suicide . . .

Yet it must be said that not only did everyone who worked for him find him to be kind and generous, but they would surely agree that he achieved more during those years when he was at his best than the rest of us achieve in our entire lifetimes.

(Shortly after his death I was interviewed on television and asked: "Have you ever contemplated suicide?" I was so furious at this patent exploitation of his going that I looked the gentleman straight in the eye and replied coldly: "Suicide, no. Murder, yes!" . . . The interview came to an abrupt close!)

Anyway . . .

So I gambled on trying to be a comic actor. Since the West End had nothing to offer at the time, I accepted an offer to appear in a production of *Tons of Money* at the New Theatre, Bromley. Oddly, it was a play I'd done with the Shooter's Hill Old Boys Dramatic Society. The play itself was about a man married to a dizzy wife who inherits a fortune – but can't claim it because a relative pops up saying he is the rightful heir. He adopts all manner of disguises, including that of a vicar – as does the rightful claimant. . . . Then the real vicar turns up. That sort of thing.

The leading lady was a brilliant newcomer, Sheila Hancock, and the play itself was quite a success during its limited run.

So I was encouraged to think that my decision had been the right one, especially when the next offer that came along, in August, was to go back to Juan les Pins to make another film: *A Touch of the Sun*. In it I played a porter who takes over a Riviera hotel and gets involved with con men. . . . The cast was certainly distinguished, including Dennis Price and Bill Fraser, Alfie Bass and I. Though I thought it a better film than *Jumping For Joy* (my own screen technique seemed to have improved), it didn't do as well when it came to the cinemas.

I took my own production of *Tons of Money* to Nottingham for Christmas (the theatre closed the following year, but I don't think there was a direct connection). One night I did something that was absolute heresy in the theatre at that time. It was sheer impulse – I suddenly turned to the audience, pulled a funny face, jerked a thumb in the direction of Sheila Hancock and said: "Oooh, she's a right cow!" The audience roared with laughter, although there was consternation on Sheila's part, as she didn't know it was coming. But she coped very well, considering. Since the audience liked it I went on to elaborate the technique of "coming out" of the play and addressing remarks to the audience until it included the entire cast, and then the very play itself. The point came when I almost disregarded the play (and my character) and used it as a vehicle for Mr Howerd.

It began as a spontaneous fun thing – although I didn't realise it at the time – and was indeed to feel guilty about my behaviour – I can now see that I was something of a pioneer. Not that talking to the audience was an innovation in itself: what else are Shakespeare's soliloquies? But I did it in a comic, Music Hall style, as Eric Sykes and Jimmy Edwards were later to do in *Big Bad Mouse*, and Spike Milligan did in *Son of Oblomov*. (And Joan Littlewood's *A Taste of Honey* had the cast talking only to the audience.) So I started something in my own quiet way.

Yet it was a style I never really developed as an integral part of a show until *Up Pompeii!* The reason? Well, in other people's productions one has to exercise self-discipline: you're one of a team, you have to take direction, you're there to play a character and stick to the words – and try to look interested even when you're not talking!

Anyway, when the run of *Tons of Money* came to an end Bernard Delfont asked me to go back to the Prince of Wales for a new revue, *Plaisirs de Paris*. I countered by asking Mr Delfont to put on *Tons of Money* in the West End. He replied that he'd seen the production when it was at Bromley and although he'd liked it he thought I'd be better off in his new revue – "so come to the Prince of Wales".

To top the bill again in a West End revue was enormously tempting – but my recent successes encouraged me to believe that my destiny was now as a comic actor . . . Yet Delfont's offer did have its attractions . . .

So what to do? In the end I compromised: I said that I would make a short Music Hall tour that included the acts and sketches that had been written for me in the show, and see how they went. The tour was a success, partly (or maybe mainly) because my co-star was Sabrina, whose assets were outstandingly helpful to any production (see picture!). Mind you, she did have a great sense of humour about her superbly improbable statistics, and although I liked *her* very much, I wasn't all that mad about the *Plaisirs de Paris* material.

Those of you who have voluntarily made major and fundamental changes in your own lives will understand the doubts and misgivings that now assailed me: the long days and sleepless nights of self-examination, with the pendulum of decision swinging to and fro as I argued and debated, speculated and rationalised – until my turmoil finally exhausted itself into resolve: I would turn down the Prince of Wales and continue as a comic actor.

It proved to be the worst error of judgement I was to make in my entire professional life – and that's saying something!

NINE "The Tit and Bum Show"

I went to Bernard Delfont and told him of my decision. He was very understanding, although he made no bones about the fact that he thought I was daft. But from his point of view the important thing now was to find a replacement for me. Not that I'd played him a dirty (or unprofessional) trick by walking out at the last moment: there was plenty of time for him to find someone else, and there was no problem of learning pages of dialogue as in a play – my contribution to the show consisted of a number of self-contained spots, which another comic could easily fill. Nor was there any shortage of artists wanting, and able, to top the bill at the Prince of Wales! Delfont plumped for Dickie Henderson, and the show was a great success when it opened in April 1957.

In the meantime we had to tell the Press what was happening, since advance publicity had linked my name with the show – and they knew that I'd toured with my material from it. I didn't want to give the impression that I'd flounced out in a fit of temperamental pique, nor could I baldly say: "I simply don't want to do it," and so give the impression that I was critical of the production. Yet to make a speech on my decision to become a comedy actor might have appeared sickeningly pretentious.

There was another, truthful, alternative: that I was in a state of nervous exhaustion.

For by now the strain of the painful months of indecision and uncertainty had indeed taken its toll, leaving me physically and mentally drained. My vacillating self-debate had been so intense (characteristically!) that I now found myself experiencing a reaction of terrible tiredness that manifested itself in self-pitying gloom. The decision made, I began to worry about its wisdom. I was very troubled . . .

Yes, I certainly needed a rest (although when some newspapers wrote of "nervous breakdown" they were stretching it somewhat). I went to the country for a few weeks of splendid sleep and inactivity, and returned to London in a much more positive state of mind.

The next step in my career as a comic actor was to tour *Hotel Paradiso*, the French bedroom farce which had starred Alec Guinness in the West End. After Guinness, the public must have thought me pretty flat beer – and were probably right! We didn't do brilliant business. Part of the problem was that the shrinking audiences who were still interested in me expected the "Ladies and Gentle-*men*" Frankie Howerd, and didn't altogether take to me as a would-be comic actor. But I battered on – determined to persevere with this new image.

During the tour we played Bristol, and one of the girls in the cast, Wendy Williams, introduced me to a boy friend of hers who was watching the show from the wings, and who was with the Bristol Old Vic: a tall, thin lad named Peter O'Toole. He asked me to go and see him in Peter Ustinov's *The Empty Chair*, which I did, and although his technique was raw he was riveting to watch as a personality. After the show I told him that his performance had been a bit rough round the edges – but assured him that one day he'd make it big. (And was Francis the Forecaster wrong? Yes! I said it would take him six years. . . . It took two!)

In those days his salary was small (and he roistered away most of it), so I took him out to dinner a couple of times. He was certainly grateful (and should have been – he ate like a horse!), but a couple of years later we were to dine in somewhat different circumstances . . .

The truly way-out thing that happened during the tour of *Hotel Paradiso* was a call from someone at the Old Vic in London. The conversation went like this:

"Frankie Howerd?"

"Yes."

"I hear you want to do comic parts in plays."

"Yes."

"Well, we're putting on The Tit and Bum Show. Interested?"

"I *beg* your pardon?!"

A weary sigh. "*A Midsummer Night's Dream*. You know – the one with Titania and Bottom in it. So we call it The Tit and Bum Show." Anxiously: "You do know the play?"

Now what *did* I know about *A Midsummer Night's Dream*? Answer: nothing, except for a vague recall of the hilarious scene at the end – the play within a play – which I remembered the kids putting on at Shooter's Hill Grammar School. I hadn't been in it, but I retained the memory of hooting with laughter when I saw it . . .

Now while there are times when I dither, there are times when I am impulsive; and on the strength of that 1936 memory I took one of my gambles:

"Do I know The Tit and Bum Show? Do I *know* it? Of *course* I know it: intimately! Indeed, there are times when I talk of little else. And I'd be delighted to help out the Old Vic if they feel my presence would give them a boost."

A dry: "Good."

"Er . . . Is there any need to ask the part I'll play?"

"None at all."

"I thought not. . . . But I hate to think of the bad jokes that are going to bounce around."

"Instead of Bottom, would you rather play Oberon, King of the Fairies?"

"No thank you."

"Good day."

"Goodbye."

I put down the telephone, and the enormity of my decision winded me as though I'd been thumped. I thought:

Above: With Sunny Rogers – a sketch in *Pardon My French* at the Prince of Wales.

Below: Yes, it's Frankie – as Little Millie Ponders in *Night of 100 Stars*.

Above: Me as Bottom – with Moira Shearer I meet the Queen after a Gala Night at the Old Vic.

Below: With Sabrina – her assets were quite outstanding!

Above: In *Charley's Aunt* with (*left to right*) Joy Rodgers, Jane Brown and Wendy Williams.

Below: Some of the laughter in *Charley's Aunt* didn't amuse the producer.

I meet local children during
my first Forces tour in
Cyprus.

Above: At the time of my down period – a picture taken during that painful Press interview.

Below: What's My Line wasn't my line at all! With me are Isobel Barnett, Muriel Young and Stephen Potter.

1957 – With my mother and sister, Betty, at a wedding reception.

Above: A Funny Thing . . . With me in this scene are Robertson Hare & Kenneth Connor.

Below left: Again in *A Funny Thing* . . . After the dark years I was back in a West End theatre.

Below right: Panto at Southsea with Joy Beattie . . . It could have been my last show ever.

Above: In Borneo. With me is Shirley Abicair, "*White goddess*".

Below: Also in Borneo – I often had to make myself heard as best I could!

"I must be stark, raving mad. Me – playing Shakespeare!" Then: "But I suppose the Old Vic know what they're up to . . . *Or do they?*" A further thought: "There was no mention of money" – and I nearly had a heart-attack when I learned the salary was £30 a week (including matinées).

But the die was cast, as we Shakespearians say.* The Press were told, and there were indeed the predictable jokes, such as: "For Howerd to attempt to go straight by playing Bottom is the end." And one opening night telegram said: "Here's to a warm hand on your opening." On another tack the *Daily Sketch* said: "It is news calculated to fill earnest lovers of Shakespeare with a profound sense of doom."

Charming!

Mind you, there *was* a surface madness in the Old Vic asking me – and in me agreeing to do it. First, I had trouble discovering what the play was all about. Shakespeare may have been a great scriptwriter, but he *was* a bit stylised, wasn't he? He didn't exactly have yours truly in mind for Bottom, did he? Not one "Ooh" or "Aah". Further: I have problems learning lines at the best of times, but to have to memorise Ye Olde Englishe was sheer murder. It was a foreign language to me. Yet rehearsals were scheduled to last only six weeks. There were many times when I kicked myself for my impulsive acceptance of the role.

The rehearsals began towards the end of 1957 under the direction of Michael Bentall, with a distinguished cast that included Joyce Redman, Paul Daneman, Ronnie Fraser, Edward Hardwicke, an unknown Nancy Kwan, and the very well known Coral Browne. (She played Hermia, which I found impossible not to pronounce Hernia.)

At the beginning of rehearsals I was incredibly shy at having to mix with distinguished Shakespearian performers. Not only because they were classical actors and actresses, but I hadn't lost my youthful capacity for wide-eyed

* What? It's attributed to Julius Caesar? Between you and me it's well known in the profession that he stole most of his material from Shakespeare.

fascination at the sight of other stars. I'd still hang around the fronts of theatres on opening nights, or cinemas at gala premières, and watch the stars go in.

I remember my first meeting with Noël Coward at some Café de Paris opening night. He rushed up, and with a great "Dear boy!" kissed me on the cheek. It was an integral part of his natural flamboyance, but I was terribly embarrassed. And I was frightened by his wit, which immediately transformed me back into a gauche and shuffling schoolboy. Then again, you will recall that everyone called him Master – only I never could. Since I didn't consider Mr Coward right (and I'd never have dared call him Noël), I avoided direct address. Guv'nor or Boss would have been all right, but not Master. Why not? It was the imprint on my subconscious of my early religious training. There was only one Master: Jesus Christ. And much as I admired Noël Coward I wasn't going to raise him to that level . . .

Back to the Old Vic. As I say, I was twitchy when I went to the first rehearsal, with no idea of the reception I'd get from these distinguished Shakespearians, but my fears proved to be utterly groundless. Everyone was charming, unassuming and sendy-uppy to the point of irreverence. A period costume, for instance, was always referred to by the men as a frock: "I like your frock, dear" – not said in today's "gay" sense, but as a send-up. It was almost a Music Hall approach, and I'm reminded of something Vincent Price once told me: "You can make a horror film only if you're absolutely frivolous about it between the scenes and send yourself up – just as you can't live in a state of morbidity off stage because you're playing King Lear. If it's said that comedy is a serious business, so – off stage – tragedy can be wildly hilarious." (Mind you, even *on* stage, both tragedy and comedy can provide unintendedly hilarious moments.)

One thing about *A Midsummer Night's Dream* struck me as odd: because the play is almost in three distinct parts for the cast – court, rustics and fairies – we rehearsed pretty well in separate, self-contained, groups, and I never did discover what the overall plot of the play was about!

Despite the friendliness of the cast, I ended the first week of rehearsals regretting what I'd taken on. At the end of the second week Bentall regretted it, and by the end of the third week we were both knee-deep in regrets. For my part I felt that the Shakespearian scene was alien to me and that I'd made a dreadful mistake. I simply couldn't grasp the technique. Certainly it was comedy, but it was in a style that seemed terribly confining to a performer like myself.

One night I was given a lift home after rehearsals by one of the set designers, and I told him that I was depressed because I didn't think I could do it and so was going to be a flop.

"In that case," he said angrily, "get out of the production."

From me an astonished: "Eh?"

"Get out," he repeated. "How dare you threaten the livelihoods of the other actors and actresses because of your incompetence? You've no right to be on the stage with them if you're going to flop. Get out!"

He may have meant the production, but I got out of the car! I was furious – for what I'd expected was sympathy, reassurance and kindness! Instead of which I'd been castigated for my unprofessionalism. Me – unprofessional! That was the cruelest insult I could have received. Yet it did the trick, for as I walked the rest of the way home I thought: "Right, you sod, I *will* have a go!"

So came the turning-point which transferred doubt into determination.

On Bentall's side, the worry was that I wouldn't fit in: be able to discipline myself. As he put it: "This is Shakespeare. You can't Howerdise it. You can't alter the text." I assured him that I had no intention of even attempting to alter the text.

Nor did I, despite what people were later to imagine. The fact of the matter is that Bottom's great play scene is loose in terms of possible interpretations. It's very much like a Music Hall sketch (as the Crazy Gang demonstrated when they did it). Without me altering the words, there were a great number of *visual* possibilities in it: for instance, when the cardboard moon kept hitting me I'd give it one of my glares – and there were a number of similar opportunities for *visual* gagging. But never did I introduce an "Ooh" or an "Aah". In fact the *Daily Telegraph* was to say: "I feel sure Mr Shakespeare would have approved of Mr Howerd, not only for his acting but for his loyal obedience to his author's injunction: 'Let them that play your clowns say no more than is set down for them.' " (I was very grateful to the Bard for that injunction: I had enough trouble learning the words that *were* set down!)

Once I'd mastered the Shakespearian technique (and understood the language!) I realised that there was a great deal of myself in the part of Bottom: a bumpkin with delusions of being a great actor. Also when the play within the play is cast – Piramus and Thisbe – Bottom covets every part: the lion, Thisbe, Piramus . . . he fancies himself playing them all: it took me back to my old concert party days as an amateur!

An odd moment during rehearsals: a young photographer came to take pictures of me, but I was so worried and wrapped up that I wasn't very communicative or helpful. Years later I had the opportunity to apologise for my offhandedness to the now Lord Snowdon.

The show came on just after Christmas, 1957, in circumstances that are dreadful for a performer: we opened "cold". In other words, instead of an out-of-town tour, followed by West End "previews", we had just one dress rehearsal – then it was curtain-up.

Before it rose, Betty was out front and heard the comments made about me by the Shakespearean purists in the audience: "It's dreadful having Music Hall comics in this sort of play". . . . "A stupid publicity stunt". . . . "He's ruined the play, of course." Thank God I couldn't hear them: I was terrified enough as it was, standing in the wings bent double with nerves.

Facts are facts – I got away with it! The Press were extremely kind (possibly as an over-reaction to their earlier forebodings – as though surprised I could sit on a horse, far less ride it). *The Times* said my Bottom was "most poetic" (!). Certainly the role brought me back into the public eye: not that my fans suddenly became Shakespeare addicts, but my performance brought with it enormous publicity value.

Yet I came to think that my going to the Old Vic wasn't all that wise. For while today artists can be more varied in what they do – and be accepted (even admired) for a flexibility of talent – in 1957, acting and show-business were far more compartmentalised. For me to go from Music Hall to plays, culminating in Shakespeare, gave many people the impression that I'd gone all up-market. The Old Vic suggested Culture, with a *very* capital C.

So good publicity was not necessarily good public relations. A typical reaction came from a producer in Australia who wrote: "We'd have liked Frankie to come over. . . . Pity he's gone all cultural." I experienced an uneasy feeling that I was heading for trouble . . .

(On March 18th, there was a Gala Night at the Old Vic, and the show ended with that play scene from *A Midsummer Night's Dream*. The Royal Family were there, and told me afterwards that they'd enjoyed it.)

Despite rumblings in my mind about the wisdom of my change in direction, I was committed to another so-called cultural venture: Molière's *The School For Wives* on TV, in which I played a scheming, jealous old lecher in his sixties. Now the Old Vic is the Old Vic – when you go there you've a pretty shrewd idea of what you're going to get. But for a large proportion of the TV audience, the name Molière meant nothing, the title didn't matter – what they expected was the familiar Frankie Howerd. They didn't get it. Instead they got me, as a pompous old man, complete with bald wig, in a mannered seventeenth-century satire. The sound of switched-off sets was like a thunderclap across the land.

I knew I was beginning to flounder, but fame has a certain

momentum, and I was offered a radio series. Although it had nothing to do with "acting", but was a straightforward comedy series, I jumped at it. Called *Fine Goings On*, the cast was a strong one, including Dora Bryan and that great boxer-turned-character-actor, Freddie Mills; while the scriptwriting team was truly formidable: Johnny Speight, John Junkin, John Antrobus and Dick Barry. Perhaps there were too many of them, for while we all tried hard it didn't click with the listeners. A more apt title for *Fine Goings On* would have been *Quick Coming Off!*

Then another offer: to star with David Tomlinson in the film *Further Up The Creek*, a sequal to *Up The Creek* and in which I would play the Chief Petty Officer role created by Peter Sellers. The trouble was that *Further Up The Creek* was made too soon – a matter of months – after the original, and so the public had not had a chance to work up an appetite for it. It followed on far too quickly. Also, from my point of view, the nearness in time meant that I couldn't be judged in the role *in my own right*, but was inevitably compared with Peter Sellers' characterisation. (In a nutshell, no one nominated it for an Oscar.)

So, although I may have been a success in *some* of the plays and *some* of the films in which I'd appeared, the situation in the latter half of 1958 was far from cheerful. I'd got myself into a position in which I was neither fish nor fowl, nor good red herring. Large numbers of the general public had found new favourites (and I'd alienated myself from most of the remainder), while my future as an actor was misty. I was aware that I'd lost my way through bad judgement – or was over the hill and slipping down the other side. Whichever depressing fact was true, my self-confidence was now evaporating – and fast. So what was I to do?

An answer was offered by, of all people, the S. A. Gorlinsky organisation. I say "of all people" because Gorlinsky was a concert agent who presented famous opera stars like Maria Callas and Victoria de los Angeles; but now he wanted to do a musical. Called *Mr Venus*, and written by

Alan Melville, it was originally thought of as a vehicle for Norman Wisdom. But Norman didn't want to do it, so they came to Frankie. I read the script and although my career was in the doldrums, and I had no other work in sight, I had to say that it really wasn't me.

"Try Max Bygraves," I suggested. "He'd fit in ideally with the material. But it's not my cup of tea."

"But we want you," said Gorlinsky. "And this isn't just a provincial tour – it ends up at the Prince of Wales."

To return to the West End in this sort of show was just what I was after now, but professional honesty compelled me to say: "I still think Max would be better: I wouldn't do it justice."

"We'll rewrite your part for you. How about that?"

"On that basis . . . Well . . . Yes . . . If you're sure it'll be OK, I suppose so . . ." Secretly I still doubted the wisdom of my decision, but as so often happened in my career I lacked the courage of my own instincts.

The plot concerned a man who arrives from Venus (Anton Diffring), preaching love. Nobody understands him, so he comes to me, working in a pub, and uses me as the vehicle to spread the message. (Looking back, I realise that the very concept of the story was well in advance of its time: all this business of love and peace and flower power and hippies with bells on their toes did hit the imagination – but not until about eight years later.) Paddy Stone had done a brilliant choreography, Russ Conway composed the music, Norman Newell wrote the lyrics – and once my material had been rewritten to more closely suit my style and personality I thought that I might indeed have found a passport back to the big time.

The show was distinguished (or extinguished) for an unusual reason: it had no overall director. Partially this was my fault: because I was a bit uneasy about the show, and wanted to protect myself, I asked to do what I'd done in panto and revue – direct my own "talking" scenes. But even apart from this, there was one person to look after the rest of the dialogue, another to supervise the dancing, and someone else to take charge of the singing. It was a curious jigsaw, with not one section of the show knowing what the others were doing. Yet at the time none of us thought it odd – least of all me. But odd it certainly was, as each section went its separate (and intense) way.

So to the Manchester Opera House in September to start a pre-London tour – and with a very embarrassed Anton Diffring. For as Mr Venus, his costume proved to consist of just a sequined jockstrap, high-heel and platform-soled shoes, and a pair of wings. He looked like a great big fairy queen lost on the way to the Christmas tree. (I, thank God, wore ordinary clothes.)

Having recovered from the shock of Anton's costume, we discovered – on the day before opening – that what we'd been rehearsing didn't match the scenery! For instance, I'd rehearsed with sets in which doors opened and closed, but the designer's proved to be little cardboard cut-outs. As we moderns call it (for want of a better word – or finance!) "symbolic". So all our stage movements were chaotic.

If this wasn't bad enough, we then found that the dancing didn't fit in with the dialogue, and the dialogue scenes didn't really fit in with the musical numbers, and neither fitted in with the scenery or costumes. *Nothing* synchronised.

We were all in a right old state – especially me, for such a situation was all I was short of at this stage of my career. We howled and argued and raged until exhaustion brought common sense: in the absence of an overall director (or Gorlinsky) we'd have to sort it out as best we could ourselves.

On stage was the scenery for the first half of the show, so we worked through the night attempting to synchronise the singing to the acting to the dancing to the scenery – and by the time the sun rose over Manchester like a mocking, bloodshot eye, we were exhausted, yet had the feeling that we'd knocked that first half into some semblance of shape and sense.

But what of the second half? Certainly we were all in need of our beds, but were prepared to forgo that luxury in favour of further rehearsals. Unfortunately, however, the stage hands weren't available! – so while we could attempt to sort out our performances during the second half, the scenery against which we would play was a magnificently enigmatic question mark.

By the time the curtain went up we were all pretty frail (even I was too weary to be twitchy!) yet in the theatre – as, I suppose, in other professions – there is a reserve of energy and enthusiasm for the big occasion, and as far as the audience was concerned we were all smiling and lively and full of the joys of spring. It really was a touch of the laugh-clown-laugh cliché.

The first half went fairly smoothly, but the question in all our minds as we performed was a simple one: what happens after the interval?

The answer was too crazy even for *Monty Python's Flying Circus*.

That second half had an enormous number of scene changes, but the stage hands had no idea what went where (or why) – while the cast could only pray to God that our last-minute rehearsals would indeed fit in with the way-out impressionism of the designer.

So OK – during the interval the scenery was sorted out and put into position (with much noise and disputation which the audience could not fail to overhear) and the curtain went up. . . . And OK again – we stumbled through the scene without too many dancers being knocked over by actors gesturing towards non-existent scenery as they declaimed lines that interrupted a passionate love song . . .

End of Act Two, Scene One. What now?

When the curtain came down the audience was treated to an interminability of back-stage noises and scuffles and arguments as we tried to identify and get into position the props for the next scene. . . . Winded and wilting, we staggered on, did our stuff – then the curtain came down and the entire crazy business was repeated for the next scene . . .

And so it went on: every scene a wildness of back-stage chaos.

It was a marathon of madness. At first the audience was

bemused, then bored – then booing. In the end there was virtually no audience as hour followed hour and they went off to their beds or early Mass. By the time the disaster's final curtain came down it would have been a courtesy to serve breakfast to those faithful enough, or obstinate enough, or curious enough, or stupid enough to have sweated it out.

We grabbed a few hours of sleep, then met to decide what we could do to salvage it all. A call to London resulted in them sending up an overall director, Eleanor Fazan – but by then I was ready for a padded cell as I ran around quacking like an eight-legged duck, telling everyone what was wrong and trying to put it right – and probably doing more harm than good in the process.

After a few days we pulled the show together (as far as anyone could pull it together) and we didn't do too badly at the box-office. The same at Liverpool. But I still wasn't madly happy about the show: it just didn't come together as an entity. My doubts were pushed into the background, however, when it came to the sheer physical problem of playing at Cheltenham: some bright spark had booked us to play at a cinema where there was hardly any room on stage for *any* scenery, classic or symbolic. Nor could any be hoisted to the flies – there weren't any!

We were told to do most of it "in curtains", which meant that some scenes would be performed in front of the curtains, and some behind – on an almost bare stage. But there were virtually no wings for entrances and exits! It was more chaotic than Manchester.

To make matters worse, being a cinema there were few dressing rooms. They brought a caravan to the car park, and some of the cast changed in that. Others used the corridors and toilets. I was lucky: being the star of the show I had the manager's office. (Mind you, being crushed together in what served as the wings did mean that as we awaited our entrances the cast got to know one another quite intimately! Especially poor Anton Diffring!)

It was at this time that *Further Up The Creek* came out –

and the notices did nothing to improve my morale . . .

I sent frantic messages to London urging that we extend the tour to polish it up a bit before opening in the West End. But the management was so anxious to get *Mr Venus* into the Prince of Wales they told me "not to worry". I sent a desperate telegram: HAVE ANY OF YOU ACTUALLY SEEN IT?

In a panic, they decided the solution lay in a rapid rewrite to streamline the plot. At a moment's notice, Eric Sykes, Johnny Speight and Galton and Simpson were brought in – and although they were great writers, Alan Melville was understandably upset and asked for his name to be removed from the credits. The result was a cannibalised mess, for only four days were allowed for the rewrite – and rehearsals! – before the London opening. (Part of the rewrite involved the axing of one actor's role so that Anton Diffring, instead of being the onlooker from Venus, now fell in love with the girl and carried her off – presumably to Venus – leaving me to cope with the critics!)

Further complaints were useless: on October 22nd, 1958, we opened at the Prince of Wales. I was aching with nerves, and was so taut during the first half that when the interval came – and for the first time in my career – I spent it downing great swigs of brandy. The second half was much the better for it!

The first-night audience had heard, inevitably, of our troubles on tour, and were anticipating disaster. Nor were they disappointed. There was some applause at the end, but jeers and boos dominated the night. To again quote the *Daily Telegraph*: ". . . a dull, flat and vulgar entertainment with no beauty, no style, no comic resource and defying even Mr Howerd's power to make it acceptable."

Although the critics were kind, and let me off with a warning, a flop is a flop, and you can imagine the effect it had on the fragmented remnants of my morale. I was in no way surprised when, after three days, it was decided that the show would close. It folded on November 7th after a run of seventeen days.

Oddly, as soon as I heard that it was to close, I relaxed on stage. Since there was nothing to lose, I started to fool about with the show – and it went down enormously well. Again I have to refer in advance to *Up Pompeii!* and the technique of making mock of it all. But at this stage it was simply what I had done in *Tons of Money* – only more so: *I came out of the show* and laughed at it. Sent it up. For instance, when a joke didn't earn a titter, instead of going on with the dialogue I'd turn to the audience and say: "What did you expect – wit?" Or a rather arch: "Please yourselves!" And again the cast came in for rude asides, and Anton Diffring's costume was a godsend.

All in all, I played *against* the show, as though its faults were part of a deliberate plot against me: *I* was being sabotaged by *them* – the cast, the scriptwriters, the management – and was striving to rise above it all. On the very last night we threw all caution to the wind, went mad, thoroughly enjoyed ourselves – and so did the audience.

Had it been the *first* night things might have turned out so differently. Yes, it was very sad, especially since we were a very happy company.

Before the show opened I'd been asked to do some of the scenes from *Mr Venus* on *Sunday Night At The London Palladium.* Although I was now hardly in a position to dictate to the bosses of television, I none the less refused: honesty compelled me to say that apart from the overall quality of the show, excerpts from musicals never seemed to work on TV. They'd tried it before, to help publicise a show, and failed. Big-stage set pieces just didn't come over on the small screen. One scene from a play – yes: but not a scene from a big, panoramic musical. In any case, although the spot was a marvellous one – top of the bill – how much of the show could one put over in twelve minutes? I said I'd rather go back to my old patter act and include some of my numbers from *Mr Venus.* And so it was agreed.

I rehearsed and rehearsed until it was possibly the most polished act I'd ever done: brisk, hopefully witty, and impeccably timed. At the final rehearsal I was congratulated by everyone in sight (which did my ego no harm at all).

But a fortnight or so had elapsed since the invitation to appear on *Sunday Night At The London Palladium* – and I did my act the very night after *Mr Venus* had finally folded.

As a result, when the curtain went up, I was suddenly overcome by a wave of positively maudlin sentimentality for the disastrous show. I got all sloppy and ethereal. (It was like that scene in *Cinderella* when Cinders, all emotion and ham, tells Buttons she can't go to the ball – only this time it was as though I was playing Cinders, not Buttons!)

When I got to my material from *Mr Venus* I got so bogged down with wistfulness I overran by three minutes. Bad enough, but my performance – whether for an extra three minutes or three hours – was awful. As the *Daily Mirror* put it: "Frankie faded" – and the *Daily Mirror* was absolutely right.

I'd blown it in a big, big way, and it was to be a long, long time before I was invited back to the London Palladium. For the producer didn't consider that I'd been wistful – just plain lousy.

TEN Summer in Scarborough with "Thing"

I was in a bad way – and knew it. My last widely *popular* success (thus discounting *A Midsummer Night's Dream*) had been *Charley's Aunt* – and that was nearly four years ago: a positive aeon of time in the competitive world of show-business. So once again the question: what was I to do? If, as I still believed, my sort of act was *passé* as far as the public were concerned, yet that same public weren't prepared to accept me as an actor, then I was in danger of moving in ever-decreasing circles until I disappeared up my own career. So this was no time to think of bad judgement and bad luck: I had to do something *positive*. And as I walked and pondered it occurred to me that what I must do was get back on to television – but in a role that was a compromise between patter and acting. The answer: a situation comedy.

I had a long talk with Johnny Speight, who was now a solo writer, after being with that Shepherd's Bush co-op for some years. Johnny devised a pilot for a virtually one-man series. Each would last half an hour, and the first had me alone in a bed-sitter when an anonymous letter arrives saying that someone intends to kill me – and I go to extraordinary lengths to barricade myself against the intruder. . . . In the end I discover that it's all a ploy by the landlady who hopes to get rid of me by scaring me out of the house.

I thought the story was good and the "stream of consciousness" dialogue (or rather monologue) was superb, but I was sufficiently intelligent to realise that at this stage of my career I needed an absolutely first-class director: a man of good judgement who'd help restore my morale and self-confidence by virtue of *his* expertise and self-confidence when he put the show together. For such things *are* communicated: when someone has a doctor in whom he has faith he's often half-way to a cure. To extend the analogy: I wanted a top Harley Street specialist – and got a first-year student! In other words, a trainee director! (I don't know if he's still about somewhere or other, so I won't mention his name.)

When the show went out on December 16th, 1958, the audience reaction was poor – so the BBC, quite understandably, dropped any idea of extending the pilot into a series.

Ironically, as far as the Press were concerned, it wasn't the director or myself that got kicked – but Johnny. Said the *Daily Mirror*: "He packed in quite a few chuckles. . . . Deserves a stab at a series of his own – but the material must be better. Howerd deserves it." Poor Johnny took the can back for some of my faults, and an even larger number of the director's. (I don't know why I say "poor Johnny" – he went on to write superb material for Arthur Haynes before hitting the jackpot with *Till Death Us Do Part*, while the trainee director and I sank almost without trace!)

Now the skids were really under me. For Christmas I went to the south coast for a limited run of the old farce *The Perfect Woman*. It wasn't a great hit by any means, and I didn't do it because of residual yearnings to become a great comic actor – there was nothing else on offer. I knew by now that I wasn't getting anywhere with this sort of thing, but I needed some sort of work. I was floundering all right (as well as left and centre). I had no sense any more of direction or purpose.

My family? They were concerned for me, of course – but what could they do?

I also had the support of enormous loyalty from my new personal manager, Dennis Heymer. Basically he's a Mr Fix-it, a super Jeeves who can drive a car and get me there on time, who deals with hotel bookings, supervises lighting and stage props, advises on my performance, timing and technique, and rehearses my lines with me. He's a keeper-out of unwanted visitors, and soother of troubled brows – in other words, from that day to this – a Godsend! Also, when you say that your performance was awful, he's there with a soothing: "It wasn't all that bad" – then, when you've come to accept that it "wasn't all that bad", he says: "Actually, it *was* awful!" (It's known as breaking it to you gently.)

The first bloke I had as a personal manager worked for me for five years. He was good, too – until he got stage-struck.

"I've been watching you," he told me, "and I think I can do this comedy stuff myself."

"Oh yes," I replied, fearful for his sanity.

"Oh yes," he assured me. "I'm convinced I could do an act."

"And the best of British luck!" said I.

The last I heard of him, he was a lorry driver.

I felt that he had no talent for performing, but he fell into the trap of hanging around back-stage for so long he came to *think* it was simple. Ironically, despite his years watching artists perform, he failed to grasp that the secret of their professionalism was to make their acts *appear* effortless.

The guitar manufacturers were pushed into the top echelon of industry by kids who saw the Beatles and thought it was simple. Thousands of women rushed to buy type-writers following the success of Enid Blyton, because they thought that writing children's stories was kids' stuff. But they soon discovered that it wasn't – and also that it's no good imitating the Beatles or Enid Blyton: you've got *to be* the Beatles or Enid Blyton.

However, after this chap, I had another Mr Fix-it, then Dennis arrived on the scene. Introduced by friends, he was one of those people who seemed to have tried his hand at a dozen careers, but was basically interested in the theatre. Indeed he claimed to have acted as an amateur. (Later, having seen him perform, I was to wonder how amateur you could get!) Also, although he had a keen eye for the birds, he had no domestic ties, which meant that he'd be free to travel around the country with me. But the trouble was that he'd come along at just the wrong time: circa *Mr Venus*. As I told him: "I'm going through a bad patch. The way things are I can't even offer you a sensible salary." He must have been in a worse way than me: he still took the job.

Now my career may have been in a rough old state, yet there was still some residual momentum of fame, for despite the disasters (or maybe everyone else at the time was working for the other channel!), on January 28th, 1959, the BBC gave me yet another chance: a half-hour comedy show, *Shakespeare Without Tears*.

It went well – Heaven be praised! Said the *Daily Mirror*: "Frankie struck his old form with a very funny half hour"... And since nothing succeeds like success, I was at last offered another TV series – after a break of seven years. Frankie's morale zoomed upwards – but not too high: my self-confidence, my faith in myself, was far from restored by one half-hour success.

Before *Fine Goings On* got under way, Tom Sloan, then head of Light Entertainment, said to me: "We're going to give you this series, but you've got a very bad reputation for altering scripts. You must give me your word of honour that you won't change anything."

"What's all this about a reputation?" I countered. "All I've ever done is discuss with scriptwriters ways of making a script more Howerdish, or I've *interpreted* a script. I don't know where this 'reputation' comes from – unless it's because I've gone wild a couple of times at the tail-end of a stage run when there was nothing to lose."

"But you must promise not to do *anything* with this one. You accept it the way it's written, or you turn it down."

In what position was I to argue?

And what did I get?

Two writers – an American and a Canadian. One had never written for me before; the other had never even heard of me, far less seen me perform! All they knew was that they wanted to write a series – *a* series – for British TV, irrespective of the performer. Result? Excellent scripts – but they just weren't me. Think of any comic – Ken Dodd, Morecambe and Wise, Mike Yarwood, Tommy Cooper, Bruce Forsythe, etc. etc. – and you associate him with a specific style: a *type* of comedy. Material has to be aimed for his particular needs. Yet these two transatlantic lads were writing for a vacuum: a series that may have been comic in itself, and which may have suited *someone* – but was certainly not me.

But what could I do? I'd sworn a solemn swear to Tom Sloan.

As if this wasn't bad enough, at the moment when my career needed a powerful lift by the scruff of its wilting neck – I got another trainee director!

The outcome? You've guessed it – another calamity. I did my best, but obviously it wasn't enough.

Once again I was in need of a rest; some sort of a holiday. But I was conscious of the pennies now (or the future lack of them), so there was no wild talk of the French Riviera – Dennis drove me to the Welsh mountains where he'd been raised, and where he reckoned he'd teach me to ride a horse. I thought it a great idea: I'd always felt nostalgic about my wartime service in Wales (and was still sentimental about the girl I'd known at Pen-clawdd), while I'd read somewhere that horse riding was great for shaking-up the liver.

We stayed just outside Brecon, and despite my fear of heights (a seemingly enormous horse and an apparent Himalayan range of mountains), I came to love horse riding – until the last of my three falls.

The trouble was that we'd borrowed these beasts from a local farmer, not hired them from a riding school, so their tack (as we equestrians say) wasn't all that marvellous. The first cropper came when the reins broke. I fell, howled – and hit the earth with an almighty thud. I was bruised and frightened, but was back in the saddle next day (intrepid Francis!) – when a stirrup broke. More grazing and bone-jolting, and I realised that more than my liver was being shaken up!

The third calamity occurred when we were on an (apparently) quiet climb. The horse was huffing and puffing (for I was quite hefty) – when without warning it suddenly forgot its tiredness and took off like the clappers down the side of the mountain. I tried to control the creature, but as I learned later, it was his dinner time, and there was no stopping him. Now, I was neither a John Wayne nor a Harvey Smith: just a novice who didn't know how to cope as this immensely strong animal charged down and down and down. . . . I experienced sheer, blinding terror: every fibre of mind and body fused into a scream of panic as the horse bolted down the mountain . . .

Instinct must have made me pull at the reins . . .

They broke . . .

This time I wasn't just thrown off, but fell on to an outcrop of rock, bringing the horse down on top of me, kicking me in the head as it came . . .

He scrambled up, but I lay there frozen by a shrieking agony of pain. Time is meaningless at such moments: for what seemed to be an eternity I suffered a thousand torments as I saw myself broken, crippled, paralysed, dying . . .

In fact only thirty seconds passed before I struggled to my feet. Dennis rode up, found I could stand (thank God) and galloped off for an ambulance. Then a numbness set in, and unaware of pain now, I staggered down the mountain after him.

Miraculously, the hospital at Brecon found that though I was cracked and sprained all over, only my wrist was broken. They plastered me up like a stand-in for Boris Karloff and let me go.

The psychological effects of the shock I suffered were to be long lasting, and in no way helped the nervous tension I was experiencing at that time. (Nor the worse days that were to come.)

My next date was a summer season at Scarborough. No nonsense now about topping the bill: I was grateful to co-star with Cyril Stapleton and his Show Band. He'd been there the previous year and had enjoyed a great success – and this made me feel in my own mind that maybe it was dangerous for him to go back so soon: triumphs are not always repeated automatically.

But who was I to argue?

Between being kicked in the head by a horse and going to Scarborough, someone said to me: "There's a marvellous fortune-teller you've just got to see."

"Fortune-teller?" I replied. "Me? But I've no fortune to tell."

"You must go to see him, Frankie. He's brilliant. The stars, you know."

"But I'm not a star any more."

"No – he reads them. The stars in the sky. Although hundreds of the other sort of stars do consult him. . . . And you get a whole hour for three guineas."

At this stage of the game what had I to lose (apart from three guineas)? So I went to see Maurice Woodruff – even though I knew that psychologically one only goes to such people to be cheered and reassured. Nor was I disappointed.

He shuffled his pack of cards and gave me a pencil and paper. "Write all this down," he urged. "It's very important that you remember it."

First, however, he told me things about my friends and family that were certainly true. I was impressed now – if he was correct in these matters, why shouldn't he be equally accurate about others? "Others" meaning the future – and in this particular he told me of the glowing success that the next years held for me, beginning with an almost obscenely successful triumph at Scarborough.

I left Maurice Woodruff with my feet not even touching the ground.

"How did it go?" asked Dennis anxiously.

"Nothing to worry about," I assured him. "Everything's going to be fine. An absolutely marvellous future."

"Thank goodness for that," he breathed.

"Exactly. So off we go to Scarborough with happy hearts."

Needless to say, everything happened in exactly the opposite way to which Woodruff predicted. He was one hundred per cent wrong. The years that immediately followed were an unmitigated disaster. How he got his extraordinary reputation among show-business people and the Press I'll never know. Only one thing is certain: he put me off professional fortune-tellers for life.

I might add that the best person I knew at this sort of thing was my mother. Apart from occasional fun with tea leaves, she did have her "feelings" – those curious psychic flashes. Nothing too specific, and nothing to order. There was that remarkable moment of intuition at Lewisham Hippodrome, and there had later been the day when she suddenly interrupted a conversation with me to say: "You'll meet Royalty . . . Under an arch . . . A big arch . . . And you'll be wearing a funny-looking garb. I don't know why . . ."

"Eh?"

She nodded, but would not – could not – add more.

I thought of Marble Arch, with me watching a procession go by (although the "funny-looking garb" baffled me), then forgot all about it.

Two years later, at that Old Vic Royal Gala, when the curtain came down on the finale I was standing next to ballet-dancer, Moira Shearer. Something caused me to look up, and I saw the vast proscenium arch of the theatre. My mother's words came back to me, and since I was dressed as Bottom, everything fell into place, including that "funny-looking garb" . . .

However, to Scarborough . . .

I was determined to be a success there. I was going to

be nice to everybody. My behaviour would be impeccable. I'd be charming, polite, helpful, uncomplaining: in a nutshell I'd be my most lovable self – humble to the point of obsequiousness, and with no arguments about dressing rooms or names at the top of the bill, and with forelock-touching deference to management.

So much for good intention: without exaggeration, it proved to be the unhappiest show I've worked in during my entire career . . .

The first problem could be described in what is known in legal terms as an Act of God – a heatwave. Blazing sunshine day after day – so who wanted to go to the theatre for the six o'clock first house? Or even the eight o'clock second house if it was still daylight and blazing hot?

Also, the show was not the most stylish of productions. In those days seaside landladies would be invited to opening nights on the basis that when visitors arrived at the boarding-houses they'd ask: "Any good shows to see?" – and with luck yours would be recommended. Ours wasn't.

While back-stage arguments and bickering dissolve if the seats out front are filled with bottoms, so, by the same token, empty seats lead to recrimination and the apportionment of blame.

In show-business, as in other professions, you are sensitive to what might be termed the vibrations. So even before anything was said out loud I was aware of a bad atmosphere: there was a sort of ominous tingling of my nerve ends as I sensed that as far as some of the others were concerned (though not all), I was going to be the whipping boy – everything would be my fault.

After a fortnight, I put it to the management: "What's wrong?" – hoping that a friendly chat would bring the rumblings out into the open, clear the air, and so lead to a happier, more relaxed ambience in which to work and live.

"What do you think's wrong?" came the counter-question.

Despite my earlier self-promise not to complain, my professionalism forced me to say (although with great diffidence): "Well, apart from the weather, the show could be improved in the way it's put together. The lighting——"

I was interrupted by a shaking of heads. "The trouble is that you're too vulgar."

I uttered a squeak of an "Eh?" Then: "Look, my stuff isn't even original! I've done it all before – and without even the tiniest frown of complaint about vulgarity."

"It may be all right for down South, but it's too vulgar for Scarborough."

"For goodness' sake give me an example!"

"Your entrance."

My entrance. . . . In those days the usual seaside entrance was to come on and say: "How are you? Are your cars parked nicely?" but as I've explained, my technique was to come on as though straight from the street or beach and launch into a story of an encounter or misadventure. At Scarborough I came on wrapped in a towel, wearing a big pair of boots and carrying a boat's tiller – with an account of how I'd been buried on the beach by some children and had lost my clothes.

"Your entrance. It's far too vulgar for here. What you should do is come on and say: 'How are you? Are your cars parked nicely?' "

"This strikes me as odd," I replied.

"Why odd?"

"Well, we did rehearse the show, didn't we? And we've now been running a fortnight, haven't we? Why wasn't it mentioned earlier? For I do wish to please. Had you told me, I'd've done something about it."

"Well do something about it now. Tonight."

"Of *course*," I replied, positively bowing as I made my exit.

When my rage simmered down, I wondered: "What on earth can I do as a substitute, with the curtain due to go up in just a couple of hours?" It was impossible to write, memorise and rehearse new material in such a short period of time, and "How are you? Are your cars parked nicely?" wouldn't get me very far.

I racked my brains – and came up with a sketch I'd done in *Dick Whittington* at the Palladium in 1952–3. It was ideal as a last-minute substitute, since it was all in mime and gave me the opportunity for a flamboyance of comic gesture and face-pulling. It involved a small boy (me) who leaves his lollipop on a park bench, and a courting couple come along and sit on it. The main part of the sketch concern my ruses to get it back – by putting my hand round and under the bench, by attempting to get them to move, and so on. But they are so utterly involved with each other, they aren't aware that anything's going on. It was a purely visual joke. So I got a couple of the members of the cast to enjoy an on-stage cuddle, and did my stuff.

The audience responded quite well – but "Thing" in the management was livid. He interpreted every single gesture and facial expression I made in such a way that I was the most obscene, degenerate, uncivilised unmentionable that ever trod a stage!

"B-but it was devised for pantomime," I howled in protest. "For the kiddy-winkies. When I did it before it was an enormous success. It's from a children's show!"

A narrow-eyed: "Which pantomime?"

"*Dick Whittington* at the Palladium."

A triumphant: "Ah-ha!" Then, darkly: "We've heard about the sort of kids they've got in London. . . . But we're telling you this: up here it's too filthy even for adults."

If I wasn't even allowed to use a harmless pantomime sketch, what the devil *could* I do? I sensed that it wasn't a matter of Scarborough's moral standards: *whatever* I attempted would be wrong, as far as "Thing" was concerned.

And so it proved.

The most way-out joke I told was an old one (naturally!), and it went something like this:

I went to see the doctor about this pain in my back. Ooh, it was a shocking pain. And I queued for three hours. That's right – three *hours*. And there was this woman sitting behind me, and she was in a real temper. A right old state. So I said: "What's the matter with you then, moaning and groaning all the time?"

And she said: "What about my children?"

I felt a guilty flush creep over me. "Your children? What about your children?"

"They're at home waiting to be fed. I can't hang around here."

So I said: "How many children have you got?"

And she said: "Sixteen."

"Sixteen? Six*teen*? Look missus, you'd better get a telly to keep your mind occupied."

"Oh, I wouldn't have any more," she said. "Not now that I've got me new aid."

"Aid?"

"Yes: hearing aid."

"Hearing aid? What's that got to do with it?"

"Well, before I got it I could hardly hear a thing. Not a damn thing. We used to lie in bed of a night, me and 'im" (I didn't ask who 'im was – that was her business), "and I could hardly hear a thing the man was talking about. I felt like a fool lying there. And he knew – cheeky devil! He used to turn to me and say: 'Yvonne' " (frankly, she looked more like a Nellie to me), " 'Yvonne, shall we go to sleep now, or what?' And I used to shout: '*What?*' " . . .

Even with a few Howerdisms thrown in it wasn't the world's funniest joke (as you'll have gathered), but it certainly wasn't one of the world's bawdiest. Yet for "Thing" this was seen to be a joke dredged from deep down a bottomless pit of filth. ". . . And what's more, how dare you use that name?"

"Name?" I was puzzled. Then: "Oh, you mean Yvonne. I use it because it's so inappropriate. She's obviously a Nellie, so to call her Yvonne – which has a posh-sounding ring to it – adds to the humour of the joke."

A doubtful: "Mmmm. Are you sure that's the only reason?"

"What other reason could there be? Don't tell me it's the name of the Mayor's wife."

It transpired that "Thing" thought I used it because it was a filthy *double-entendre*, Yvonne sounding like "'Eave on!" How can you cope with minds like that? It was a joke I'd dragged out in desperation, having told it around the Music Halls years earlier – with no complaints. But it was far too fruity for their show (or so "Thing" said).

I was now so demoralised that I was terrified of telling *any* joke.

The show struggled on through that hot summer, and the back-stage tension was appalling. There were complaints to London about me from the management, and the producer came up. My material was chopped and changed yet again – and then "Thing" decided to bring in another comic "to help me out"! It made no difference – the show carried the stigmata of doom. Mind you, I'm not saying that I didn't bear a good deal of the responsibility. After all, my morale at that period was low, and my nerves were in a bad way after the incident with the horse, so maybe my sense of insecurity communicated itself in some measure to the others. But the fact remains that *all* the problems of the production were laid at my door. I wouldn't be surprised if they didn't secretly blame me for the weather.

Yet I like Scarborough as a town (indeed, I've played there since and have been very happy), and the moors around are truly majestic. During that summer of '59 they afforded a great escape, and my mother loved their beauty when she came up for a holiday. We walked and talked and discussed; and, as ever, I was able to draw temporary comfort from her seemingly inexhaustible reserve of spiritual strength. And her weeks in Scarborough are also to be remembered because they marked a turning-point in both our lives.

For her it was the last time she was really physically fit. For me? Well, the show closed – the unhappiest ever. So much so that for the one and only time in my life I said goodbye to the cast during the interval, and left at the end of the performance without saying a word to the management. Despite heavy fog I just wanted to get away.

I drove south morose and dejected beyond words, suffering a terrible feeling that Scarborough marked the end of an important chapter in my life and that things would never be the same again.

Nor were they.

ELEVEN A Long Night in Eltham

As with other professions, show-business challenges like a mountain. Among its climbers there are some who never get beyond the base camp, while others (of choice or necessity) settle for one of the intermediate resting-points along the various paths to the summit. Perhaps these are the sensible ones. Those who are clever enough (lucky enough, ambitious enough) to reach the peak, stay for as long as they can and then – ideally – make their own way down (i.e. retire gracefully from the scene). But there are other methods of descent: you can be pushed off the top, or simply lose your footing. Descent can then be a non-stop dead-fall to disaster, or a slow slither as you grasp at brittle rocks, try to check your downward slide – and attempt to haul yourself up again . . . Me? I was now half-way down the mountain the slow way, occasionally pulling myself up a couple of feet – then slithering down a large number of yards. I was trying to halt and reverse this downward trend, but the footholds were narrow and the fingerholds treacherous . . .

What I needed after Scarborough was a complete change of scene: not just a holiday or a rest, but an entirely different power source (to change metaphors) with which to attempt to recharge my professional batteries. It occurred to me that New York might hold the answer, so I dug into what little capital I had left and crossed the Atlantic.

An agent was arranged to look after me and take me around, and the first thing he took me to see was the *Ed Sullivan Show*, televised from an old cinema. During rehearsals everyone was very kind, pointing out the cameras, and where Ed would sit, where the audience and orchestra were placed – as though I'd never seen a TV studio before. (It may have been a long time since I performed from one, but I knew what they looked like!) An added irony was that from what I could see, Britain was technically far in advance of America at that time.

While in New York, I bumped into Hermione Gingold, who proved to be a fan of mine. With particular memories of my "deaf pianist" act, she thought we could work together in a revue she was due to appear in on Broadway: *A to Z*.

"You're joking," I said.

"Joking?" she replied in that marvellous voice of hers. "Why joking?"

"Because this is the sort of break I've come to America in search of: to get away from the downward spiral I've got into back home. I need something new."

"What about a face-lift, darling? Or a new joke? . . . Or is that going too far?"

Since she was the hostess on that occasion, and since it was her show I wanted a part in, I let her win that exchange.

I met the director and producer, very much the twitching new boy again. They pointed out that I wouldn't receive a lot of money, since I wasn't known in America, and I told them that I understood this, but that it didn't matter: it was the break I was after.

The producer put up various ideas, and I suggested (modestly) modifications to suit my style – although angled for a New York audience. They agreed that it was better for me to stick to the sort of stuff I knew I could do, so that was fine. I then met the backers of the show, and we got on very well. At last, it seemed, I was on the right road again.

I mentioned my good fortune to a hovering reporter, and

caught a plane back to London in high spirits: once again the Yo-Yo of ego was spinning (tentatively) upwards.

Two weeks later I received a letter: they didn't think I was suitable, after all.

Why? There was no explanation. I wrote back a long letter saying (almost) that I'd appear naked, or make my entrance jumping from the Empire State Building, or that I'd flog my few assets and *pay them* in order to appear. . . . But no: that was it – they didn't want me.

Again – why? Had my shy nervousness implied lack of confidence? Had my talk to that reporter suggested cockiness? (Surely not in the publicity-orientated world of show-business – especially the American variety.) Had I somehow mishandled the whole affair? I'll never know. Suffice to say that I didn't get the part. And suffice to say that *A to Z* lasted three performances – so that's one flop for which they can't blame me!

There was the teeniest glimmer of hope towards the end of 1959 when I did my first panto on television: *Mother Goose*, with me as the Dame. Produced by Richard Afton (at the time of writing a highly individualistic TV commentator on the *Evening News*), it was well received.

Then, after the up, the increasingly familiar down. Maurice Winnick, another band leader turned impresario, put on a version of *Alice In Wonderland* at the Winter Garden, Drury Lane. I was asked to play four parts: the Mock Turtle, the Mad Hatter, the Caterpillar, and one other which I forget. It would be more merciful if amnesia permitted me to forget the entire show. In the words of Bernard Levin, then drama critic for the *Daily Express*, it was "a horror". It also proved to be the last production at the Winter Garden before it closed for ever: Frankie Howerd, the man who gave the Winter Garden the deep freeze.

It took me only a week into the run to realise that the show was a dead duck, so again I "came out" of the production and threw caution to the winds. If the audiences weren't responding to the literary qualities of Lewis Carroll, they could have the "Mad Hattery" of F. Howerd instead!

The smaller the audience, the wilder I went – and by the time we'd finished, the Trial Scene at the end would have shamed the Goons. If I say it myself, between us we turned the show into an uproarious success (unless you'd come to see *Alice In Wonderland*) but – as ever – it was too late.

Despite his involvement with my appearance in *Alice In Wonderland*, Maurice Winnick told me that he was to produce a TV version of the popular radio panel game, *Twenty Questions* – a variation on the old *Animal, Vegetable or Mineral* – and would I audition for the panel?

"I've got to be honest," I replied. "I need work, but I just haven't got the quick sort of mind for this kind of show. It's not me at all. Believe me, I've still got vivid memories of *What's My Line?* – and so have older members of the public."

"Will you at least come for an audition?" Winnick persisted.

I shrugged. "What can I lose?"

Some were to take my reluctance for arrogance – for I later learned that celebrities by the dozen were banging on Winnick's door begging to be included on the panel!

Anyway, I did the audition, with all the old stuttering, stammering twitchiness which, for me, was implicit in such occasions – but Winnick actually liked it. Would I do one more? So I went away and, with the help of Dennis, practised guessing "the next object". For the programme consisted of the panel being given twenty questions in which to identify some absurdity: a carrot, an Aeolian harp, the second palm tree on the left as you enter the Sahara from the north, the electrical flex on Harold Macmillan's hot-line telephone, or the wart on Oliver Cromwell's nose. Somehow I passed that second audition and was in.

The panel consisted of Stephen Potter, Muriel Young, Lady Barnett and myself, with Stuart Macpherson as question master. Before the first broadcast I said to Stuart: "For God's sake have a go at me during the programme. Because otherwise I don't see how I can get any titters – and these days I need them badly. So I'll look at you and make faces, and you'll glare at me, and I'll say 'Big head' – and so on. Let's not take it seriously."

Which is what happened – and from my point of view I did indeed get a few laughs. But others didn't like it, and Maurice Winnick came to me and said: "You're making this into too much of a comedy show, which it isn't meant to be. Instead of a quick-fire succession of questions and answers, you're turning your role into a cross-talk act with Stuart."

"It's the only way I can do it," I replied.

"Just the same, please tone it down."

My attempt at less flippancy didn't work, for I am just not quick-witted enough to be able to shout with triumph after the nineteenth question: "The garter Queen Victoria wore on her left thigh during the baptism of Prince Edward." (Cheers all round.)

As a result, Maurice Winnick came up with his master-stroke: "Sorry, Frankie, but you're too big for the show."

"Big?" I yelped. "*Big?* Do you realise that I'm visibly shrinking?"

But what's the use of arguing?

As it transpired, the show didn't transfer well to TV, with or without me. For none of the panel could be seen properly: there was just a long shot of us behind a table, and a babble of voices. I don't think it was ever brought back for a second series.

By now the dead weight of the joyless days was taking its toll. I sank into a state of deep melancholia, convinced that I would never find my feet again. My diary for 1960 was an unrelieved blank, save for a series of once-a-week summer concerts at Folkestone. Not only wasn't I earning money, but I'd saved little – and on top of everything else the Inland Revenue suddenly came up with a demand for thousands of pounds in back taxes! It was a shocker from the blue, because it went back years, and since tax returns were gibberish to me, I'd left such matters to other people. Someone had clearly fouled things up in a big way, and for the first time in my life I found myself in debt. It was too

Whoops Baghdad with
gorgeous Anna Brett and
Hilary Pritchard.

Sir Max Aitken presents me
with a silver key for a
"belated" 21st Anniversary.

Above: Off to dinner with Liz Taylor after her visit to *Way Out In Piccadilly*.

Below: At the White City with the Gabor sisters: Zsa-Zsa (*left*) and Eva.

Above: How thoughtful we look! With Ray Milland between scenes in *Nightmare Park*.

Below: After my surprise appearance at the Royal Show – with Princess Margaret, one of the Supremes and Pet Clark.

The Wind In The Sassafras Tree . . . I had every reason to look pained.

The Great St. Trinian's Train Robbery – with a posse of schoolgirls after my blood.

With those two great scriptwriters, Ray Galton (*left*) and Alan Simpson.

late to kick myself for my lack of responsibility. The question was: how to pay? There was only one answer: about eight years earlier I'd bought a country cottage near Reigate in Surrey, and by selling this and by cashing an insurance policy, I was able to get the tax men off my back and so stay solvent.

It did nothing to uplift my spirits, and since I virtually didn't drink, spirits were unable to uplift *me*!

In terms of houses, I'd still been living in that flat in Holland Park – until 1959 when Dennis said to me: "You're daft. I know the rent's low, but at the end of it all it'll have accumulated to a fair old total . . . and you'll own nothing. Now that things are sticky, you need to invest whatever money you can spare in a freehold: that way you'll always have a roof over your head." In principle he was right, of course, and I bought a small mews cottage off Holland Park – but I didn't realise that the overheads were to prove an almost immediate burden!

Money became so tight that I said to Dennis: "For goodness sake go and find yourself another job. I just can't afford to pay you."

"Don't worry," he replied. "One day you'll get on your feet again."

"I doubt it," I said. I took a deep breath. "Look – there's only one thing for it: you're fired!"

He refused to go. "I'm staying," he insisted. "One day you'll earn enough to pay my back wages."

I was deeply moved by this display of loyalty, but attempted to hide it under a joke: "As long as you don't charge me compound interest!"

We struggled along on £10 a week each, and apart from his basic loyalty, I learned a couple of years later that there was another reason for his staying . . .

Anyway, with no work that needed personal managing, Dennis now became virtually a male nurse. For I was gradually sinking into a spiritual crisis, and I became crushed and wretched and lost in a bleak and endless void of misery.

Did it add up to a nervous breakdown? It was never

officially described as such, although it must have skirted that situation, even though the most the doctor diagnosed was "a very bad nerves problem". (At one time I suspect that he thought I was suffering from that occupational hazard, a drink problem.)

There were times when I snapped out of the worst of my sense of grim helplessness, but even during these "better" periods I was still edgy and demoralised. What hurt most, in a way, was the terrible feeling of rejection: not by family or friends, but by managements – yet I didn't really blame them for their behaviour. In fact I think I can honestly say I was never to feel bitter about it, for I realised that much of the situation was due to my own failings as a performer and the awful errors of judgement that I'd made. After all, it's not called show-*business* for nothing: a producer has responsibilities to the shareholders, via the customers. What matters is how many seats are filled, how many viewers see a show. If the public chose not to watch a performer, who's to say they are wrong? . . . Nevertheless, I *was* rejected – and it hurt.

I walked a lot (sometimes for hours on end), watched TV, played draughts with Dennis, or just sat waiting . . . waiting . . . waiting for the telephone to ring.

I also went to church a great deal – St Barnabas in Addison Road. Not so much for the services, but during the day when it was empty I could sit alone at the back and pray. This brought an enormous measure of comfort, for with prayer goes meditation, and such a channelling of thought towards an *acceptance* of a situation can have a powerful (if temporary) therapeutic quality. As for the prayers themselves, I asked for courage, for help for myself and those around me – and for work. Not to be a star (I'd faced up to the fact by now that I'd probably had my day in that role), but just work – as long as it was in show-business.

It was difficult to accept that well before the usual age of retirement I'd been made redundant: but that's what it amounted to. I had horror glimpses of going back to an office job for which I was so ill-suited – yet I had to do something, since my finances were dwindling and in those days there was no social security for the self-employed.

One day I went to see Tom Sloan at the BBC, to ask if there was any work about. He said: "I'll see what I can do – but you'll have to take an audition." To have an audition for *Twenty Questions* was one thing – but to have to audition *as a comic*. . . . It showed that now I really was back at the bottom of the heap. Anyway, I heard no more about it – and it was the last time I was to go begging for work.

To add to my distress, my mother was now very ill. It was a condition of the bones, and their wasting opaqueness caused her the most excruciating back trouble. Although she didn't complain, she was in obvious agony, and walking was reduced to a lip-biting hobble.

Empty days dissolved into empty weeks into empty months – then came a glimmer of light in the valley of darkness that was 1960: I was offered by Emile Littler to top the bill (believe it or not) as Buttons in *Cinderella* in London (just!) at the famous old Streatham Hill Theatre. The pay was low, the run was scheduled for only six weeks – *but it was work!* (although I didn't have a single date in 1961 to follow it).

My state of nervous depression, my sense of failure and rejection, were too deep to be dispelled by this one booking, nor can I pretend that in the circumstances my performances were up to my highest standards. But I tried, and as a result it was a happy and successful show – although there was a fraught moment.

I'd been sleeping badly, and one Sunday night, having set the alarm in good time to get up and ready to leave for the two-thirty matinée, I took a sleeping tablet. . . . The next thing I knew was Dennis hammering and screaming at the front door: "Frank! Frank! Where are you? What's happened?"

I half-opened an eye, tottered to the window and croaked: "What's the matter?"

"It's two-twenty!"

"Oh-my-gawd!"

I staggered downstairs, and as Dennis made a frantic phone call for them to hold the curtain (they couldn't – it was too late), I put an overcoat over my pyjamas and shoved my feet into a pair of Wellies that were in the hall. Then, without so much as a drink of water, and still bleary-eyed, I collapsed into the car.

Only a Divine Chariot could have got us across London in ten minutes: we had only a battered old Ford. But by some manic driving (thank God I was too dopey to be aware of it) Dennis did manage to make it by two-thirty-nine. Allowing for the duration of the opening numbers, this left me with just sixty seconds to get on stage.

There was only one thing for it: I pulled on my costume trousers, but still wearing my pyjama jacket and Wellies, reeled on to do my stuff. I was on stage for fifteen minutes before I could make my first exit, have a glass of water, and finish dressing. (Fifteen minutes may not sound a long time, but it is when you're jabbering away and singing with your throat absolutely parched. As for my eccentric costume – it may have raised a titter among the audience, but the producer gave me a right old telling-off.)

As a result of the panto, people in the business became aware that Frankie Howerd was still in the land of the living – even if on the edge of the beach with the tide coming in. So "was Mr Howerd available for radio, TV shows, TV commercials . . . ?"

Was I available?

Then, for one reason or another, these same people would back out: "He's not suitable" . . . "He's not box-office any more" . . . It was absolutely heartbreaking to receive these offers, rouse myself from lethargy into a state of near-excitement – and then be dropped down again into the depths.

For instance, at about this time I was offered a part in a film with Bruce Forsyth. It would have been a positive godsend, but my then agent, Roger Hancock (brother of Tony) came to see me in a state of extreme embarrassment: the deal had fallen through. I had to exercise tremendous self-control not to break down in front of him. Instead, since he was so upset for me, I poured him the last of the gin from the "hospitality bottle".

So what had gone wrong this time? The official reason: "Frankie Howerd is too much like Bruce Forsyth." Considering that I'd started my career a good deal earlier than Bruce it was strange to be told that *I* was too much like *him*! A very odd excuse, indeed, but the truth was related to me later: "Frankie Howerd? He's great!" Then as the effect of the brandy wore off: "Well, he *was* great." Finally: "Yes, he used to have a good name. But now he's a bit of a has-been, isn't he?"

If they'd said that in the first place, it would have been bad enough, but not *as* bad: at least I wouldn't have had my hopes so falsely and cruelly raised.

So film parts were reduced to what are politely called "cameos" – a half-day's work for a fleeting appearance (if it didn't end up on the cutting-room floor). One such booking was in the film *Watch It Sailor* when I was to be seen (if you didn't blink) as a church organist. And it led to the most painful Press interview I've ever given. Jack Bentley of the old *Sunday Pictorial* (now the *Sunday Mirror*) heard I was doing this spot, and came to the studios with a photographer in the hope of a story for his paper and, by implication, some publicity for me. A very kind gesture – and very much needed – if only I knew what the devil to say when he asked: "What are your plans for the future?"

For I had no plans for the future. More accurately, perhaps, the future had no plans for Frankie Howerd! To admit this in a newspaper would have been too embarrassing. And Jack said it would be of no help to me if he were to write a down-beat story. Yet I had to say something, and although I hate lying to the Press (they're too clever for you in the long term), I temporised: I avoided the future and revealed for the first time the story of my horse-riding accident. True it had happened a couple of years earlier, but nobody had found me sufficiently interesting to interview in any sort of depth in the interim, so it had a news value, and the little lie I told was to update it to post-Scarborough, and use it as an excuse for my not having worked. (It's true that the nervous shock of the incident *had* contributed in some measure to my present mental state, but I made it carry all the blame.)

Jack wrote: "I'm lucky to be alive at all," said Frankie. "While horse-riding in Wales, a stirrup broke. As I fell, I was kicked on the head. I had serious concussion, and because of recurring blackouts I was resigned to giving-up show-business.

"The trouble was kept secret because I can't bear sympathy and fussing. Consequently I retired into the background and underwent treatment. It wasn't until late last year that I really felt fit. So I dived straight into the tough routine of pantomime at Streatham, and its great success completed the cure. Now I'm all set to give the customers new kicks."

So Jack got a story and I managed to avoid reference to the virtually empty desert that was my diary.

One moment of light relief at about this time came when the young sculptor, Frederic Brown, finished the bust he'd made of me. It had taken him three years, and was three times larger than life. (I don't think he asked me to sit because he was in search of a latter-day Adonis – rather because he was in search of a challenge!) All he was going to charge me was the cost of the casting – £70 – but what was I to do with the great bronze beast?

I offered it to my mother. She looked at it doubtfully, and decided it was too big. "But maybe it would make a door-stop."

I was outraged. A doorstop? *A doorstop?! Me – a door-stop!*"

"You're right," said my mother. "People would only trip over it. . . . Maybe we could scoop-out the top of the head and turn it into a sort of Toby jug for flowers."

"*Scoop out the top of the head?! . . . For flowers?!*" I was near apoplectic.

Misunderstanding my fury (or did she, I wonder?), my

mother said thoughtfully, "The best thing would be to scoop out the top of the head, put it at the bottom of the garden and use it as a bird bath." (My mother was very fond of birds.)

"And the dog would find it useful," said Betty helpfully.

It was one of the few occasions in my life when words – any sort of words – failed me.

As it turned out, the discussion was academic: I didn't have the £70 to spare – but I've sometimes wondered whether I ended up as the centrepiece of some millionaire's prize collection, or was melted down to be re-cast as one of Harry Secombe's chins . . .

My next date was on *Juke Box Jury*. Had I been in any position to pick and choose, I'd have turned it down. Pop was a subject about which I knew absolutely nothing (although I've always thought "Tiptoe Through The Tulips" to be a great tune), and once again, as in *What's My Line?* I was unable to cover my ignorance with witty ad-libs.

Maybe it was the result of the publicity effect of the Bentley interview, or Roger Hancock's efforts, but one day the Palladium phoned. At first I thought it was someone playing a sick practical joke – but no: "Would you care to do a *Sunday Night At The London Palladium* on TV on March 5th? Mind you it's . . . um . . . bottom of the bill."

How are the mighty fallen. Last time, top of the bill – this time, bottom. But I leaped at it. No false pride in Francis any more!

"Of course, you'll have to do an audition."

"Sure," I said, put down the phone – and groaned. For there were those dreaded words again: "You'll have to do an audition." I really was considered a has-been now, who, if he wanted to prove himself, had to pass an audition to demonstrate that he had even a vestige of talent left in him.

The years seemed to slip away on a reversed video tape of Time as once again I stood in an office, suffering a dreadful inferiority complex, shaking like a leaf, and stammering and stumbling as I did my act before an audience of one –

the same producer who'd pronounced me "lousy" after my *Mr Venus* fiasco on TV.

"That's fine," he said when I'd finished. "Fine . . . Just one thing."

"What's that?"

"Last time you were here you overran. So please keep it to five minutes, eh?"

"Sure – and I'll try not to be wistful."

He looked at me blankly.

Incidentally, David Whitfield was top of the bill, and this brought back memories. For when I was top of the bill at Great Yarmouth in 1950, Hughie Green arrived one Saturday to do a concert with his *Opportunity Knocks* discoveries. Among them: David Whitfield. Well, that's show-business (to coin a cliché).

I did my five minutes, and was so terrified of over-running, so scared of offending. I raced through my act and actually did it in five minutes. If this sounds a contradiction, it isn't: five minutes really means six or seven – to allow for the laughs and applause. But I was in such a state from the accumulation of the long months of insecurity; was so down, was so aware of my final decline by that audition, and so basically enervated by self-pitying wretchedness, that when I went on stage I did my act in an almost incomprehensible gabble. "Uninspired," said the *Daily Mirror*, and that newspaper was being remarkably generous.

Val Parnell, ironically, welcomed me back to the Palladium as an old friend, and invited me for a meal at the canteen (as I called the rather swank stalls bar) as though nothing had changed in my circumstances. In that sense he was absolutely fair: if I was bottom of the bill it was because it was supposed that was all I was worth – but such a professional appraisal in no way affected his feeling of personal friendship. As a person he still treated me as though I was top of the bill.

Roger Hancock shopped around to get me a summer season for 1961, but nobody wanted to employ me. Not one management – until he finally found a theatre at Great

Yarmouth owned by Jack Jay. Yet even he got cold feet when (as I later heard) an important London agent said: "Frankie Howerd? Why on earth have him? He's finished. Dead as a doornail. Get someone else, instead." But (to his credit) Jack stuck by me, although (understandably) he protected himself by bringing in Tommy Steele to top the bill, while I was relegated to a "supporting artist". However, it was work – work I'd been praying for (literally) – and at least he didn't ask for an audition; in fact he was very kind and encouraging.

I'd never met Tommy Steele before, and so had no idea what he'd be like. I thought he might prove to be a cocky little big-head: after all, he was the kid who'd made it in a great way, while I was a relatively old-timer at the bottom of the slippery slope. . . . Not a bit of it! He was an absolute charmer: kind, diffident and helpful. Indeed, although he topped the bill, because I was on and off the stage all the time while he did his one big spot at the end, he insisted that I have the Number One dressing room, because it was nearer the wings. I was genuinely touched by this.

As at Streatham, I'm not saying that my performances were the greatest ever: mental turbulence precluded such a possibility. But I tried hard, the show went well, and was very happy back-stage. Other names in Great Yarmouth at the time included Bruce Forsyth, Bob Monkhouse and Arthur Haynes, and all were tactful and kind – treating me as though I was on their star level and that there had been no changes in my fortunes since we'd last met.

But then it was back to London and the telephone that never seemed to ring . . .

Inevitably, as interminable day followed interminable day, my thoughts began to dwell more and more on the past: of the heady years of so-called fame and glory – *Variety Bandbox*, top of the bill in the West End, Royal appearances. It certainly seemed that I'd had something in those early days, but somewhere along the way I'd gone wrong. But where exactly?

I became obsessed with puzzling out the reasons for my

personal and professional disintegration – and something of a solution came to me after a visit to my mother in Eltham. When I left her, saddened by the progressive decline in her health, I turned up the collar of my coat and started walking. I spent the entire night wandering the empty, drizzle-washed streets, and almost by instinct I returned to the places I'd known as a child – the area around Arbroath Road and the Nine Fields . . . Gordon and Shooter's Hill schools . . . the church of St Barnabas . . . the church hall; each reminding me of people and events: concert parties and dances, outings to Herne Bay, Sunday School, Tilly of Bloomsbury . . . And I tried to compare the Frank Howard of those early days with myself that night, for although I was aware of the false images created by the selective amnesia of time, there was no doubt that those days of comparative innocence were days of happiness.

As a little boy, and as a youth, I'd fondly believed (in my ingenuousness), that success would solve all my problems, and those of the people around me. A happy ending was bound to follow.

So where had it all gone wrong?

I remembered the birth of my determination to become an actor, and how I'd practised signing my autograph ready for the day when I'd become famous. . . . And I thought, not in an ordered progression of reason, but as a jumble of ideas and images: had I been *too* obsessional? Were my standards of values all wrong? And that being so, shouldn't I accept that if it's all over, as it seemed to be, perhaps it might not be such a tragedy, after all? Does my fall from professional grace really *matter* that much? My mother is ill, my family and friends grieve because I am so unhappy and depressed – and aren't these people more important than the hope of a summer season?

This led me to think that my obsessive determination to succeed in show-business – the very burdens and ego and all-consuming demands of it – had made me fail badly as a human being: had severely flawed my personality so that it had never truly developed outside of the strait-jacket confines of my professional career. My perspectives had become distorted: a combination of fanaticism and inferiority complex had given me nothing to aim for or cling to but fame . . .

And I realised that even the measure of fame that I'd gathered *hadn't* brought me happiness, nor solved any of the problems I'd so naïvely supposed it would. I recalled how, even when I was a star of the day, my mother had privately told my sister that she wished I'd give it up: solely for the reason that, "It seems to make him so unhappy . . . and has he got a clean vest on?"

If my mother was aware of the haunting power of the driving forces of ambition, she was also conscious of the unhappiness that resulted. It was a paradox: she wanted me to be happy in the theatre – she shared my love for it – but could see that my fixations and emotional turbulence had brought the exactly opposite result. . . .

And then I suddenly stopped dead as another, truly frightening, thought came to me: what if, in fact, my talent did not match my delusions, after all? That my talent was a sudden flash in the pan – a tiny spark that had burned itself out?

So I walked and walked, with this great tumult of thoughts and images tormenting my mind: a kaleidoscope of people and places, of success and failure, of the likelihood that I was now a burned-out case, and of the flaws of personality that had resulted from my egotistic engrossment with ambition.

I know that it's banal to talk of serving one's time again, especially if one could do it armed with the lessons learned from the sum total of life's experience, yet I could not help having this yearning. I suffered an aching longing to start afresh.

If that long night at Eltham brought any answer to the question: "What had I lost on the way?" it was not the one I'd expected – although it was obvious and simple enough. The answer was not so much career: that was incidental to a greater loss – *myself*.

That, I felt, was what I'd really lost on the way.

This realisation may have come with the dawn, but the creation of a new self was not an instant, B-film thunder-clap, followed by Frankie walking towards the sunrise accompanied by a heavenly choir. Life is less romantic than that: brought to the surface, the ingredients of my turmoil sank back into the melting-pot of my subconscious for a slow and painful remoulding . . .

The next booking I had was a concert to celebrate the Urban District Council's new hall at Cheshunt, Herts.

TWELVE I Join the Establishment

Apart from my family, my friends stood by me. Among others, Barry Took, Johnny Speight, Eric Sykes, Galton and Simpson and Marty Feldman all tried to help in various ways, such as by offering me material free of charge. Splendid – but where was I to perform it: busking outside the Met, Edgware Road? To some extent I'd even avoid seeing these chums – particularly if it meant going to Orme Court off Bayswater Road, where Sykes, Speight, Galton and Simpson and Spike Milligan shared a suite of offices, and where I was supposed to have an office, too. For there they were busily working, telephones ringing offering them jobs, large sums of money being bandied about. . . . It was all too embarrassing. Not that I said anything, but my very presence was like a begging bowl.

Once Eric Sykes kindly rang the new Palladium boss, Leslie Macdonnell, and asked him if he could find me a spot in one of his shows. When I heard about it I thanked Eric, but said No: partly because I was so lacking in confidence I didn't think I could do it; primarily because I had no intention of accepting charity. I wanted work, but only if I was genuinely considered to be worth it, and if it was work I thought I could cope with: and at that time I certainly didn't think I could cope with the Palladium again.

There were still people who inflated my hopes with

promises that came to nothing. One character did it with such frequency that I came to say of him: "You can always tell when he's lying – his lips move."

Financially, my family were in no position to help me, nor did I want them to: I was a grown man who had to arrive at his own solution, work out his own destiny. My friends offered money – even Sunny Rogers, who had "fed me", both off the stage and on, for a number of years, though too shy to approach me direct, went to Dennis and through him offered me some of her life's savings. It was a beautiful gesture, but I couldn't accept it: not only was borrowing no solution to the problem, but I had a horror of being in debt – another imprint from my youth, for no matter how poor we were my mother had always paid her way.

Then there was the occasion when I said to Marty Feldman: "The phone never rings. I can't go on living for ever on dwindling capital. I can't wait for non-existent offers. I've really got to face up to the fact that I'll have to give it all up."

"Don't give it up," he urged me. "Because you have got talent."

"There aren't many people who think so," I replied. "Including me."

"You mustn't pack it in," he persisted. "I'll tell you what – come and live with us until things improve."

"No," I said. "I can't do it. I can't sponge."

But it was a great demonstration of friendship on Marty's part.

Writing at the time with Marty was award-winning Barry Took – who, as a comic, had toured with me at bottom of the bill when I topped it. He, too, did his best to boost my morale. He'd invite me for meals and urge me not to be too despondent. "You *will* make a comeback," he'd assure me. "You *will*." Although I appreciated his faith in me, I just couldn't believe it.

In terms of meals, I bumped into the now famous Peter O'Toole again. He greeted me most warmly, and we had dinner at the Carlton Tower Hotel. The irony was that this time I was the one to eat like a horse, and he was the one who paid!

In a curious way, my fall from grace had not been too *physical*. What I mean is that even when I was a big name I'd never moved into a bogus-Georgian mansion in Surrey with a swimming pool at the bottom of the garden. Equally, of course, I'd never had expensive or pretentious tastes in food and wine. I may quarrel, but I've never picked a Beaune with anyone! (Jokes like this have never exactly helped my career!) So in these respects there wasn't a great deal to give up. Now it could be argued that by the very nature of my life style being so modest, I must have had a lot of money tucked away. So why was I now so broke?

Well, it must be remembered that even when I was a big draw I was under contract for most of the time, so that while I was earning a few hundred pounds a week, people like Danny Kaye were getting £4,000 – and that was twenty-five years ago, when taxation was less punitive. So when I could have stashed it away I just wasn't earning it. Then came that swingeing tax bill.

I remember Max Bygraves telling me how naïve I was about money, and how stupid I was to permit myself to be exploited. "You're too gullible," he complained. I realise now how right he was . . .

And what did the public at large think had happened to me (if they thought of me at all?). One answer came when I was making my comeback and a newspaper columnist said to me: "It's marvellous how you've done it, for let's be fair – everyone knows you had a drink problem." And a local shopkeeper said: "Great to see you back at work – we were all sorry how you'd become a down and out on National Assistance." So that, it appeared, was a cross-section of opinion. Well, things may have been bad, but I was hardly a down and out (and not yet on National Assistance!), and as for a drink problem – I simply couldn't afford one!

I worked again at the end of December 1961 – in panto at Southsea. And while I was there I was asked if I'd attend the 1962 *Evening Standard* Drama Awards presentation at the Savoy Hotel in London. If this sounds an absurdity in terms of my professional situation, we have to go back to 1958 . . .

In that year I was playing Bottom at the Old Vic, and was invited to the Awards as a guest. I was very nervous about it, since it was a "posh" occasion, and among those present were people like Laurence Olivier, Rex Harrison, John Gielgud, Alec Guinness, Sybil Thorndike, Edith Evans – you name them and they were there. And all "legitimate": I was the only one of the other sort! I was horrified when Max Aitken, Chairman of Beaverbrook Newspapers (who own the *Evening Standard*) sent a note to my table asking me to "say a few words". Now there had already been twelve speeches – including contributions from such brilliant masters of the art as Robert Morley – and as you know by now, I'm no great speechmaker, and certainly abysmal when I have to say anything off the cuff. So I was about to reply "No thank you" when, to my horror, I was announced – and had precisely ten seconds in which to think of something to say.

Somehow I stumbled and bumbled through it, people applauded, and when the evening was over, Max told me that I'd been very funny.

"Kind of you to say so," I replied, "but don't ever do that again, unless you warn me in advance."

Now this was the period when I was beginning to go downhill, so I was astonished to be asked back the following year. I went, this time armed with a carefully rehearsed and memorised speech (which was, in fact, a potted act) – and my worry now was that I *wouldn't* be called on to say a few "spontaneous" words. Fortunately I caught Max Aitken's eye and he got the message. It was sufficiently successful for my appearance at those *Evening Standard* Awards to become an annual invitation (even if I had to send myself up by saying that my presence "was my only West End appearance of the year, like an annual pilgrimage to Mecca").

But this year, 1962, I decided that although Max Aitken was still very loyal to me, I couldn't go, for I'd accepted that I'd come to the end of the line, and that Southsea was to be my swan song. What was the point of working just three months of the year – if I was lucky – and spending the other nine in self-pitying misery? The time had come to make a clean break.

In fact, before Southsea I'd tried to negotiate buying a tiny night club near where I lived – not a swank affair, but a pleasant little eating and drinking place – and thought I could just about scrape up the money for it if I sold my house. But the deal had fallen through, and now I was thinking of taking a pub, if I could get a brewery to back me. Since Dennis's parents had been in the trade I reckoned they could help me run it.

An excuse not to go in 1962 would have been easy enough to find: the weather was awful that winter: a treacherous amalgam of ice, fog and snow – so it would be understood if I said that it would be impossible for me to get to London in time for the awards.

Then another thought came to me: I *would* go – and for one special reason. If I was quitting show-business, I'd have one last fling. I'd make my farewell appearance in evening dress, in posh surroundings, in front of a good class audience!

It was a bitterly cold and icy night, and when the curtain came down at Southsea, Dennis drove like a man possessed to get me to the Savoy at midnight, just in time to make my speech – although in order to face the ordeal I drank half a bottle of Scotch on the journey!

And I'm pleased to say that my farewell speech *was* a success – with the help of that Scotch – even if it did include that chestnut about the deaf woman at the doctor's.

People came up to say how much they enjoyed it, including the winners of that year's award for the best musical, *Beyond the Fringe*: Peter Cook, Dudley Moore, Jonathan Miller and Alan Bennett. None had seen me perform before (they were probably too young to have had the opportunity!) and I was touched (whisky or no whisky) to have impressed these talented youngsters.

Peter Cook told me they were involved in a new club

that was to open, The Establishment, where they would put on "satire" (the new "in" thing), and would I appear there? Neither cabaret nor satire were my style at all (and in any case I was giving up show-business), but after half a bottle of Scotch I'd have agreed to play on the moon!

Next morning, in the cold and hungover light of day, I dismissed it all from my mind, and on the way back to Southsea I went to Eltham to see my mother and tell her of the events of the night: the success of my speech-cum-act, and of the people who'd won awards.

She looked at me oddly and rather sadly. "You'll get an award one day – and not too far into the future – though I won't be there to see it."

I gaped at her.

"What are you talking about: 'won't be there to see it'? You mustn't say things like that . . ." Hoping to hide my uneasiness in an attempted jest: "As for an award, the way things are going I'll be lucky to be awarded an old age pension!"

We chatted a while, and then I continued on my journey back to Southsea . . .

While the panto continued its run I was staggered to be told that for the production of Lionel Bart's *Oliver!* on Broadway my name had been put forward to play Fagin.

"*Me!*" I shrieked. "For one thing I don't believe it, and for another I'm not interested. When this show's over I'm opening a pub."

It was Dennis who said: "OK, so you're going to open a pub. Fine. But can't you postpone it long enough to have a look at this *Oliver!* set-up?"

I shook my head. "I just don't care any more."

"Oh yes you do."

He was right. Of course I cared deep down – for my giving up show-business was only an acknowledgement of the fact that it was giving me up.

"Look," said Dennis, "you proved at the Savoy that you can still do it when you try and are given the opportunity.

So why not follow it up. After all, is Broadway such a dreadful thought?"

I allowed myself to be talked into it, and went to see the Director, Peter Coe, and the Producer, Donald Albery. There were those who were to say that I was daft when I told them: "I've got to be honest towards myself, to you, to the show and to the public. I need work, but with the state I'm in, I'm not sure I can do it. So to be fair, can I suggest this: that I rehearse for a few weeks, then you see me and make up your minds?"

This was considered by many to be extremely eccentric: I should have simply taken the part and hoped for the best. But I was merely attempting to do the decent thing all round. So after the panto, and with cautious optimism, I went to the New Theatre where *Oliver!* was playing, and between shows rehearsed the role of Fagin with the cast.

Then came a phone call saying (you've guessed): "Forget it."

Now what had gone wrong this time? The answer at least held a quality of originality . . .

I'm so used to playing Frankie Howerd (for what that's worth!) it takes me time to get into a character part (*vide* Bottom). So at the beginning of rehearsals I wasn't attempting to act or sing or move as a complete entity, but spent some days trying to get the gestures right, other days working on the vocal tones, a further time concentrating on the lyrics – and so on, ringing the changes as I went.

It transpired – or so I was told – that the producer of the American version, David Merrick, had arrived one day, sat in the gallery and watched just one section of my rehearsals: either the gestures, or movements, or singing, or vocal tones – certainly at that stage it would have been impossible for him to have witnessed a complete run through. But on the strength of what he did see he said: "No." I felt it to be a bit unfair, for had I known I'd have tried to give a proper performance. But what could I do?

Everything collapsed again into dust and ashes – so back to the negotiations for that pub.

But I reckoned without my new agent, Beryl Vertue, who had taken over from Roger Hancock. This former typist from the Shepherd's Bush connection was incredibly tough with me.

"The first thing I'm going to do," she said, "is get you back to work."

"No way," I replied, with an emphatic shake of my head. "It's all over. Finished. Done with. If you want to do me a favour you can come and buy overpriced champagne at the pub I'm about to open."

Long before Women's Lib was ever thought of, strong men took to the hills when they heard Beryl Vertue was on her way. Coldly, evenly, she said: "You-are-going-to-continue-in-show-business-and-you-are-going-to-do-well-again."

"Poppycock," I replied. "Give me a single instance."

"For instance the Blue Angel."

"The which?"

"Blue Angel. It's a night-club in the West End, and I've got you a booking there for a month."

It was so ludicrous, I had to laugh.

"Look," I said, "even if I had any intention of remaining in the business – which I haven't – I can't think in terms of the West End. And as for cabaret, it's the one thing I've always known I *can't* do. It's too intimate for my sort of style."

"But you've done it," she replied.

"*Done* it? Where? How?"

"At the *Evening Standard* Drama Awards. What was that if it wasn't intimate cabaret?"

Beryl is a dreadful bully – thank God! So I agreed to do it, provided everyone thought I was suitable, and that there was no audition.

Now Max Setty, owner of the Blue Angel, for all that he was an extremely nice man, also had reservations about me being able to do cabaret (or anything else, for that matter!). "Well," he said. "Yes . . . Um . . . Yes . . . But would you try it out first?"

"I will not *do* an audition," I insisted.

With the help of my friends, I got together an act – then Setty telephoned to say that the artist doing the cabaret that week was ill, so could I fill the gap for one night? As a ruse he'd not make the announcement to the audience that the man was ill until the last moment – but since Frankie Howerd was sitting in the audience, would he volunteer to fill the gap?

I agreed – but when I saw the artist who was supposed to be ill standing at the back of the room for all the audience to behold, I realised that I *had* been conned into doing an audition!

Fortunately my "non-audition" went down very well. It proved, as Dennis said, that I still could get the titters given the opportunity and incentive (i.e. money!), that I could do cabaret, and that if I could summon up the courage and the luck, there might yet be a glimmering of hope for me this side of a saloon bar.

So I took the booking: a month of cabaret at the Blue Angel, starting in May 1962.

At about this time Galton and Simpson had parted from Tony Hancock – more accurately, Tony parted from them, feeling he wanted to extend himself. Having written for him for years, they were understandably shaken (although I don't think they appreciated their own value as writers). They floundered around a bit at first, not certain what would become of them, then came to me and said: "We think we could write for you."

"I'm sure you could," I replied. "You've done it in the past."

"A TV series," they said. "For the BBC."

"It would be a blessing if you could," I told them. "But I'm hardly the blue-eyed boy at the moment. Especially with Tom Sloan of the BBC. He'd never wear it."

"Don't you think we've got enough prestige with the BBC?"

"I'm sure you have. I'm the one nobody wants to know."

"We'll put you back on the map again," they said confidently. "Don't worry."

"Well, I'll tell you what: if you can get the BBC interested, I'll do a pilot show for nothing."

"In that case," said Galton and Simpson, "we'll write it for nothing. So there's no reason at all for the BBC not to do it, is there?"

They were wrong. They went to see Tom Sloan – and sure enough, the very mention of my name (as a performer) gave him an attack of the vapours. He wanted no part of me – even as a gift. Instead he went ahead with another idea: six *Comedy Playhouse* try-outs, one of which you may subsequently have heard about: "Steptoe and Son". So who is to say that Tom was wrong?

I wasn't surprised, but Galton and Simpson were genuinely shocked – until then they'd never fully realised how low my stock had sunk.

Cabaret at the Blue Angel was all very well, but it offered no long-term solution, and again I questioned the wisdom of permitting myself to fight what appeared to be a lost cause.

Then came a truly gigantic hammer-blow: on June 7th, half-way through my engagement at the Blue Angel, my mother died.

Emotion and feeling dissolved into an utter and absolute sense of emptiness: I felt that nothing material – but nothing – mattered any more. I'd lost someone I'd loved, its shock heightened by the fact that although I'd watched my mother's decline, I'd never realised (or had refused to acknowledge) just how ill she really had been. And it was also my first experience of death near at hand since my father had died.

Wandering through the house at Eltham I opened, by chance, a little tin box she'd kept in her bedroom. In it were pictures of Betty and Sid and me as children, school reports, and some newspaper cutting about me that she'd gathered over the years. I'd had no idea they were there. Downstairs I saw in the cool corner of a cupboard a jelly: she'd made one every week-end – and I had to shut the door quickly. . . . It's strange how tears can be unexpectedly evoked by such mundane objects: even a jelly . . .

My mother had shown no special favours in the apportionment of her love. (Once, asked: "Aren't you proud of Frankie?" she'd replied matter-of-factly: "I'm proud of *all* my children"), and in return it's true to say that Betty and Sid and I were all equally shattered by her passing. But there are aspects of grief which are essentially personal in terms of memories and often of guilt evoked – and therefore grief is essentially lonely. There is a certain point beyond which it cannot be shared or communicated – as so many of you will know and understand . . .

As is so often the case, it took my mother's death for me to truly appreciate her goodness and her sacrifices over the years. . . . And it brought back yet again the realisation that career and fame are meaningless if one tends to take one's friends and family and loved ones for granted in the pursuit of ambition.

And I then learned something that indeed made me feel humble: how, apart from loyalty, Dennis had stuck by me because of a promise he'd made to my mother. She knew, naturally enough, of the bad patch in my career, and was aware of how my health was suffering. . . . But although she kept it well hidden from me, she was also conscious of the gravity of her own health situation, and not knowing how much time she might have left, she'd asked Dennis to stand by me and look after me. Dennis said he would – and he did . . .

Life is filled with mad and mocking paradox. For while my mother's passing made me feel that I didn't care about *anything* any more, *the very next day after her death marked the turning-point in my fortunes* . . .

I received a message: would I appear on Alma Cogan's *Startime* on ITV? I said: "No – I can't be bothered any more," but Beryl Vertue was adamant.

"You've got to do it. You've got to make an effort. You've got to snap out of yourself."

So I did it, and it was a success. (Odd how women have

been such great influences in my professional life: my mother and sister; Beryl Vertue, Joy Russell-Smith of *Variety Bandbox*; Winifred Young who coached me for *Tilly of Bloomsbury*; Mary Hope who tried to get me into RADA* – even my pianists have been guardian angels in their fashions.)

Then I was asked to appear on TV in a *Billy Cotton Band Show* . . . I was offered a radio series written by Barry Took and Marty Feldman . . . And Peter Cook telephoned to say: "Don't forget The Establishment."

"We-ell," I replied cautiously, "you were joking, weren't you? After all, you'd all had a couple of gills at the time, hadn't you?"

"We weren't joking. We'd like you in September."

I thought: "Shall I do it? *Can* I do it? OK, so I've played the Blue Angel. That was cabaret. But I'm not a young, swinging, with-it, satirical comic – I'm a rather moth-eaten Music Hall comic (albeit without a music hall!)."

But when I put these points to Beryl Vertue she said: "For one thing, you need the money. For another, you *can* do it, because you *have* done it."

I was baffled. "I *have* done it? Where? How?"

"Think back again to those *Evening Standard* Awards. What was your material there if not satire?"

"It's not the same," I protested.

Beryl came up with the clincher: "You gave your word, and you can't break a professional promise."

So I agreed, but first, in July 1962, I made another film: not a "cameo" part this time, but the lead role as Ko-Ko in *The Cool Mikado* at Shepperton – an updated version of the Gilbert and Sullivan classic.

The director, producer and writer was the then unknown Michael Winner, and his very first words to me were: "You must understand that I'm a genius." Before I could utter even a gurgle, he went on: "Who makes your suits?"

This time I managed a falsetto: "Eh?"

* And Tessa Le Bars, my long-suffering secretary and business executive for the past eleven years (poor soul).

"The one you're wearing is very badly made. That's what makes you look so fat."

I thought: *What a very strange man . . .*

Not only had he written the film, and was to produce and direct it, but he was also making it very much on the cheap (judging by my salary!) Yet I was prepared to do anything on what promised to be the road to a come-back.

At Shepperton I had one of the star dressing rooms: Judy Garland occupied the other, since she was also at the studios making a film with Dirk Bogarde. It was a great thrill to be able to meet Judy Garland – only I never did. Not one day did she turn up for work: the entire crew waited – but she never arrived.

In attendance, waiting for Judy, was her hairdresser. In the absence of coiffure, she drank endless cups of coffee. I put it to her: "Instead of sitting there in danger of caffeine poisoning, how about giving me a short back and sides?"

She looked me up and down – and ordered another large coffee: black and strong . . .

As for the jazzed-up version of *The Mikado*, it was to get a shocking press – and deservedly so. I remember that during the making of the film Bill Connor (Cassandra of the *Daily Mirror*) lambasted Winner – "this pipsqueak who dares to desecrate Gilbert and Sullivan" – and the stories Winner put out about "doing something modern with this dreadful old musical" not only outraged Gilbert and Sullivan fans, but antagonised the Press in general by its pompous and cocky attitude. Winner revelled in it all; for he'd deliberately made his attacks on Gilbert and Sullivan for the publicity they would evoke.

As for the script, let me give you a sample joke:

Me: "Do you serve wild duck here?"

Waiter: "No, sir."

Me: "Well bring me a tame one and I'll irritate it."

(Yes, you're right: it *was* an old Marx Brothers gag.)

The cast contained some famous names: Tommy Cooper, Pete Murray, Mike and Bernie Winters, Kevin Scott, Dermot Walsh – but none of us knew what was going on for most of the time. Pete Murray recorded in his autobiography the madness of it all, and Winner's unpleasantness, while Bernie Winters, in the autobiography he wrote with his brother, tells of the occasion he nearly thumped Winner in the teeth. (I can vouch for the truth of this: I egged him on – although, being a coward, I did my egging from some yards to the rear!)

As far as my performance was concerned, Winner seemed to confine his direction to screaming: "More go, Francis! More go! We must have more go!" So I went: becoming progressively more and more frenzied – although the script was such that what I was going *at* remains a mystery to this day.

In a curious way, working for Winner had a comforting quality: it was reassuring to know that there was someone around even madder than me!

The film was a disaster, the finished product having all the appearance of being compiled in a wind tunnel. Nobody could make any sense of it, and I can say without equivocation that not only was it the worst film ever made, but was the one production in show-business that I'm positively ashamed to have appeared in. Compared to it, *Mr Venus* was a composite of *Cabaret*, *West Side Story*, *My Fair Lady* and *The Sound of Music*.

It was intended to be *avant-garde* and surrealistic. In fact it was absolutely incomprehensible gibberish. "A new technique," said Winner. It was certainly that! All I can really remember of my part is that for some reason it called upon me to be dressed as a Chicago gangster most of the time. I had a touch of the intuitions and thought: "This man is never going to be heard of again. He'll sink without trace." But in that respect my intuition was having an off day, Winner went on to make such successful films as *The Nightcomers*, *Scorpio*, *Chato's Land*, *The Mechanic*, *The Stone-killers* and *Death Wish* – and my own wish is that he'd employed me in one of these instead of as a teething ring!

There was no West End showing for *The Cool Mikado*. It went out on release as part of a double-bill. They tried to keep the Press away, but those who saw it were blistering.

There's now a standing joke among my family and chums when I put in an indifferent performance: "Well, at least it's not as bad as *The Cool Mikado*." Or there's a threat: "If you don't behave yourself we'll make you watch *The Cool Mikado*."

Some time after the making of the film I was having dinner at the White City, and the waiter brought me a note. It read:

Dear Mr Howerd:

I have been a great admirer of yours since I saw a film of yours called "The Cool Mikado". Is there any chance of this being re-released?

A Fan.

I turned round, saw Michael Winner at a table behind me, and sent back the reply:

Dear Sir:

If I make any more films like that you won't be A Fan, *but my* only *fan!*

Since then we've met on several occasions, and in a very friendly spirit. The last occasion was a few weeks before I started on this book; an amiable meeting in a restaurant, when I asked: "If you make any more successful films with Charles Bronson, could you find a part in one for me?"

He replied: "That's a good idea: we might do *Son of Death Wish*. . . . There's only one thing."

"What's that?"

"You must find a good tailor."

I fled.

Anyway, after I'd made *The Cool Mikado* I was due to appear at The Establishment, and I was absolutely petrified, for the previous artist there had been Lennie Bruce – that controversial, drug-taking, four-letter word cult figure among the sophisticated "in" set of the day. How was square little me to follow him?

There was only one answer: to ring up Johnny Speight

and plead for help. He gallantly came to my aid, and we devised some material for the first thirty minutes of the show. He cunningly suggested that I should base my act on truth – that I was quite out of place there, that I hoped the audience would understand my predicament, and that I would do my best in the circumstances. Having thus disarmed the audience (I hoped) I then took a wild swing at everything and everybody in sight. . . . Apologising all the time for having to do it!

Even then, before his '*Till Death Us Do Part* days, Johnny was very adept at firing barbed shafts at the Establishment.

In the second half of my act I had little choice but to fall back on something I knew – a Music Hall act. Here, again, I felt the best method of getting away with it was to be truthful: so I explained what I was about to perpetrate, and how the audience could best cope with it.

"This place is shaped like a coach" (which it was – all long and narrow) "so I want you to imagine you're a coach party, get comfy and let yourselves go." I even had the sauce to bring in Madame Blanchie Moore, complete with piano!

And it worked. For many, Music Hall was so remote they took it to be even more "with it" than satire! So my run at The Establishment was an outstanding success, and the fact that I performed twice nightly added to the Music Hall flavour. I felt sincere regrets when it came to an end (feelings which had nothing to do with money or fame), and promised to go back. Sadly, I didn't have the opportunity: the place closed within a year.

Even Ned Sherrin, producer of the BBC's *That Was The Week, That Was* came to see me *three times* (on complimentary tickets, I suspect) and said: "You must appear on the show."

In terms of real success The Establishment didn't bring me great acclaim with mass audiences, but it got my name back into the newspapers; and did an enormous service in terms of helping to restore my self-confidence. The chain of Fate, or luck, had been remarkable: Max Aitken had been loyal to me and so had invited me to the Drama Awards . . . I was determined to pack it in, but to go out with a mad fling . . . Peter Cook and company had been there to see it – and bingo!, I was on the road back!

Although life was less gloomy now, when I did *Puss In Boots* that Christmas at the New Theatre, Coventry, I wasn't yet sufficiently back in the public eye to be top of the bill. It starred Sid James "with" Frankie Howerd. Still, I couldn't expect too much too soon. I had the Number Two dressing room, but was happy enough: Sid and I had always been great pals, the money was better than Southsea, it was fun playing to an audience of children again, and I felt that life was moving in the right direction.

It was another shocking winter, yet we played to good houses, and once more I was invited to attend the *Evening Standard* Drama Awards presentations. Again Dennis had to drive me to London through ice and snow but (as ever) got me there on time.

I was armed with a speech – yet Max Aitken (or, more accurately, his panel of judges) managed to throw me completely out of my stride. For to my absolute stupefaction I found that *I* had won an award. Certainly it was for nothing I'd achieved during 1962 (if they'd had an award for Best Cinema Actor, my role as Ko-Ko would have far from qualified) – no, it was an award for "services to the theatre". It carried my name and the words: "Wit, Philosopher and Friend".

I climbed to my feet, and as the assembled stars generously applauded, I experienced a gut-tightening emotion as I remembered the words of my mother just a year earlier: "You'll get an award one day – and not too far into the future – but I won't be there to see it."

I tried to tell this story to the audience, but half-way through I broke down and wept. The tears just poured down and down my face, and I rushed from the platform.

Later I was to feel shockingly embarrassed about my ill-judged behaviour at what was meant to be a happy and relaxed occasion.

THIRTEEN A *Very* Funny Thing Happens...

During the run of *Puss In Boots*, the producer, Pauline Grant came to see me.

"Frankie," she said, "you know that show *A Funny Thing Happened On The Way To The Forum*?"

I nodded.

"Yes. It's supposed to be doing enormous business in America. One of those saucy romps. Not so much kitchen sink as Roman Bath." (In fact Marty Feldman had told me about it a year earlier. "It would be ideal for you," he'd told me. To which I replied: "Chance would be a fine thing!")

"Well," said Pauline, "it's going to be produced over here."

I groaned. "Don't tell me they want me to play one of the eunuchs."

She shook her head.

"John Gielgud's in New York. He heard about the London production, and has told them that you'd be a good choice to play a lead."

My instinct was to say: "You're joking" – but I could see that she wasn't, so I could only gape. It seemed too good to be true. Finally I managed: "Me? . . . Back in the West End? . . . A lead in a new show? . . . It's impossible!"

Again she shook her head.

"How do you know about it?"

It appeared that the London presenters of the show, Richard Pilbrow and Hal Prince, on John Gielgud's recommendation, had approached Pauline to ask: "What's he like to work with? Is he difficult?"

And Pauline (the marvellous creature!) told me later that she'd replied: "On the contrary, he's very co-operative. And he's been very helpful to Sid James who's never played pantomime before."

"Yes, but is it true that he desecrates scripts?" (How that myth had got around!)

"Never to my knowledge," she assured them (fingers crossed), and added her recommendation to that of John Gielgud. "So the authors of the show, Bert Shevelove and Larry Gelbart, are in England and are coming to Coventry to see you at work."

I was staggered, for if this deal came off it could well mean what we so fondly call a "come-back" . . . Yet I was cautious: for one thing, fame for its own sake was not the blinding objective it used to be; for another, I hadn't got the part yet!

One night, before the curtain went up, I was told that Shevelove and Gelbart had arrived in Coventry, and were sitting out front – and other thoughts were swallowed by doubts and trepidations. These men had never seen a British pantomime. Its very concept – part variety, part fairy-story, part spectacular, part audience participation as they joined in the choruses and shouted replies to the asides of the performers – was quite unlike any form of entertainment they could have known. To confuse them further, the principal boy was a girl, and the Dame was a man! So how could *Puss In Boots* serve them as any yardstick of my suitability? And to make life difficult for *me*, my nervous awareness of their presence in the audience caused me to give a very tense and self-conscious performance.

At the end of the show I expected to be given the message: "Sorry, but we've had to rush back to London." But no – apparently they'd loved every minute of *Puss In Boots* (proving, yet again, what marvellously contagious enjoyment panto really is). For all their dignified intellectualism, they'd joined in when the song sheets came down from the flies, booed the villain, ate ice cream during the interval, and even laughed at me.

They came back-stage (where I was in a right old state of the trembles, I can tell you) – and on the spot offered me a lead role as Pseudolus.

I nearly broke down in front of them.

Then one said: "There's a proviso."

"What's that?" I asked.

"You mustn't alter the script."

I'd have promised anything – even to playing it full frontal. Anyway I gave my word, and stuck to it – anything I altered I first obtained permission for: I didn't even make *visual* asides without approval. (Although there were times when I was tempted . . . Ooh, how was I tempted!)

When the Press announced that I was to take the lead in *A Funny Thing* . . . I was flooded with mail. Not only from people in the business, but from members of the public saying how pleased they were for me. I was deeply moved.

Then, in March 1963, I was offered no less than three TV shows within a fortnight. One was with Billy Cotton, which involved me in a sketch with Adam Faith . . . The next was a situational comedy by Galton and Simpson called *Have You Read This Notice?* – about a man trying to get a watch through Customs: *although it was the very script turned down a year earlier by Tom Sloan!*

Both shows went very well.

The third was to talk about the Budget on *That Was The Week That Was*.

This TV show, fronted by David Frost, represented *the* peak of the "satire" boom, and my invitation to appear on it resulted from those three visits its producer, Ned Sherrin, had made to The Establishment.

Understandably, I got panicky. I said to myself: "You're bloody stupid. This isn't your cup of tea at all. You're an idiot. The budget's on Thursday, you broadcast on Saturday, so how are you going to cope? What are you going to do?"

I went to Beryl Vertue and said: "I'm in a right old state about this. Have I done the proper thing? For it isn't too late to back out."

"Personally I think you should do it," she said. "You can't let them down. You promised."

So I thought, and came up with this answer: out of three TV shows, if the third (even though the most prestigious) flops, then two successes out of three isn't a bad average. After all, you can't win 'em all! So I took one of my gambles.

Again Johnny Speight was an enormous help, and I also telephoned everyone – but everyone – I knew in the business asking for topical, budget-angled jokes: Eric Sykes, Dennis Norden, Galton and Simpson, Barry Took, Marty Feldman. . . . They all rallied round with one-liners, and I worked them together with Johnny Speights' material into a script which sent-up Reggie Maudling's Budget.

Now the irony about my performance was that the show went out so live I actually rehearsed in Ned Sherrin's office while the early part of the programme was being transmitted – when I went on stage the other performers had no idea what was coming (I wasn't too sure myself!) as I sat on a stool in front of the cameras and just chatted away as though having an intimate gossip.

David Frost sat watching me – giggling away. The trouble was that he had to follow me with some acid comments on the early editions of the following day's papers that had just arrived – but instead of reading them he was utterly absorbed with my act. (OK – so it sounds big-headed, but ask David if it isn't true!) When I finished – and remember that there had been no rehearsal with David present, so he didn't know *when* I was to end – the camera flashed back to him . . . but he'd been so busy watching me he hadn't read one newspaper. (I know this sounds like the ravings of an egomaniac, but facts are facts.)

Anyway, the camera flashed back to David Frost and he looked a bit worried, not having read his papers.

Many people saw it in a different way: that because I'd gone down well, David had looked daggers of jealousy. In fact the reverse was the truth. He was the first to congratulate me, and was delighted that I'd gone so well. It was just the way the cameras happened to catch him – with his papers down, as it were.

The fact that this appearance made such an impact with Press and public completely bewildered me. From my point of view all we'd done was to cook-up a "turn" suitable for this particular style of show. Yet I now found myself a cult figure on a national scale. It shook me rigid. I was even asked to take part in University debates, but turned down all such invitations – as my mother used to say: "It's better to be thought wise than to demonstrate that you're really a fool."

My triumph on *That Was The Week . . .* was probably the greatest surprise of my entire show-business career. I was meant to do eight minutes, but laughter and applause made it last a full thirteen.

While my stints at the Blue Angel and The Establishment had taught me the art of working to a small audience – to drop the brash Music Hall style and *underplay* – so I discovered via *That Was The Week . . .* that modern TV methods now allowed me to sit on a stool and appear in intimate, confidential camera close-up.

It was a technique I tried to develop about a year later when Galton and Simpson wrote a series for me deliberately exploiting this sitting-on-a-stool method of presentation – in other words, have a cosy gossip (often behind people's backs) in a style that was to become a major feature of *Up Pompeii!*

Although I was becoming a bit of a name again, I was not too proud to accept the money for a "guest appearance" in the film *The Fast Lady.* It starred Stanley Baxter and James Robertson Justice, and introduced Julie Christie to the screen.

The director was Ken Annakin, and he explained that the climax of the film was a crazy car chase. My role was to be positioned in a manhole in the middle of the road examining

. . . well, whatever it is men do examine in manholes in the middle of the road.

"What happens," said Ken, "is that you raise the manhole cover to come out – but a car whizzes past, so you duck down again. . . . Then you lift the cover once more – but another car comes hurtling past, so down you go. . . . And so on. That's the sequence: car after car rushes by, so you never get out of that manhole.

"You'll have to listen carefully for my directions, because we don't want any accidents."

I was in such fervent agreement with this that it's seldom been known for an actor to be so utterly co-operative to direction!

The street was cleared of spectators and I went down the manhole. But it was very deep, and as I explained to Ken, I couldn't hang on to the rungs stapled to the wall for what might prove to be hours on end. So they poured rubble into the hole to provide me with something to stand on. The trouble was that they used so much rubble I was forced to double-up, crouched on my knees, elbows in, the palms of my hands at head level. They put on the manhole cover, and it was quite eerie being doubled-up there in almost total darkness, for the only illumination came from needles of light through the tiny (and mostly blocked-up) ventilation holes.

We had a number of runs through. "Now!" Ken would shout, so I'd lift the cover and peer out – and a car would hurtle past, its wheels just skimming the edge of the cover as I held it above my head. The drivers were brilliant stuntmen (thank God!), but it's amazing the things you do when you're acting that you'd never dream of doing in real life – *except, of course, that I was doing it in real life!* (Roger Moore was to tell me how, when making *Gold*, he had to hurtle down a lift shaft at a tremendous pace with flood water pouring over him. "I thought it's all right acting," he said, "but I'd never do this for real. . . . Then I realised I *was* doing it for real!")

Anyway we rehearsed a few times, then Ken Annakin said: "That's fine. Now we'll shoot it on camera."

So once again I awaited my cue . . . Lifted the manhole cover . . . A car whooshed by . . . Down I went. I repeated the operation – but when I tried it a third time the manhole cover wouldn't budge! (It transpired that when I'd lowered it the second time I hadn't replaced it properly, and a following car, going over the edge of the cover, had wedged it tight.)

There I was, crouched in acute discomfort in that hole, the rubble digging into my knees, with just those weak slivers of light filtering down: it was like a premature burial. . . . My stomach began to turn, and I suddenly realised that apart from all my other troubles I suffered from claustrophobia!

A voice said: "Don't worry, we'll try and get you out."

"*Try?*" I howled. "What do you mean, *try*?"

I heard scrapings and mutterings and bangings, and another voice said: "It's stuck solid, and these holes are too small to get hooks through . . ."

I suffered a mounting wave of panic at this feeling of being buried alive. I was agonised by cramp, blinded by sweat, and had to bite on my knuckles to prevent myself from screaming . . .

Hours of sheer, shivering horror seemed to pass – but it was, in fact, only twenty minutes before they finally levered off the cover and hauled me out. They helped me straighten my limbs and asked: "How are you?"

I must be a great actor, for I managed an airy: "Me? I'm fine – but I'd like to sit down for a minute if you don't mind." I tottered behind a hedge, collapsed, and lay there until I had the strength to go to the pub for a large brandy.

Later Ken Annakin said to me: "You were remarkably brave. You kept so cool."

I managed a bland smile – but prayed there'd be no re-takes!

1963 was to be a busy year, for my next engagement was in Manchester to do the opening cabaret at a new club there, Mr Smith's.

There were two houses, rare for a club, and during the

break they kindly supplied supper. On the opening night, during the interval, a journalist from a music magazine asked if I'd mind having my photograph taken with an admirer. "He's a new, up-and-coming, pop singer, and the publicity might be of some help to him."

"Sure," I said. "Bring him round."

So he came to my dressing room and I was introduced to a charming, well-mannered young man called Paul McCartney. "What do you do?" I asked.

"I'm with a group in Liverpool. It's called The Beatles."

"Oh yes," said I politely . . .

In May I flew to New York to see the American version of *A Funny Thing Happened On The Way To The Forum.* I left London on a Saturday at lunch time, and because of the time difference seemed to arrive there at Saturday lunch time. This business of jet lag is not a fiction: after the journey I felt both utterly exhausted and disorientated – I needed to take to my bed and have a nice, long sleep. But no: the management had booked me a seat for *A Funny Thing* . . . at eight o'clock that night – when, apart from this feeling of mental unreality, my body clock was registering a very, very tired four a.m. the next day!

If that wasn't bad enough, I found that my seat was bang in the centre of the front row, with the overspill of the stage lights in my weary eyes – and the entire company, from Zero Mostel down, knew I was there. It was very embarrassing, because I'd hoped to sit at the back and get a *general impression* of the play – look at the action, listen to the text, analyse the production. So sometimes I watched, while at other times I sat with my hand over my face, listening and diagnosing – getting the *feel* of the show.

The result? Zero Mostel complained that I hadn't laughed, and so hadn't enjoyed the show – a statement that was reported in the next day's *New York Times* and relayed to the Press in Britain.

Of course I'd laughed – but I tried not to get too involved with Mostel's performance lest I became brainwashed into copying it. In any case it's difficult at the best of times to sit in the front row shrieking your head off when you know that everyone on stage is watching you.

I went to see Mostel to explain all this to him, and to tell him that he was marvellous (which I sincerely thought he was), then went back a couple of nights later to see the show while standing at the back of the theatre – and I did have a good laugh since I wasn't there to analyse quite so closely (nor was I so desperately tired!).

I returned to England to do summer season at the Plaza in Jersey, and during my stay I took the opportunity to learn the score of *A Funny Thing* . . . It was a difficult one, with music and lyrics by Stephen Sondheim who wrote the lyrics for *West Side Story* and has since written *A Little Night Music*. One of the things that made it tricky was its modernistic quality – the orchestra wasn't always playing what I was singing. We vocalists call it contrapuntal (I think!). At first I thought I'd never master it, but at home rehearsals Sunny Rogers thumped it out (flat as ever), while a girl friend in the show sang the soprano parts, and Dennis (God help us) "sang" the tenor lead. It may have been an overall musical disaster, but by sheer hard work I mastered my end of it. Bert Shevelove came over and we went through it for him.

"OK, that's fine," he said, although to the surprise and sorrow of Sunny and Dennis, neither were offered long-term, million-dollar contracts.

While I was doing this summer season in Jersey, The Beatles came over for some cabaret and asked if they could see the show. I went to the manager and said: "Can you find some seats for The Beatles?"

I know it's a corny joke today, but in the summer of 1963 the manager of the Plaza was genuinely horrified. "Beetles? Here? In the theatre?"

I explained that they were a pop group.

A relieved: "Oh, are they? But we're sold out, so they'll have to stand at the back."

I was embarrassed, thinking they might not be prepared to do this: but they did.

That night a girl in the show decided to throw a party, and I asked The Beatles if they'd like to come. They said they'd be delighted. Some forty people turned up, and the point came when Dennis said: "You ought to go and talk to those Beatles. They look so lonely on their own, huddled in a corner. They're so out of it. After all they don't know anybody, and you did invite them."

"You're right," I said, and went over to them and chatted, and tried to get them to mingle a bit.

So that was that. Next day, their engagement over, they returned to the mainland.

I saw them again just a few months later when I went to watch Alma Cogan at the Talk of the Town. They also turned up that night – and there was no standing unrecognised in corners now! Nor were the screaming kids in the street waiting for Frankie Howerd or Alma Cogan! Suddenly, in a matter of weeks, they'd captured the imagination as no pop group had done before . . .

It may seem ridiculous, but while I was at Jersey I felt just a little bit sad about going back to the West End as the star of a show. In a way I'd grown accustomed to not being a "name" any more – as long as I was working. There weren't the burdens or the stresses: if I flopped as a solo performer, or in a supporting role – OK, I flopped. But I was aware of others now: if I flopped as one of the *stars* of a show I'd bring an awful lot of people down with me. It was a paradox: one part of me enjoying the sheer release from this sort of responsibility – yet a resurrection of the feeling that perhaps I did have talent and *did* want to reach the top again.

Anyway, back in London we began proper rehearsals at the end of August 1963. The show was to be directed by George Abbott, the doyen of American directors of whom everyone (so I was told) was terrified. In his entire career nobody had ever dared call him George. It was always Mr Abbott. He was a tall, austere man in his late seventies: remote, unemotional and uncommunicative.

I was advised that he was a stickler for punctuality, and

when he said he wanted to meet the cast at ten-thirty a.m. – he meant ten-thirty a.m. So we assembled on the stage of the Strand Theatre at ten a.m. (to be on the safe side) – and he strode in at ten-thirty precisely, like a schoolmaster ready to tame an unruly class, followed by his lady assistant.

There was no attempt at: "Hi! . . . Good to see you . . . Great . . . How goes it?" putting-at-ease: after a few brisk and perfunctory words we started reading our parts.

I read mine in my own way and the rest of the cast (bless them) laughed a great deal. When I finished, Abbott said: "That's fine for a start: now we'll do it properly."

Properly? I was completely flummoxed, but since he didn't elaborate on what he meant, I continued doing it in my own style.

We staggered on, and settled down to a daily pattern: his assistant would take rehearsals in the morning while he played golf; and he'd arrive at about two p.m., stay for a couple of hours, make a few terse comments – then off.

As I say, he was not a communicative man. There was no sense of *rapport*. He was not the sort of person to whom you could go for a cheerful chat or with whom you felt you could discuss a problem. (I was told that Zero Mostel had experienced the same blockage with him.) In the end he proved to be such a cold fish I became convinced that he disliked me.

Yet he was a springy old boy who used to like to take the young ladies in the cast to supper, and I was astonished when one of them, Isla Blair, said to me: "Mr Abbott has told me how much he likes you. He thinks you're highly intelligent, and he admires the way you take direction so well." To coin a phrase, my flabber was never so ghasted, for although I was a star of the show he'd hardly said a word to me – far less uttered a compliment.

Mind you, he had his problems. We were a British cast, with styles, voices, mannerisms and methods known (and we hoped loved!) by British audiences, but none of which meant anything to Abbott: such highly individual performers as Jon Pertwee, Kenneth Connor, "Monsewer"

Eddie Gray and Robertson Hare. For instance, Abbott thought that Robertson ("Oh calamity!") Hare's splendidly unique voice was *most* odd, and wanted him to change it to a flat American delivery. In a way, I could understand his attitude (although I'm not certain that flat American was the accent actually used in ancient Rome.) In the event, Robertson Hare continued as Robertson Hare (for which British audiences were extremely grateful).

So we battled on, although there were moments when I regretted being in the show at all. Was it, I wondered, my cup of tea, the way I had to submerge my style of delivery and facial expression? And also riding on my back was that spectre of possible failure: *because* it was a come-back, *because* the publicity build-up was enormous, *because* so many other people depended upon me, and *because* it was a difficult piece of theatre, the strain was tremendous. But at least I confirmed (as in *A Midsummer Night's Dream*) that I could take direction: so I just got on with it.

Our pre-London run began in Oxford. It went very well – except for my opening number: the prologue, performed in front of the curtains and called "Comedy Tonight". It was one of those fast lyrics reminiscent of Gilbert and Sullivan, with a lot of complicated counter-harmonies. It was not only intricate but long, lasting for about seven minutes: part singing and part talking, explaining what the show was all about.

So I went in front of the curtain . . . Applause . . . I began the song – and dried-up! I was so bedevilled with nerves my mind went blank. I tried again – and attempted to bluff it out. But after a few minutes of singing gibberish I ground to a halt. I just didn't know *what* to do. Inspiration came: "Excuse me, Ladies and Gentlemen, but I've got a bit of throat trouble. Would you mind if I got a glass of water? *Would you?*" I didn't give them a chance to reply, but rushed to the wings and the prompter. He, poor soul, had been hissing at me, but with the orchestra playing I could hardly have turned to him and said: "Would you mind raising your voice a bit?"

Anyway, I saw the words on the prompt sheet, went back on stage, the audience gave me a sympathetic round of applause – and off we went again. This time I got through it – and do you know, I learned that Zero Mostel had had precisely the same trouble on his opening night (only he didn't think of that glass of water).

Next day George Abbott called the cast together and was positively friendly towards me (not only did he say "Good morning", but bowled me over by asking if he could leave his mac in my dressing room). He told us where he thought this was wrong and that was wrong, and said to me: "You know, if you could get rid of those Music Hall mannerisms, you'd make quite a musical comedy star."

"Well," I replied, "if I may say so, Mr Abbott, those mannerisms may be strange to you, but they're known to the public over here. I've been guilty of them for hundreds of years, so I think people rather expect them of me. . . . And let's be fair: I haven't introduced one of these so-called mannerisms that hasn't been approved by you."

Then to Manchester, where the show was also a success, although we were all still working to improve and polish it. Yet every time I spotted Abbott in the theatre I gave a tense performance: I was absurdly intimidated by those steely eyes staring at me through his spectacles. But he was a shrewd old bird. One night in Manchester, after the first house, he announced to the cast: "I'm off to London, so I'll leave you to it." As a result I was much more relaxed when I played the second house – and then discovered that the cunning old devil had been sitting at the back watching me!

And I certainly admired him as a director: he knew exactly what he was doing, and did it superbly.

Life wasn't all that easy for George Abbott, quite apart from his bafflement with the variations of the English language spoken by the people in the show. For after all, there were five comics, all distinguished in their various ways, and all trying to work together as a team. It was very difficult for any one not to attempt to upstage another, by pulling a face, for example, while that other person was doing a joke. In my experience it's extremely hard to listen and watch even two people at the same time. The answer, of course, is for one to talk while the other is still and silent – but this is harder than it may appear. Morecambe and Wise are a superb example of successful interplay, as were the Crazy Gang.

And so to London . . .

A Funny Thing . . . was due to open on October 3rd, and on October 2nd we did a charity performance in the presence of Princess Margaret and Lord Snowdon. It seemed to go all right, and when it was over George Abbott called us all on stage.

"Thank you very much," he said. "You've all worked very hard, but I think you'll get controversial notices. Half the Press will like it, the other half will hate it. . . . I'm off to America now."

We gave him a sincere round of applause, out he went – and the cast performed a collective double-take. We suddenly realised: "He's gone. He won't be here for the opening night of his show. How odd." I've never known anything like it, but maybe he was nervous, too – and in any case there was nothing more he could do with the show. It was up to us.

On the morning of the opening I finished the last of my Press interviews, trying to define something that defied definition – what it felt like to be making a West End comeback. Writer Wolf Mankowitz was around and said: "I do hope all goes well tonight. You know, it's extraordinary the enormous number of people I've spoken to who are really rooting for you. You've got the hopes and best wishes of everyone in the profession." Since I'd been something of a recluse in recent years, I was both surprised and touched.

The hours before opening found me in my familiar state of nerves. Apart from anything else, I had in front of me a part longer than Hamlet's (or so it seemed). Not only did I open the show in front of the curtain, but I was off-stage for only three minutes of the play's two and a half hours. To say it was "gruelling" is putting it mildly. Also there was that very business of opening the show. Not only was it long and complicated, but the tradition was for the chorus, or something similar, to break the ice – work up the show, get the audience in a relaxed and receptive mood – and *then* a star made his entrance. But in this show I was the first person to confront the audience. It was a dreadful strain, especially for a come-back.

So the evening came, and I was petrified – and not just with first night trepidations now. Memories of my last West End opening crowded in – *Mr Venus* in 1958 – and I was terrified of what might happen. Also, the publicity build-up having been so enormous, I was pretty certain the Press were there in force, with plenty of space in the papers waiting to be filled, and what this could mean to me personally (for good or bad).

I came down from my dressing room in my toga – and was perspiring enough without its woollen weight, I can tell you. (Later, when I dripped sweat all over the stage, it was changed for a cotton one, but on that opening night I was swathed in wool.)

Now following my prologue the curtain was to come up on a scene involving four twittering eunuchs. I stood with them behind the tabs, listening to the orchestra tune up and the excited buzz of a very distinguished first-night audience – and the accumulation of emotion suddenly caused me to freeze, absolutely paralysed with cramp. I am not exaggerating a word. I stammered to the eunuchs: "I-I can't move . . . I'm so terrified, s-so frightened, I'm just frozen rigid. I can't go on."

One of the eunuchs, George Giles, looked at me with utter contempt. "Frightened?" he almost spat. "Frightened! What the bloody hell are you talking about? Frightened? We've been slogging our guts out all these weeks, working ourselves to death, just for this opening night – and you're frightened! Now just you get out there and stop bloody moaning!"

I was shocked. I expected sympathetic encouragement. A friendly pat on the shoulder. A few kind words. . . . Instead I got insults! Shock turned to rage and I was so livid that although George may only have been playing a eunuch, I nearly turned him into a method actor there and then on the spot.

I thought: "How dare he attack me like this? Has he no feelings? No sensitivity? How dare he?" I was so taken aback I quite forgot nerves and audience and occasion, flung aside the curtains and did my stuff.

Afterwards I was enormously grateful to George Giles, of course. He'd acted in just the right way with his "shock therapy". Without it I dread to think of the disaster that opening night might have dissolved into. (It was reminiscent of the incident when I'd had my doubts about *A Midsummer Night's Dream.*)

The show itself received a tremendous reception that opening night, and I had a tumultuous personal ovation. When the final curtain came down I was so overwhelmed I couldn't utter a word all the way back to the dressing room. It was a full ten minutes before I'd recovered sufficiently to allow anyone in . . .

Dennis and Betty and a girl friend of mine were the first to arrive: too nervous to sit, they'd watched the show from the back of the theatre. Then others came round with very kindly comments. There seemed to be hundreds of them – and the one problem with hundreds of people is hundreds of drinks. I reckon that opening night cost me my first week's wages in champagne and Scotch! (But I far from begrudged it.)

Later I opened the telegrams that had arrived. I'd not read them before the show because the repetition of "good luck" . . . "good luck" . . . "good luck" would only have added to the burden of responsibility. But now I looked at them, and included was the most original first-night message I've ever received. It had been delivered by hand from the TWA airline office – a TWA menu on which George Abbott had scribbled as he flew the Atlantic: *All the best. Thank you. George A.*

I was glad that he was to be proved wrong in one

particular – when he'd said: "I think you will get controversial notices. Half the Press will like it, the other half will hate it". . . . For the critics were virtually unanimous in praising the show. Even Bernard Levin, who'd now moved to the *Daily Mail* (and had panned *Alice in Wonderland* when on the *Express*) was generously enthusiastic about me.

So it really had happened. I'd made a West End comeback . . .

FOURTEEN Sir Francis, and Viscount Feldman

A Funny Thing . . . was to run until July 1965, and it was a very happy show. It was full of great characters, among the most memorable being Eddie Gray, a compulsive practical joker, who'd sometimes do the most outrageous things (maybe as a result of his years with the Crazy Gang). He lived in Brighton, as did one of the girls in the show, and if they travelled up on the same train he'd give her a lift in a taxi from Victoria. On one such occasion, as he got out of the cab he undid his fly and pushed his shirt through the gap. Then, and in deliberate view of the taxi driver, he pushed a pound note into the poor girl's hand and said: "Thank you very much: I enjoyed that!"

As I've said, the show was long and I was on stage for most of the time. It became very tiring, and after some performances in which I felt I'd been rather lethargic, I went to see the doctor. He diagnosed that I – red-blooded Francis – was suffering from anaemia. Fortunately it responded quickly to treatment.

What made life particularly exhausting at this time was success itself: once again I'd been "discovered" and so was in popular demand. Yes – even *Sunday Night At The London Palladium* wanted me back, and I'm pleased to say that they didn't ask for an audition. Instead, on April 27th, 1964, I did a twenty-minute spot at top of the bill and it went down very well: partly because my self-confidence as a performer had been restored, and partly because of a superb script by Sid Hills and Dick Green.

I also did two television series for the BBC during 1964, both written by Galton and Simpson, and this involved me working a full seven-day week: at the Strand Theatre, Monday to Saturday, learning the TV material between times, then rehearsing and recording on Sundays.

The first of these series (apart from getting me on the cover of the BBC's little magazine, *Radio Times*) consolidated the style I'd tried out on *That Was The Week* . . . – a projection of my old gossip act, but modified for a TV audience: bewildered me sitting on a stool and nattering on about how I'm the victim of "Them" or a nameless person referred to as "Thing" . . . although the audience were made quite aware that these anonymities were, in fact, the producer of the show, or the head of the BBC, or the Prime Minister, or the Establishment in general, or whatever. (It was a style I was later to take to the Royal Variety Shows with my send-ups of Bernard Delfont.)

I'd start off innocently enough: "Now listen, brethren, before we start this eisteddfod, I'd like to make an appeal. No, it's not an appeal for money – you've been robbed enough as it is. No, you feel such a ninny stuck up here on a stool if no one laughs . . . Now, who can manage a little titter? . . . You could? It isn't easy to get your titters out on a wet Wednesday . . ." (And, of course, there'd be absolute outrage on my part if the word "titters" was misunderstood – which it usually was, may I say!)

Then I'd tell of my misadventures – and the point of the act was to make the audience laugh (God willing!) at my grievances, but to pretend to be furious with them for doing so. . . . "No – don't laugh. No don't. No, don't laugh. Listen! Pull yourselves together. You'll make me a laughing stock . . . Gawd help us – this is going to be a rowdy do! . . ."

And, of course, the more an audience is rebuked, the more it laughs (or is meant to!).

Of necessity, this is very much an over-simplification of

what it was all about: as I've said, an entire book in itself could be written attempting to analyse the different styles of various comedians – and in the long run an awful lot depends on our scripts.

Anyway, Galton and Simpson wrote two superlative series for me in 1964 – and another powerful memory of that year is a *Blackpool Night Out* on TV with Tony Hancock.

I'd worked with Tony on radio, of course, but I hadn't seen him for years, for we didn't meet socially, and his success came when I was virtually out of the running – and if I didn't go out and about creating a public "presence" when I was at the top of the tree, I certainly didn't attempt to put on a bold front by mingling with the famous when I was down in the depths.

Anyway, Tony said he wanted to do something in the show with me, and when I went to see him back-stage at the Talk of the Town, he was now the one suffering a bad patch after his break with Galton and Simpson, and also as a result of the adverse publicity he'd had because of his marital and drink problems. He was pleased to see me – but produced an act for us to do together which he'd certainly done at least twenty years earlier, and in which I was to play his stooge. Not that that worried me: what did worry me, apart from the dated quality of the material, was that it was extremely difficult to play a Music Hall part that's been specifically designed for someone else.

So I made non-commital noises, then went to the producer of *Blackpool Night Out* and said: "What Tony's got in mind just won't work. It was written for someone else, and for me to play it (apart from it being dreadfully old-fashioned) would be bad for us both. Also, it's so long I wouldn't be able to do the patter act you also want." After some discussion it was agreed that the best thing would be for me to do a solo act and then Tony and I would swop a few jokes in the finale.

When we met again in Blackpool, Tony was in a very wound-up state, and didn't look at all well. He seemed to be suffering from emotional stresses, and before the show, alone with him in his dressing room, I said: "I'm sorry you're going through a difficult patch. If there's anything I can do, don't hesitate to ask."

He thanked me, but said "No."

Now it's a custom of mine (and other comics) to make jokes about people on the bill. In *Up Pompeii*, for instance, when poor old Max Adrian came on astride an ass, I'd say: "Hello – here comes Charlton Heston." Or if I was doing a sketch with a very bad actor, it might be: "Thank you very much, Laurence Olivier." A wizened little man would be referred to as James Bond, and when a pantomime Dame came on I'd say: "Here she is – Raquel Welch." By playing against the type you'd hope to get a laugh. And I've often been at the receiving end of such subtle witticisms myself.

When Tony Hancock came on for the finale at Blackpool, I could have said: "Here comes Dracula," or "Here comes the Invisible Man," but it happened that the then enormously popular TV characters of the day were Batman and Robin. So I said: "Ah – here comes Batman" – thinking he might say: "All right, Robin" (which could have earned a titter since you could hardly think of two characters less like Batman and Robin than Tony Hancock and Frankie Howerd). But he didn't rise to the bait, and I learned later that he was terribly upset about me calling him Batman: such was the sensitivity of his mental condition he associated the name with "batty" or "batty-man". I was truly shaken, for I'd never intended any such implication.

Four years later, in Australia, he committed suicide. I was saddened, both for the man himself, and for the loss of a truly brilliant comic talent. He'd put up a gallant fight against mental illness, but in the end it overcame him.

It's too easy to present all comedians as tragic souls. . . . It's a cliché, but it isn't true. Straight actors and accountants are just as likely to commit suicide as funny men . . .

It's a fact: all professions have their strains and stresses, but in show-business they are often more extreme and more publicised.

Anyway, while in *A Funny Thing* . . . I also found time to

make a film with The Beatles: *Help!* directed by Dick Lester.

"It's a guest spot, but not a 'cameo'," he assured me. "You'll have a full ten minutes playing a drama coach. Are you interested?"

"Sure," I replied. "Send me the script." He did, I read it – and then had to admit that I couldn't make head nor tail of it.

"Well," said Dick, "You're playing a two-dimensional character. It's a caricature."

"*Really?*" said I, as though now enlightened. "The thing is that this script calls upon me to say these fantastic sentences in a style and technique that are absolutely bewildering to me – and I've got vividly painful memories of an epic called *The Cool Mikado*. So will you promise me that if it doesn't turn out right you'll cut it out of the film, and we'll forget the money?"

"Sure," said Dick, so off we went.

The Beatles' idea of making a film was quite original! For instance, I'd been trained to arrive at studios at seven a.m. for make-up and then continue until the day's work was over – but they just came and went as they pleased, much to the bafflement of everyone else present. Things got held up for the daftest reasons. For instance, one day Paul forgot his bathing trunks, and while nobody was certain why he needed them, production was delayed until a car was despatched and brought them from his home. It wasn't that The Beatles were showing big-star temperament – they were, in fact, quite charming lads. It was simply their attitude of irreverance towards everything and everybody. And, of course, while the film was being made the studios were in a virtual state of siege because of the thousands of screaming fans outside the gates.

When it was all over I was still baffled and bewildered by my role – I wasn't certain *what* I'd done. Then I got a phone call: "We hope you don't mind, but your part has been cut."

"Oh? Which part of it?"

"All of it."

Three people gave me three different explanations. First, since *Help!* was much too long, something had to go, and as the film could survive without my role, out it went. Secondly, that I was too good for the rest of the film. Thirdly, I just wasn't right for the film. I leave it to you to decide which of the three excuses *I* accepted!

But there was a happy ending – they didn't ask for their money back (and I certainly didn't volunteer it!).

One day during *A Funny Thing . . .* Dennis was hovering around the box-office at the Strand Theatre when three old ladies were buying tickets. He heard one say: "You know, Frankie Howerd lives near me. I often see him walking around the park. Oh yes, quite often. And do you know, he always looks so scruffy. Really scruffy. Not *dirty*," she added quickly. "I must make that clear: not dirty. Just scruffy. The poor devil looks as though he hasn't got two ha'pennies to rub together. So do you think it would help him if we bought more expensive seats?"

When Dennis relayed the story to me I said: "Blimey, I know I'm a bit untidy, and I know I'll never win a Best Dressed Man of the Year award – but here I am in the middle of my great come-back, and I still give the impression of being a down and out. I've gone from rags to rags!"

That afternoon I bought a new suit.

Clothes played their part when I decided I needed a break from the show, and Marty Feldman suggested that with his wife, Lauretta, I and a girl friend should join them for a week-end in Paris, with Dennis coming along since he was also in need of a break. Because of *A Funny Thing . . .* it had to be a short week-end: a late plane after the second house on Saturday night, then back relatively early on Monday.

Since it was an impulse thing we didn't both about what clothes we took – nor did we have time to book hotel rooms in advance. We thought we'd just chance it – and found Paris jam-packed with tourists. We went round and round the town, trying hotel after hotel, and finally found rooms at a modest establishment off the Champs-Elysées. It was very cheap and we soon understood why: we were expected to occupy our rooms for an hour, then make way for the next occupants! The management was really put out when we said we proposed staying until Monday morning. (There was much unprintable badinage among our party as we sat on the stairs listening to spanky-times.)

I was anxious to see the show at the Lido: traditionally a big and superb cabaret as you wined and dined – although madly expensive. Now we hadn't brought the clothes for such an occasion (certainly I hadn't brought my new suit), while Marty, the world's most eccentric dresser at the best of times, hadn't even packed the clothes he'd intended to bring: his wardrobe consisted of a pair of jeans, a pyjama top and a brocade smoking jacket. "Don't worry," I said. "Leave it to me."

So I strolled up the Champs-Elysées to the Lido, and employed my best French. "Now écoutez. Je suis un grand acteur Anglais. Je suis dans *Un Très Drôle Chose Occuré En Route Au Forum*. Je suis——"

In impeccable English I was told: "I'm sorry, monsieur – we're full tonight."

I muttered an (Anglo-Saxon) imprecation and returned to the hotel. "I'll show you how it's done," said Dennis. "I'll go with Marty and I'll fix it."

"How?" I asked.

He winked. "I'll flash a few francs – that'll do the trick."

So these two scruffs went down – and were tossed out on their ears.

It was then Lauretta's turn to come up with an idea: "If there's one thing about foreigners it's that they're enormous snobs."

"You're right," I said.

So she reached for the telephone, called the Lido, and said in that marvellously posh and languid voice of hers: "The Lido? . . . Oh, Sir Francis Howerd is in town. I'm calling from the George Cinq Hotel." (Since it was the swankiest in Paris, she covered the phone with her hand and said: "I hope to God they don't phone back to check," then continued): "Now he wants to see your show, but wouldn't *dream* of coming unless he gets a good table. . . . Oh, and by the way: he has a *most* important party of people with him. So what would be the best time to arrive?"

A great flurry at the other end of the telephone, then: "Sir Francis 'Owerd, madame? . . . Yes, madame. . . . Of course, madame. . . . We 'ave zee one marvellous table we keep for 'eem. I suggest 'e come at eight-thirty of zee clock."

"Thank you so much," Lauretta drawled. "And do make certain the service is impeccable. Since he is in Paris for only the one night, we don't want to create a bad impression, do we? *Mmmm?*"

"Certainly not, madame."

So far, so good, but I said to Dennis and Marty: "It's silly for us all to go together. They simply won't let us in with you two looking like a pair of yobbos."

"Us? Yobbos?" Marty yelped. "What about you?"

"Me?" I replied haughtily. "I am an eccentric baronet."

So Lauretta and I went on ahead to the Lido as Sir Francis and Lady Howerd. When I asked for "Sir Francis Howerd's table", the poor old *maître d'hôtel* ushered us to it walking backwards and doubled up as though suffering a crucifying attack of lumbago. (By the time we got to the end of that long and narrow room he probably did have lumbago!)

So we sat, and five minutes later the others arrived. As they walked in the *maître d'hôtel* frowned at them suspiciously and demanded: "Where do you think you're going?"

Marty, his preposterous eyes whirling like Catherine wheels: "We are guests at Sir Francis Howerd's table."

The *maître d'hôtel* shook his head. "I'm sorry, sir, but you can't go there."

Dennis now: "But we're with him."

A disdainful: "*You?*" of recognition – but to make certain, a waiter was sent to my table to ask: "Are these people with Sir Francis?"

I made a great play of peering across the room. "Oh yes," I drawled. "That's the mad millionaire, Viscount Feldman, his mistress and my valet." With weary hauteur: "They may sit."

And that's how we had a splendid night out at the Lido . . .

In July 1965, my contract for *A Funny Thing* . . . expired, and although I was sorry to leave a show that had brought me such a very helpful come-back, I was very tired from the sheer physical effort of it. Dave King took over – but he, poor fellow, went sick, so it was decided to close. An understudy played the role for the last week, but for the final performance I said to the management: "I'll come back and do it free, as a gesture of thanks." (There was then talk of my appearing in the film of the show, but nothing came of it: the argument was that American audiences needed a known name – Zero Mostel.)

But I didn't rest for long: in August I was asked to go to Borneo to entertain the troops who were keeping the peace there because of some confrontation between Borneo and Indonesia. I took with me zither girl, Shirley Abigail; conjuror, Al Koran; Sunny Rogers, and Dennis to stage manage the shows. Poor Sunny. I said to her: "Look, there are no pianofortes in the jungle, so you'll have to take an accordian."

"A *what*?"

"Accordian."

"But I can't play one."

"You've got just a week to learn."

Being small and slight, it was all the poor soul could do to hold the instrument. And as for playing it when the bellows were extended . . . in that one week her arms stretched to such a degree she could almost scratch her ankles while standing to attention! But she did learn to play the accordian (and almost as badly as she played the piano).

Our first stop was for three nights on the island of Gan in the Indian Ocean where the RAF had a staging-post.

There were about two hundred lads – and one woman. A neighbouring island was packed with members of the opposite sex, but our boys were not allowed to visit: the natives made it quite clear that any serviceman who did land would be decapitated (for a start).

Gan was hot and humid, but had a remarkably unspoiled beauty. With its palm trees and golden sands and blue sea under a cloudless sky, it was a Robinson Crusoe dream of an island. The Commanding Officer was extremely kind, finding room for us in his quarters, had fans installed to provide some comfort from the heat, and I thought: "This is truly Paradise."

Next morning, as I was about to go for a walk, barefoot, along the warm and lovely sands, the C.O. said: "You'd better wear shoes."

"What for?" I asked.

"The moray eels. If you walk among them and they bite you, you'll die."

"That's nice."

"Oh, and if you fancy a swim, you will keep your eyes open for sharks, won't you?"

"Do you know," I said, "I think I'll have a quiet sit-down instead under a palm tree. . . . But tell me, why have they got metal bands round them half-way up?"

"Ah," said the C.O., "that's because of the rats. We've got really huge monsters on Gan."

"Oh, thank you very much."

That night Dennis went to the Naafi for some cigarettes, and after three minutes came back screaming. "There's . . . there's bloody great black things flapping about out there. *Enormous*."

"Don't worry," said the C.O., "they're just giant fruit bats."

So much for Paradise . . .

We then flew to Malaya for some concerts in the jungle there. It was pretty rough, since the guest houses in which we were accommodated were covered – walls, ceilings and floors – with lizards, and the rats and primitive sanitation did nothing to cheer me. On top of this my ankles had swollen in the heat, and my back was playing me up: residual, but severe, pains that I sometimes suffered as a result of that accident with the horse. I wasn't sorry to get to Singapore.

We were met at the airport by a young officer in the Royal Engineers – all very pukka with a little stick under his arm and a little sprinkling of hair on his upper lip – who announced that he was to fly with us to Kuching in Borneo, and be our escorting officer. As we drove from the airport to the Singapore hotel he said: "I've got a coach laid on when we arrive in Borneo, and the schedule's all been finalised. On the first day, at 02.00 hours we'll be at so-and-so, then at 04.00 hours at such-and-such, and at 08.00 hours . . ." And so he went on, while I just gaped at him. It was like the briefing I'd had for my first route march at Shoeburyness. "It's a busy schedule for you performing chappies," he concluded as we reached the hotel "Any questions?"

"Just one: would you come up to my room?"

When we got there I said: "Let's get one thing clear. For the duration of my tour I've been given the honorary status of an officer by the War Office. Now what rank are you?"

"Lieutenant."

In one of the greatest examples of self-promotion I said: "Right – I'm a general. . . . So, for a start, don't be so patronising about us 'performing chappies'. We're not in the Army, nor have we been paid to come out here. That's number one. Number two: I'm not going the length and breadth of Borneo in a clapped-out old coach. I've got a bad back and I can hardly walk, so we'll need a car. Not a Rolls-Royce, but a car. Look – when Bob Hope goes abroad to entertain the troops he has a fleet of planes. All we want is a small car. Because apart from my aches and pains we want to be reasonably fresh when we arrive for a concert, so that we can put on a decent show. All right?"

He gulped and nodded.

"As for your schedule," I continued, "you seem to have us in a dozen places at once for every day of the tour. However, since it's arranged we'll do our best, because we don't want to disappoint the lads. But just don't try to regiment us as though we are a bunch of Albanian buskers. Any questions?"

"Oh . . . Mmmm . . . No."

"Ever looked after a concert party before?"

"No."

"You'll find it's not as easy as it sounds. You're in show-business now, and it's tough – not like the Army."

He laughed then.

We were to do a show in Singapore, and found the lighting arrangements all wrong. "We just can't stand around," I told the lieutenant briskly. "Go and get a ladder." He did – and lo and behold, two hours later he was still hanging by his heels from the rafters, helping to adjust the lights. . . . And from then on he was absolutely marvellous, realising that a concert party such as ours involved more than just walking on, doing a turn, and walking off again. As he admitted after the tour: "I didn't realise there was so much to it: lighting, spotlights, getting the audience in and out, changing clothes – and when you repeat it five times a day in different places . . . *phew*!"

He was a godsend.

So to Kuching, where we were joined by a BBC team who were to do a TV documentary about the tour: *East of Howerd.* When I'd agreed to it in London I hadn't realised the physical drain the tour was going to make on me – without the BBC dragging me out at dawn to film me buying melons.

I don't want to sound too sorry for myself: we were away from England for a month, but the troops we entertained were doing full terms of duty in those humid Borneo jungles. They were great lads, delighted to see us, very appreciative of our efforts, and so made the tour immensely worthwhile.

The jokes were, of course, aimed for that particular audience. (Sample: "My being here is all a terrible mistake

. . . No, don't laugh . . . Really, I shouldn't be here at all. You see this colonel fellow at the War Office said: 'I say, Howerd, care to go to Borners?' And yes . . . Well . . . I thought: 'That'd be nice – a summer season at Bournemouth' . . .")

To get to the denser parts of the jungle we travelled by helicopter, and my morale was in no way improved when a senior officer said to me in the dry, elliptic, Sandhurst, matter-of-factness that these people have: "Problems with these helicopters, what? . . . Must be the heat . . . Dropping like flies."

The only witty riposte I could think of was: "I always thought flies flew."

What's certain is that every time we travelled in a helicopter we had to sign a form absolving the Army from any responsibility (presumably financial) should any disaster befall us, and name our next of kin. (But I managed a brave smile for the shadowing BBC cameramen!) Somewhere in the archives there must be a total of about five hundred "Wills" of mine.

The helicopters took us to remote jungle clearings of tents and nissen huts with sandbags around their perimeters – and the soldiers, with their traditional sense of fun, would nail notices to the huts in which we changed: "London Palladium" or "Prince of Wales Theatre". And in these remoter places there was often the need for ingenious improvisations on our part. I remember that once Dennis "borrowed" the flare lights from the airstrip to illuminate the show, otherwise we'd have played in total darkness. On another occasion he took a headlight off a Rolls-Royce, and with an extension flex used it as a spotlight, which he held with sweating brow and roasting fingers for an hour and a half.

Then there was the noise. Borneo is certainly the noisiest place I've visited in my life. For twenty-four hours of the day the twitters and screams and growls and roars of insects and birds and animals came from the jungle – and, without a mike, performing was sheer murder. Nor was the situation helped when Dyak head-hunters came to watch from the back of the stalls (as it were) – accompanied by their bleating goats. Not that the Dyaks flocked to see me (although my noble head was certainly worth the hunting) – Shirley Abicair was the first blonde they'd ever seen and was regarded as something of a goddess. But Al Koran was treated with even greater awe: apart from the connotations of his surname, he was a brilliant illusionist, and when they saw his art as a prestidigitator (how's that for a word?) they almost fell down on their knees to worship his magic qualities!

So they rooted for Al and Shirley, while I had the goats on my side (I think). But I suppose the worst problem for me was attempting to do an act standing on a stage of sandbags in the middle of the jungle while helicopters arrived and took-off. The dust and noise were appalling (although the havoc the helicopters played with Shirley Abicair's skirts was much appreciated!).

Then, half-way through this safari, my ankles decided to assume the proportions of balloons. A local M.O. said: "You're suffering from nervous exhaustion and must rest."

"How the devil can I rest?" I replied. "I'm here to work – and with a shockingly tight schedule." . . . But it must be admitted that although I've never begrudged doing a tour for the services (after all, one's only giving back a measure of one's good fortune), on this occasion, what with the travel and the unaccustomed jungle climate, I was drained.

Back in London I thought I'd take a really splendid holiday.

I had a few pounds in the bank again, so with Dennis, Betty and a girl friend, I decided on a trip that would take in New York, Las Vegas, Los Angeles, Acapulco and Mexico City.

Now I'd done my share of air travel, including those visits to Korea, the Middle East and Borneo – but suddenly, just as Dennis had bought the tickets, I was smitten with an absolute terror of getting aboard an aeroplane! I just couldn't face it. As I put it to my doctor: "I don't know why, but I've got a phobia about flying."

"Lots of people have," said the doctor.

"But I've never had it before."

"Well, you've got it now."

"What do I do?"

"A lot of people drink to give themselves courage," said the doctor. "Or I can give you some tranquillisers."

I settled for the tranquillisers.

When we arrived at the airport I was shivering with nerves as though it was again the first night of *A Funny Thing* . . . Said Betty: "This is ridiculous. We'd better cancel the trip."

"We c-can't do th-that," I stammered. "N-not at this st-stage . . . I'll take some pills." So I swallowed a handful of tranquillisers – a later count showed that I'd gulped down eighteen!

The plane took off, but I was still rigid with fear. I thought: "I'd better have a couple of drinks, after all" – but they had no effect: I remained frozen with tenseness. We landed at New York, and as soon as the wheels touched down I relaxed – and then the combination of pills and alcohol hit me.

But hit me!

I weaved and staggered across the tarmac, and when an official asked: "What is the purpose of your visit?" I could only reply something in the nature of: "Yerrs-gurgle-guggle-glugglc-glurp."

"Is that so?" I was taken to one side, where he attempted to question me further, while Customs Officers went through me and my baggage with a fine-tooth comb. They must have been convinced that I was doped up to my eyeballs – and so I was, although not in the form they imagined. When all they could find were my tranquillisers, and after explanations by Betty, they let me through. I went to my hotel and slept for forty-eight hours. So I never did see New York that trip – by the time I awoke it was time to go!

On route to Las Vegas the countryside over the Grand

Canyon has breathtaking beauty – or so I'm told: I made the entire journey with my eyes tightly closed.

With the aid of tranquillisers, on to Los Angeles, and then to Acapulco. As we took off I kept my eyes on the "No Smoking" . . . "Fasten Your Seat Belts" lights – when they went out I knew it would mean that at least we were safely up and away. The "No Smoking" light went out – but the other didn't. I beckoned a passing stewardess and asked why.

In a confidential whisper: "Not long ago we hit an air-pocket over these mountains, and as the plane dropped someone was flung to the ceiling and broke his neck. So we feel it better if passengers keep their belts on . . ."

If there was one person on board to whom such confidential information should not have been given, it was me! So while the others sat relaxed – reading, smoking, drinking, chatting, dozing – I swallowed every tranquilliser left in the bottle.

When we landed at Acapulco the first thing we discovered was that all the hotels were packed: we'd arrived bang in the middle of the Acapulco Film Festival. In the end we had to take a villa outside the town on the edge of the swamps. Its only windows were on the inside walls of the building which was built around a courtyard, but since these windows didn't close the insects nearly drove us mad.

One night there was a heavy thunderstorm. When it was over the villa was so humid I went for a walk down the path through the swamp to the sea, then home again: a pleasant ten-minute stroll in the moonlight. But on the return journey I saw a young man in a jeep, just driving backwards and forwards across the road, and I thought: "Oh dear, we've got a right one here: a drunk on our hands."

He shouted something in Spanish. I replied: "I don't understand," and he yelled in English: "Don't come near."

"Why not?" I shouted back.

"There's a snake. The rain brought it out and I'm trying to kill it."

I was about to say "Never!" or something equally

memorable, when I saw it. I give you my absolute word of honour that it was more than thirty feet long and as wide as a dining-room table. With a wild scream I broke the all-comers sprint record back to the villa.

"Snakes!" I yelled. "I've just seen the most enormous snake in the world! A monster! Horrible!"

Dennis frowned. "You been drinking again?"

"Of course I haven't been drinking! Bolt the doors! Lock the windows!"

Convinced by my panic that I had indeed seen this reptile, Betty pointed out: "But the windows don't even close."

"So what do we do?" asked Dennis.

In the end what we did was spend the night sitting back to back on the sideboard, watching for snakes, none of us daring to attempt to even doze. Next morning we caught the first plane to Mexico City.

Sitting in the plane, waiting for take-off, I saw that there was no door to the pilot's cabin, and I looked with some trepidation at the rows of knobs and dials and switches, feeling that it needed an Einstein to understand them all – then transferred my gaze to the tarmac, saw a lad in uniform who looked to be about twelve years old coming towards the aircraft, and thought: "He's a bit young to be a steward . . ."

He wasn't: he was the pilot.

The take-off was a bit jerky, and since I'd used up the last of my tranquillisers on the flight to Acapulco I rang for the stewardess and ordered a giant brandy. . . . Then another. . . . And a much-needed third as we arrived over Mexico City – for I opened my eyes long enough to see the pilot pulling at every knob and switch in sight, as though playing the Mighty Wurlitzer at Eltham Odeon. . . . The plane suddenly tilted forwards, and we descended on Mexico City in an almost vertical nose-dive! "God!" I thought, "he's not a child Mexican airline pilot, after all – he's a diminutive Japanese *kamikaze* who doesn't know the war's over!"

But he straightened out the plane with what seemed to be inches to spare, landed, and with a scream of protest from the melting tyres, brought the aircraft to a halt.

My first visit was to a doctor – for more tranquillisers.

"If you go on taking tablets like this," he said, "you'll kill yourself."

"Better to die in a tranquil stupor," I answered him, "than to be frightened to death."

"I'll give you just enough to get you back to England."

When I did arrive home, those people who said: "Lucky devil. What a fabulous holiday you must have had" never realised just how close they were to sudden and brutal strangulation.

A Beau Brummel on TV –
but off stage, never!

In Cyprus with Dennis Heymer (*far left*) and Julie Ege.

London Palladium, 1973 – rehearsing *Jack and the Beanstalk* with Dora Bryan.

Spud bashing – in a scene from *Up The Front*.

No, I wasn't in the First World War! Another scene from *Up The Front*.

My noble features were well
suited for King Richard
in *Up The Chastity Belt*.

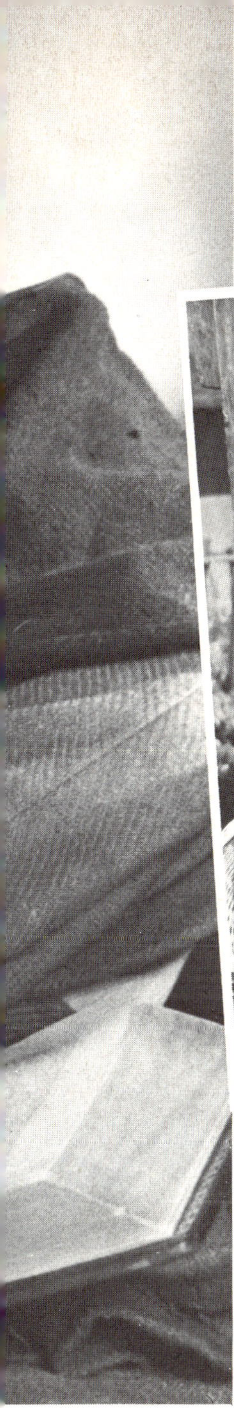

But I also played a serf –
although a blue-blooded
one!

Well, Ladies and Gentle-*men*, I do hope I haven't bored you . . .

FIFTEEN "A Powerful Stimulant"

At the end of 1965, Frank Launder made *The Great St Trinian's Train Robbery* and asked me to play the lead. It was my first offer of a lead role in a picture for many years (unless you count *The Cool Mikado* as a film), and opposite me was Dora Bryan with whom I hadn't worked since the old days of radio. The film was great fun to make, and again the climax was a chase, this time with railway trains. It was an intricate operation with me (the villain of the piece) on one train, while these dreadful St Trinian schoolgirls fiddled the levers and pulled the signals to send the pursued and the pursuers all over the place and in every possible direction. Split-second timing was vital to avoid a crash, and the sequence was shot at an Army camp at Longmoor in Hampshire where they had long tracks of railway lines, and engines and carriages and things. There was only one accident: when "my" train jumped a rail and landed on its side. Fortunately no one was hurt, and I wasn't aboard at the time.

But there is one vivid (if off-beat) memory for me about the film. I've always had a fear of being hit in the eye – maybe some hangover terror from a fight as a schoolboy. Anyway, in one scene I had to be pelted with eggs, and instead of standing there and allowing myself to be pelted, I kept thinking of my eyes and instinctively flinched: not just blinked, but averted my head and ducked. As a result, that one small scene added two entire days to the shooting schedule before it was completed.

None the less, when the film came out it broke all records, which more than compensated for the record number of eggs that had to be broken.

In March 1966, I did *The Frankie Howerd Show*, written by Galton and Simpson, for BBC-TV, and by this time I was also doing a lot of work around the clubs (of which more later). Then Bernard Delfont asked me if I'd like to star in a revue at the Prince of Wales, *Way Out In Piccadilly*, written by Galton and Simpson and Eric Sykes, and in which Cilla Black would also be appearing. I was quick to say "Yes", remembering how right he was to have called me daft for turning down his last Prince of Wales offer some nine years earlier: *Plaisirs de Paris*.

Eric Sykes directed *Way Out In Piccadilly*, and it was a tiring time for him, since apart from rehearsing it during the day he was appearing at night in *Big Bad Mouse* at the Shaftesbury Theatre. At one stage the effect of it all gave him laryngitis, and he'd sit screaming directions at us from the stalls – not one word of which we on stage could hear.

There was a tragic irony about this, because Eric suffers from an acute deafness problem. In my view it had its origins way back in 1949, when he was writing for me full-time, and I was appearing at the Central Pier, Blackpool. The show finished late, but the people who ran the Derby Baths were very kind, leaving the place open so that we could have a swim. Now the Derby Baths are formidably large, almost Olympic – certainly sufficiently grand for Johnny Weismuller to be appearing there that year in an aqua-spectacular. Anyway, after a jolly evening, Eric eyed the top board and said: "I could dive from there."

It seemed immensely high above the water, and I said: "I don't think you should."

"I've got a good head for heights," he insisted – and nothing would dissuade him.

So he dived, but hit the water badly – and it's my opinion that this was the start of his hearing problems.

It's remarkable how well he copes. There are times when he seems to have an extraordinary capacity to *sense* what people are saying, even when he's not wearing his hearing aid, and he's always remarkably courageous and cheerful about his disability. I admire him enormously. It never gets him down – in fact he makes jokes about it. On TV of course, since he writes his own material, he knows what's coming, but *Big Bad Mouse* involved a tremendous amount of ad-libbing with Jimmy Edwards – yet he always held his own. Nor is he ever left out of a conversation – and is witty with it. He's a Court Jester without an ounce of self-pity.

However, I started rehearsals with Cilla Black, and wasn't sure what to expect: although it was her first experience of this kind of West End show, I was worried that as a pop star she might think she knew it all. So I was wary of her – and it transpired that she was frightened of me. (Although how anyone could be frightened of sweet, modest, lovable Francis bewilders me.) In the event she was superb to perform with, eager to learn and very hard working. I soon realised that she was a great pro, and from the sketches we did together I reckoned she had a great potential as a comic actress.

One asset she had was a mad, piercing giggle. It was quite spontaneous (because the dear girl, in the brilliance of her judgement, seemed to think I was very funny), and it proved to be an enormous asset; for as I've said earlier, laughter has a contagious quality, and it immediately communicated itself to the audience. No matter how many times we played a sketch, she still thought me a hoot – so she hooted!

The show opened to extremely good notices, was to run for a year and I treasure a great souvenir of it: a silver cigarette box inscribed *WAY OUT IN PICCADILLY . . . 408 PERFORMANCES . . . FROM BERNARD DELFONT TO FRANKIE HOWERD WHO NEVER MISSED A SHOW*. (There are times, mind you, when I wonder if the wording is a tribute or a regret!)

Going back to rehearsals for *Way Out In Piccadilly*, I

received a message that Bernard Delfont wanted to see me. He was very charming, poured me a (small) drink and said: "You really MUST do the Royal Variety Show this year."

I said: "I don't want to be rude, Bernie, but the way you talk makes it sound as though I've been turning them down!" Then, as I sipped slowly at this thimbleful of drink (I didn't want to appear an alcoholic in his austere eyes): "But I can't do it."

"Why not?"

"It's not that I don't want to appear, but it's only a couple of weeks away and I'm not sure that you've given me time to prepare adequate material. You know as well as I do – better – that the Royal Variety Show isn't the sort of occasion when you can walk on stage having knocked together any old rubbish. It's got to be well prepared and rehearsed."

Bernie said he understood, so that was that.

A few days later, however, Bernie repeated his request. Again I pointed out the difficulties, and again he said that he understood. He walked out with a sad sigh.

A week after this I was rehearsing in the bar under the theatre when Delfont came in looking (for him) positively dishevelled: he had his jacket off (a sure sign that he was in a critical state). He then put on an act of dramatic intensity that Olivier would have envied. "Look Frank," he began, "I'm in dire trouble. I must ask you to help me out . . ." As he went on all he needed was an accompanying violin obbligato. It was a real Oscar performance, its pathos nearly bringing tears to my eyes.

When he finished I said: "You know, if you can put on a performance like that just for me, you must be a marvellous sight when you're addressing your shareholders. I don't think I've ever heard such a heart-wringing monologue. . . . I know: *you* do the Royal Variety Show with an impersonation of Sir Henry Irving: you'll bring the house down . . . *You cunning old devil!*"

And we both laughed, knowing that he'd won.

"But I'll tell you this much," I warned. "I'm going to

send you up rotten." And I did. I appeared in the second half with a script I'd written with Galton and Simpson and Eric Sykes, and much of it was about "Thing" – i.e. Delfont. In fact he was to be the star of the next *three* Royal Variety Shows that I did. A sample joke involved the arrangement of the hundreds of carnations that surrounded and decorated the Royal box – and how Delfont had arranged them personally. Every one. Dangling from his ankles at three in the morning to get the display just right. Why? The previous year he'd let someone else do it and found one carnation missing!

Another great accolade at about this time was the invitation I received to be guest of honour at a dinner given at the Grosvenor House by the Water Rats, an elite of show-business people who raise money for charity. I was introduced by Bud Flanagan whom I'd long admired as an artist, but didn't know very well as a person. In his speech he said that in all his considerable years in the business he had never known a come-back such as I had made – and I received a standing ovation. Believe me, to be acclaimed in such a manner by fellow artistes at the top of the profession is an overwhelming experience.

A highlight of the show-business calendar is the Royal Film Performance, and the selection for 1966 was *Taming of the Shrew*, with Richard Burton and Elizabeth Taylor. On the night, between performances at the Prince of Wales, I tried to make myself inconspicuous with coat collar turned up and hat pulled over my eyes, and went to join the crowds in Leicester Square: I was still fascinated by such events, and as excited by celebrity spotting as ever I'd been.

A few nights later I was informed that Burton and Taylor were sitting out front at the Prince of Wales with their entourage. When I told Cilla, she said: "Oh God" and started to tremble, and I, too, suffered an attack of nerves. It's one of the extraordinary things about show-business: how frightened, really terrified, one gets if other artistes, particularly celebrities in the trade are watching you. The edginess – the feeling that one must work harder as though to prove oneself – is almost unbelievable, although I suppose it must be true of other professions: the awareness of critically expert eyes when (say) journalists write for journalists, musicians play to musicians, or cooks prepare a meal for chefs.

I said to Cilla: "It's daft, really; this aura coming from two people who aren't even agents! And although I haven't seen him for years, Richard Burton is an old mate of mine." None the less I was convinced that I mistimed every joke that night, while Cilla swore that every note she sang was flat.

After the show Burton and Taylor swept into my dressing room, and I was quite tense – until Richard said how nice it was to see me again, and Elizabeth said that I was the funniest man in the world. I thought: "What a nice lady! And so intelligent! So perceptive!" She won me over in ten seconds flat.

They took me to supper at the Dorchester, where the Burton family had arrived in force from Wales, and where other stars had also gathered. Elizabeth proved to be a superb hostess, mixing and chatting, but not overdoing things one way or the other. Then a party of us went on to Annabel's night club.

As we danced, Elizabeth said: "I realise now that I've made many mistakes in my life."

"Me too," I assured her. "Me too."

She went on: "So many artistes make a habit of saying that if they lived their lives again they'd do exactly the same things. Not me. I've often behaved stupidly, and I regret it now. Very much!"

It was uncanny hearing her say this, because it was precisely the sort of thing I could have been saying to her – but then we were both born in March, mid-Pisces. (Question: do I believe in astrology? Answer: if I meet a fellow Piscean I like then I put it down to us being born under the same star, and so we are kindred souls; if it's a fellow Piscean I loathe then I dismiss astrology as rubbish. It's as simple as that.)

Another great honour came in February 1967, when the Variety Club of Great Britain made me Show Business Personality of the Year for 1966. It was celebrated with a lunch at the Savoy, and my great memory of the occasion (apart from the thrill of winning the award) was that I arrived late. The invitation said "12.30 for 1", but I'd had car trouble on the way from a TV studio, didn't turn up until everyone was about to sit down for lunch – yet still needed to pay a quick visit to the Gents when I arrived at the hotel. If this hadn't put me into enough of a flap, as I got out of the car a girl with a tape recorder was waiting. "I'm from the BBC and——"

"I can't stop now," I apologised. "I'm very late. They're waiting to go into lunch. So please excuse me."

As we walked through the hotel, she said: "This is for *The World at One*, so——"

"Darling, I don't care if it's for the end of the world, so please forgive me. If you like we'll do it later."

"But this is for *The World at One*," she repeated. It's got to go on the air today – *within the next half-hour*."

"Oh I see, but I still . . ." At that moment I spotted the Gents. "Look, dear, you must excuse me. I've got to go in here. It's vital."

I'll say this much for her courage and the tenacity of BBC reporters: five seconds later she was in there with me! As she stuck the microphone under my nose: "I've been told I've just *got* to get this interview."

Well, I've been interviewed in some very strange places, but never before (or since) by a lady in a gentlemen's lavatory. (I dread to think what listeners must have made of the background noises . . .)

Towards the end of 1967, when *Way Out In Piccadilly* came to an end I made another film, *Carry On Doctor*, then was asked to record a TV spectacular for Christmas. I'd done other TV spots during the year, but this one I have special cause to remember . . .

Among those taking part were Bruce Forsyth, Tommy Cooper, Frankie Vaughan and Cilla Black, and during rehearsals I came out in a shocking sweat, started coughing, and could barely stand. They took me to a dressing room at Teddington Studios and sent for a doctor. By the time he arrived I was literally lying in a great wet stain of perspiration. He said: "You're quite ill."

"I'm not feeling one hundred per cent," I agreed.

"No: you've got some sort of virus and a very high temperature. You shouldn't be here at all."

"I don't know what to do," I replied. "It's not just a matter of holding up a production – which is bad enough – but the show is due to be recorded tonight. Is the studio going to be available again? And even if it is, what about all the cast and technicians that have been brought together? Nor can I just drop out: I have a large part in the show. . . . I don't know what to do for the best."

The producer and director and others came along and said: "Don't do any rehearsals. Just have a rest and come on for the actual filming tonight."

So I lay there, weak as a kitten, taking aspirins – and when the time came for recording I tottered on stage, frail and woolly-brained, and did my best.

It transpired that I had pneumonia.

When the show was televised, one critic wrote: "Frankie Howerd looked positively sulky . . ."

When I'd recovered from the pneumonia, I went to Malta for a holiday, and on my return Beryl Vertue asked me to read a play: *The Wind In The Sassafras Tree.* It had been written by the *avant-garde* French playwright, René de Obaldia, and adapted for British audiences by Galton and Simpson: a satirical send-up of every cliché of all the Westerns ever screened – and long before *Blazing Saddles* was ever thought of. The producer was David Merrick (who'd turned me down for *Oliver!* and was reputed never – ever – to have laughed at any performer in his life).

The cast included a Kansas dirt farmer (me), his courageous pioneer wife, log cabins and buttermilk, a rebel daughter with straw in her hair, a rebel son, a goodie (a mysterious stranger, dressed all in white, who'd come riding in searching for his wife's killer), a baddie (dressed all in black), a drunken (Stagecoach-type) doctor, a saloon girl with a heart of gold – and, of course, Red Indians. Part of the giggle were the accents: ranging as they did from the lah-di-dah to the cor-blimey. And there were such situations as one of the Red Indians attempting to rape my daughter. . . . I try to stop him – and *she's* furious! After all, he was a very handsome Indian! That sort of thing: a splendid making mock of every Western ever devised by Hollywood.

My role (as a sort of cod Spencer Tracy-type character) called for me to play the heavy father in my log cabin for most of the play – but although speaking some very funny lines, was it *me*? Except for my weight, I've never been a heavy. It was a great part, but experience had taught me that I was at my best (if you forget Bottom and *Charley's Aunt*) when I was clowning, not as a po-faced character delivering witty lines while smoking a corn cob pipe. (Incidentally, in the original French version the role had been played by that great actor, Michel Simon, and he'd not been asked to smoke a pipe all day long, but drink soup. He'd had a monumental row with the management, his reason being splendidly Gallic: the broth had not been up to his high gastronomic standards, and he complained that he'd had to pay from his own pocket for soup of suitable quality.)

So there it was: a very funny play, but was I right for it? The answer was to try it out, which I did (at £50 a week) at the Belgrade Theatre, Coventry. The opening night audience loved it, but the next day's Press was a bit mixed, mainly because they thought the language a bit raw. I said to the management: "Why don't you put out notices saying that the play isn't suitable for children? That *The Wind In The Sassafras Tree* isn't *The Wind In The Willows*." So they did – and we were packed to suffocation!

Since Coventry was only a try-out, I thought I could afford to come out of the play a bit to get some Howerdisms in – send the play up a bit and address remarks to the audience (but not too much so). Merrick came to Coventry, saw one such performance – and to my astonishment thought it very funny. "After London," he said, "come to America and I'll make you as legendary as Bob Hope."

(Very nice, but I'd have settled for being Bob's agent at ten per cent!) Anyway I still wasn't convinced that I should continue with the show at all. Apart from other considerations, I had memories of previous comic acting aspirations that had led me sliding down the slippery mountain to near-oblivion. On the other hand it *would* be nice to appear again in a play in London. But could I afford the risk of a flop? . . . My basic sense of insecurity reasserted itself, and once again there was the agonising tug-of-war of self-debate . . .

Decision was simplified when the man who was to be the American director of the show, Arthur Lewis, said: "Why go to London at all? Why not come direct to America?" And I thought: "That's the answer. If I'm a success a whole new horizon opens for me; if I fail – oh well, it's happened before."

So to America, where the supporting roles were re-cast, and the play itself was re-staged by Bert Shevelove. We rehearsed, ready for our opening in Boston. . . . We completed the final dress rehearsal – and then, just hours before opening, it was decided to make great cuts in the show. I thought: "God in Heaven, this is *Mr Venus* all over again!" Aloud I said only: "You're making things very difficult."

It was murder for the entire cast, of course. Everyone was thrown. After all, you learn your parts, you rehearse – and then, just before the curtain goes up, chunks get cut out. . . . It's madness. None of us knew where we were.

More? Well, it transpired that we'd opened at the worst possible time – during an election campaign. George Wallace was barnstorming on some hard-line policy and Nixon was stomping around the place. So we opened in this harmless, if emasculated comedy, and I was startled to read in the next day's newspapers, not criticism of the authors or the direction or the cast – but quite vicious attacks on the lines of "how dare these British come over here with this anti-American play? . . . Stirring up racial prejudice . . ."

Racial prejudice? Me? I'd never be prepared to appear in a play angled in such a manner. As far as I was concerned it was a harmless spoof about cowboys and Indians. But some Americans can take such matters very seriously, and so equated the plot to a Black versus White issue. What with the election campaign being on at the time, we nearly caused another Boston Tea Party – with us substituting for tea chests.

So the management got a touch of the Great Theatrical Panic syndrome and started even more re-writing. The show was cannibalised to such an extent they even retitled it "Rockerfeller and the Red Indians" (and I still have occasion to ponder the difference *that* was supposed to make). So the two weeks at Boston were far from happy although, paradoxically, we did good business: being a Theatre Guild production, the tickets had been sold in advance.

On to Washington, where I was treated to a unique theatrical experience. After the opening night we went to a restaurant to await the dramatic critic of the *Washington Post*. If he arrived before midnight, it was a good sign; if he came after midnight it meant he'd panned the show. I thought: "I've heard of critics playing God, but this is preposterous. . . . And what happens if he comes in dead on the stroke of midnight like Prince Charming? What then?"

It must be remembered, of course, that there are no National newspapers in America, so local critics are immensely powerful. Washington had two papers and (so I was told) the man on the *Post* was the one who really mattered.

We sat looking at our watches, and pretending to eat, and – Heaven be praised! – abracadabra, he arrived before midnight.

If all this wasn't sufficiently ludicrous, he then read his review to the assembled diners. Since he raved about the show, I was happy to lead the applause (and was willing to concede that my criticisms about the cuts and re-writing may have been wrong).

While we played Washington, the President's wife, Lady Bird Johnson, came twice to see the show with her daughter – and this helped bookings, because she was escorted by enough security men to fill every vacant seat in the theatre. And on both occasions the rifles that we used to fire at the Red Indians were carefully checked by FBI men to make certain that they were, in fact, props and not the real thing.

Despite our success in Washington, the management continued to make amendments to the show. They cut and cut, until there was no play left: nothing remained that could be possibly interpreted as politically, racially, sexually, religiously, metaphysically, gastronomically, medically, geographically or veterinarily controversial – or funny! By the time they'd finished, the show had been reduced to an elongated sketch, our opening in New York had been delayed a week – and, as a corollary, our collective nerve was crumbling.

To continue the *Sassafras* Saga, just half an hour before the curtain went up in New York, the producer said morosely: "Of course you realise that Clive Barnes of the *New York Times* is here."

"So?"

"So if he pans the show it's finished. Dead. *Kaput.*"

"This one critic?"

"This one critic. He's the most powerful in all America."

"So OK. He's important. Bags of prestige. But at home – all right, *The Times* hates a show, but the *Telegraph* might like it. Then the *Guardian* could rave, but the *Sunday*——"

He interrupted with a shake of the head. "In New York it all depends on Clive Barnes."

"You . . . you're . . ." I didn't have the strength to add "joking", and if I wasn't terrified of heights, there and then I'd have jumped off Brooklyn Bridge.

Knowing me, you can imagine the effect: how I was overwhelmed with inferiority complex, stammering incertitude, and sheer terror. It demonstrated the immediate and instant solubility of fame, success and recently reacquired confidence, for the curtain went up as though I was giving a private audition to Clive Barnes! Except that I was so terrified that he might not be laughing I didn't dare look towards the left-hand side of the theatre where he was sitting – I addressed my performance entirely to the people sitting to the right of the gangway!

Yes, he panned the show all right (although to be fair he praised the cast including, I'm glad to say, myself). So Merrick's attitude was: "OK, it's off."

"For God's sake let's nurse it along a bit," I urged. "If only for a few weeks."

"No way," he assured me. "We'll cut our losses. There's a dozen other shows waiting to occupy this theatre. We fold at the end of the week." (I didn't realise it at the time, but the odds against a show succeeding in New York are an astronomical 36 to 1. And since the city has only about a third of the number of theatres that we've got in London, there's a queue of productions anxious to take your place. There's no messing around: indeed, in my week *four* new shows came – and went. One, headed by a very famous star, lasted just one night.)

Ironically, magazines and weekly reviews were to love the show – but by then it was off!

Before the opening, my old friend Sheila Hancock had sent a telegram to New York wishing me luck. Then she phoned Betty to ask: "Have you heard how he's doing?"

"No," said Betty, "but I'm ringing him in New York tonight after the show to ask him how the first night went. He's probably a bit homesick."

Sheila, witty as ever: "Tell him not to fret: we'll probably see him in a couple of days."

But when she next telephoned Betty and was told the show *was* coming off, Sheila was dreadfully upset about what she'd said.

"Don't worry," said my sister. "He'll think it funny."

And I did (in a sort of way!).

For the last two nights of the show I threw caution to the winds and enjoyed myself. I let myself run riot. Tension had gone, and I cursed the terror engendered by Clive Barnes on that New York opening night . . .

Oddly, the show had a four-minute prologue by me (reminiscent of *A Funny Thing* . . .) and one critic said: "You should have continued the prologue and forgotten the play . . ." Unkind to the play, but it cheered my ego a bit.

The show closed on October 28th, 1968, and I returned home on the last voyage of the old *Queen Elizabeth*. It was quite a thrill – the first time I'd made a sea voyage (other than crossing the Channel with the Royal Artillery), and I loved every minute of it, until our arrival in England. I did a cabaret on the last night, but the final homecoming of that splendid ship was (to me) very sad: certainly the orchestra assembled on deck to play "Auld Lang Syne", but I felt that this superb vessel should have ended her life of commercial voyaging with something of a State occasion. . . . Instead we almost seemed to slink shamefaced into Southampton in the foggy gloom of a November midnight.

Come to think of it, I felt my own homecoming matched the occasion.

For those of you who may be curious about the title of this chapter, my dictionary defines the sassafras tree as being of the laurel family common in North America, while its root is "a powerful stimulant".

Pause for hollow laughter.

SIXTEEN "Laugh, Damn You, Laugh"

Naturally I was unhappy – for the rest of the cast as well as myself – that *Rocky and the Sassafras Indians* (or whatever the show was finally called) had flopped, but I wasn't as depressed about it as I might have been. Certainly I'd allowed myself to be intimidated by Clive Barnes's awesome reputation, but I think I can honestly lay the bulk of the blame on others for their panicky post-Washington re-writes and cuts. Further: although a flop does nobody any good, I was now more philosophic about life's ups and downs – certainly I wanted to succeed, but success was no longer the obsessive fixation of earlier years.

One thing about my unexpected return was that I had no engagements in my diary: it had been hoped that the play might have run on Broadway for at least a year.

But I'd been back no more than a matter of hours when Bernard Delfont phoned me. Morecambe and Wise were to have topped the bill at the Royal Variety Show that year, but poor old Eric had had a heart attack. So would I substitute? In the circumstances I couldn't refuse, even if it gave me only a week in which to prepare, learn and rehearse a script.

"Let's have a bit of fun," said Bernie. "Nobody – but nobody – must know. There's been the most enormous speculation as to who's going to replace Eric and Ernie –

but we'll keep them guessing. We'll guard it as a big surprise."

And sure enough I found that the Press and people in the profession were having a lot of fun guessing who the substitute was going to be. The mystery really caught an edge of the public imagination. Would it be Max Bygraves, Gracie Fields, Sammy Davis? . . . The list was endless except (unflatteringly) it didn't include F. Howerd! Perhaps because people still thought I was still enjoying a triumph in New York, my name wasn't once mentioned which, in an ironic way, was a good thing – it would add to the surprise value.

I rehearsed well away from the Palladium, and on the night itself – November 17th – Delfont said: "Whatever you do, don't come near the theatre for the first half of the show, and even during the second half don't come in until you're due on stage. If just one member of the staff, or another performer, sees you, it'll be round the theatre like wildfire."

This injunction didn't worry me a jot. I've referred earlier to the unbearably mounting tension of a Royal Show. Back-stage, the wings and dressing rooms are one giant, jangling nerve, which eases only progressively as acts are completed. Then the artistes can relax over a drink – except for the poor devils who don't go on until the end and have to suffer the rising agony of up to three interminable hours of waiting.

So after my very first Royal Show I'd avoided the theatre, anyway. I'd sit in the car in my stage make-up and listen to the radio, or pace the back streets rehearsing and rehearsing. For it can't be emphasised enough that while singers and dancers and conjurors could stick to familiar routines, and stand-up comics often had to memorise fresh gags, I was among the handful putting on an entire, brand-new *routine*. Every alley behind the Palladium knew me well, and in the light of the street lamps people seeing me pacing these narrow thoroughfares wearing stage make-up, often gave me some very funny looks, I can tell you!

I followed the same pattern on this particular night (the Royal guests, incidentally being the Queen Mother and the Snowdons). During the second half, Dennis nipped round the front from time to time to see how things were going – until, after one such reconnaissance, he came back and said: "You're on," and I dashed through the stage-door.

The previous act was The Supremes, with a great and dramatic rendition of spirituals. . . . Then, in utter contrast, the orchestra struck up Land of Hope and Glory – on came Frankie in his old brown suit.

A gasp of surprise – and then very generous applause. I was so moved, so taken aback, I nearly started in the mood for tears instead of laughter.

I pulled myself together and began by saying how "Thing" – Delfont – had told me: "We've got a couple of people unable to get here tonight. Very important people." And I said: "Really?" . . . And he said: "I'm afraid – well, we want you to take their place" . . . And I said: "*Me?* But I'd feel such a fool sitting in that box all on my own" . . . And so it went on from there. At the end I wished Eric Morecambe better (which went down well since he was – and is – enormously popular), then there was applause for me.

Afterwards, when the artistes met the Royal party, the Queen Mother said: "You must have been very moved by that reception."

"I was," I assured her.

"I was so pleased," she said. "And I hope America didn't upset you too much."

I told her that one learns to get over such things.

"We've all been guessing who the surprise guest was going to be," she added – but a giggling Princess Margaret leaned over and whispered: "Ma'am knew who it was. Ma'am found out."

Now during my act there had been tremendous laughter from one of the boxes. Concentrating on my performance I thought no more than: "He's a godsend . . ."

So imagine my delight and surprise when it proved to have been Lord Snowdon – who now apologised for laughing so loudly.

"I'd be grateful if you were in the audience every time I perform," I told him.

So there was that Yo-Yo at work again: the flop of my American venture followed by a success at the Royal Variety Show. (My trouble is that I'm a compulsive gambler in terms of my career. Some gambles have come off, others haven't. Most artistes, wiser than me, have followed fairly predictable patterns, but while I know there are things I can't do – e.g. juggle with Indian clubs or play Hamlet – other challenges, although dangerous, are irresistible. It's certainly kept me fairly interesting to the Press, who don't know what I'm going to do next – if anything!)

Of course, the surprise quality of my Palladium appearance contributed in some degree to its success. In the same way, if a star is sitting in a restaurant or club and is brought up on stage, he often goes down better than the actual artiste playing there because he comes as an unexpected bonus. I saw it happen when Dean Martin, playing at Las Vegas, called Sinatra to the stage, and I've also had some of my biggest receptions in this way. This Royal Variety Show appearance had something of that quality: although the audience knew *someone* was to appear, psychologically it still had the quality of a surprise extra . . .

Apart from pacing the streets behind the Palladium, I've mentioned earlier that I'm a great walker anyway. And even when I'm not deep in thought, or memorising lines, my face, in repose, is somewhat lugubrious, with naturally baggy eyes making me appear even more morose. (One thing I've certainly lost on the way is the beauty of my youth!) The trouble is that while people don't altogether expect me to walk around the park cracking jokes with the pigeons, some do expect me to *exude* joviality, and can't bear it if I don't look happy. Journalist Ray Nunn once wrote: "In repose Frankie Howerd has the saddest face I've ever seen on a human being." So while it's great to be recognised as a celebrity, it really can be rather off-putting when people come up and say: "For goodness sake cheer up."

God knows that without a public I'd be dust and ashes, and I'm well aware of the cliché that the time to worry is when people don't recognise you – but I do wish on occasions that it would be realised that in repose my face does resemble a bloodhound that's spent too much time with Clement Freud.

(Mind you, I can't pretend that I'm hysterical with joy when I get into conversation with strangers and they ask me what I do for a living!)

Equally, while there are times when I beg not to be regarded as being on stage all the time (perhaps you may remember the story of my sitting with Margaret Rutherford on her death-bed?), so there are times when I've felt lousy but have had to be on stage. Once I did a full hour at Hackney Empire absolutely right-angled because of a slipped disc. . . . On another occasion I did an entire week at a northern club, positively cascading sweat as I staggered along with a temperature of 104 degrees. At the end of it the club owner didn't thank me for my effort – he awarded me with a great (if figurative) kick in the backside for giving five of his waitresses 'flu!

I mustn't exaggerate: most people are polite and courteous, and appreciate that I do have a private side to my life. But some occasions can be trying.

For instance, I've rarely refused to give an autograph (after all, I'd practised long enough as a small boy in Eltham!), but it's infuriating to be approached in a public restaurant, when, after a twenty-minutes struggle, I've finally managed to wrap some spaghetti round my fork. The irony is that this mostly happens when the people doing the asking have finished their own meals! Please don't think I'm flying into a tantrum – but if the butcher is closed for lunch and people would be reluctant to knock at his door demanding a pound of mince – so, by the same token, am I not permitted to fight my spaghetti in peace?

One ironic thing about autographs: men are shyer than

women and children (thank God!): it's seldom for themselves: it's for "Mum" or "My daughter", or even "I can't say I think much of you myself, but my Aunt Edna is a great fan . . ."

A propos of this I recall going to Noël Coward's seventieth birthday party at the Savoy, the peak of what he mockingly referred to as his "Holy Week", what with the Press, radio and TV tributes. Among those present were Laurence Olivier and Lord Mountbatten, and enough stage personalities to fill a dozen TV programmes. At the end of the do there was a queue of people wanting him to sign their menus – including me. When it came to my turn I said: "Would you mind?"

"Oh, it's you," he said. "Hello. How are you?"

"Fine," I replied. "But would you sign this?" With a grin, "Of course, it's not for me."

"Of course, naturally it isn't for you . . . It's for your sons, Morecambe and Wise, isn't it?"

As for my restless prowling when I'm involved in that most difficult of tasks, for me, learning lines, I've rehearsed in some very off-beat places: that graveyard behind the old People's Palace, as well as today's local park where I've often been mistaken for a maniac as I've talked to myself while making somewhat elaborate gestures. Away from the park, I can hardly march up and down the local High Street rehearsing in full sight of the traffic, so I prowl around the back doubles – and this had also led to problems. Many a time a resident has telephoned the police in the middle of the night to report a strange man walking to and fro in front of the house "casing the joint" . . . a police car has arrived, and with a weary sigh the friendly neighbourhood sergeant has said: "Oh God, it's Howerd rehearsing again."

However . . .

One mind-easing situation at this time was that my finances (not just my earnings) were now on a sounder footing than before thanks, in no small measure, to Beryl Vertue who had thrown in her lot – and those of her clients

– with the Australian whizz-kid and impresario, Robert Stigwood. I was a director of some of the companies taken over by the Robert Stigwood Organisation, and also under the corporate wing were such disparate characters as the Bee Gees, Johnny Speight, Galton and Simpson, The Cream, Georgie Fame, Lord Ted (Dixon of Dock Green) Willis and Eric Clapton. The Organisation was also to make a copper coin or two from *Tommy*, *Jesus Christ Superstar*, *Hair*, *Oh! Calcutta* and other shows and films – and while my shareholding far from made me even a mini-tycoon, it did give me a *feeling* of some measure of financial security.

Now I've said I was a "director" within the Stigwood Organisation – but I'm still waiting for something to direct. They always seem to hold board meetings when I'm away – even if it's only to discuss whether guests should be offered Maxwell House instant coffee (three pence off) rather than Nescafé (full price, but with Green Shield stamps). I'm beginning to grow a trifle suspicious . . .

Anyway, I was lucky in that, despite my unexpectedly early return from New York, I found plenty of work on offer; but the next date of any general consequence came in May 1969, when I went to Stockport, Cheshire, to star at the Poco à Poco Club on ITV.

I'd been working "the Clubs" on and off since 1962, and from an artiste's point of view they were a superb transference of the Music Hall (and with much better money than the old Sheffield Empire ever paid, even allowing for inflation), and in their fashion were a return to the very origins of Music Hall, which had had its beginnings in the early Victorian pubs where the artistes performed as mugs of ale were drunk. (This information, I would add, is the result of research, not contemporary experience!)

Club entertainment on a really big scale, as distinct from intimate West End cabaret, had long been a feature of the American entertainment scene, of course. Great performers like Sammy Davis Jnr had found fame, not in theatres, but in cabaret in places like Las Vegas and New York.

If memory serves me well, the first of the famous provincial clubs was just outside Rotherham at Greasbrough. Suddenly this hitherto unknown town became a big deal as far as show-business was concerned. There was certainly nothing posh about it then – but its management could afford to book cabarets that included artistes of the calibre of Tom Jones and Frankie Vaughan. Greasbrough became more important, financially, than the London Palladium – except that a club offered only a week's work, while the West End meant a season. Yet at the really boom time for clubs (i.e. before the Gaming Act) you could work the clubs like the old Music Hall circuit – it was reckoned that at the peak of the boom you could tour for *three years* without playing the same club twice. In fact one big town could have nine or ten clubs.

Of course some clubs were (are) smaller than others, so salaries vary, but Louis Armstrong was paid a small fortune to play at Batley (it could hold an audience of 1,500 a night) without the need for other bookings to justify his visit.

Are the clubs difficult to play? I suppose it's a matter of technique, if I'm pinned-down to an opinion. For instance, with my specialised material, I had to try to strike a compromise between the robustness of the old Music Hall and the intimacy of West End cabaret, for in a vast, modern club there are people literally within finger-tip touch, while others are at the back of a huge auditorium. To make life visually more complicated, certain clubs are constructed so that the stage is the dance floor, and this means that some members of the audience are sitting almost behind me when I perform. This makes me turn into something of a spinning top since my act demands that the customers see what's left of my once-gorgeous face. (These gyrations don't quite transfer me into a Tom Jones. The only time I get knickers thrown at me is by men – with their wives still wearing them!)

Not long ago I was doing a concert in a "real" theatre and Dennis – adopting Betty's role of making certain that I played to the house – complained that I kept looking behind me during my act: I was so conditioned to club audiences. Equally, he complained that I didn't play to the gallery: clubs having no gallery, I just didn't look up there!

Now here's something that may surprise you: although I'm a comic, I don't know any jokes. (You know that already?) At least not in the saloon bar sense. People say: "Tell us a joke, Frankie" – and I can't. Of course I tell the odd joke as such during my act, but generally speaking my performance consists of comic *routines*. Sometimes in desperation I can invent a crack, a jest, a witty (?) comment, but I've never ceased to admire people who can sit down and invent proper jokes. And I've always envied comedians who have computer-type memory banks of jokes, enabling them to go in front of TV or radio audiences, without scripts, yet exchange blow-for-blow gags with the best of them.

The greatest man for producing new jokes is Tommy Cooper. I once did a show with him and Bruce Forsyth, and during the lunch-time break in rehearsals he'd go to the pub across the road from the studio. It was so near that I could see the inn sign from the window, yet he'd always arrive back late with the excuse that he'd lost his way! He put on such an act of baffled bewilderment about his sense of direction, no one had the heart to criticise him for holding up the continuation of rehearsals. In any case whenever he set foot in the rehearsal room he had us in stitches.

He once gave a marvellously original reason for his lateness: he'd had lunch at a restaurant and had been charged thirty pence for coffee at the end of the meal.

"Thirty pence?" he protested. "For coffee?"

"Ah," said the waiter, "but you can have as many cups as you like."

So Tommy had sat there until four in the afternoon drinking coffee until it came out of his fez.

The point is that when he did go to the pub he'd come back with a load of new and funny tales that he'd been told over there. (Mind you, his method of telling improved them considerably.) I thought: "I must try this – God knows I need a few jokes." So one day I went to the pub –

but nobody told me a single story! I tried the next day, but was told tales so filthy as to be absolutely unrepeatable . . . or their tellers were so drunk they never got to the end of them. I don't know what it is about Tommy Cooper, but he certainly gets told a better class of joke than I ever do.

One source of material is sent to me by hopefully enthusiastic members of the public. The problem is that these scripts, no matter how kindly the motives behind them, almost invariably consist of pages of "Ooh . . . Ah . . . Yes . . . Well . . . Not on your Nelly." People don't realise that "Ooh . . . Ah . . . Yes . . . Well . . . Not on your Nelly" is the one thing I *can* do. What I need is original material.

Anyway, back to the clubs . . .

Another problem is that you can't really use scenery; so sketches can be difficult if you need doors to open and close. Props can be a problem, too – I once saw a trampoline artist prematurely finish his act with his head through the ceiling (fortunately plaster board, not concrete), while I've known dinner plates and bottles to go whizzing through the air like a circus clown's act when an adagio dancer misjudged the size of the performing area.

It may seem like stressing the obvious, but in terms of projecting oneself to a large audience in clubs, sound and lighting are of vital importance. All pros are more fussy about lighting than audiences might suppose: but it's understandable when you remember how much of an act may depend upon its visual appeal. (No, I'm not referring again to my profile.) Lighting can help or mar an act – or an entire show if you recall how *West Side Story* depended upon lighting effects rather than scenery. As for clubs, the strategic placing of a couple of spotlights can have a tremendous quality – just as *mis*-placing them can almost destroy an act. A classic example of someone knowing the value of proper lighting (in the Marlene Dietrich sense) is Shirley Bassey. I'm told she has a "lighting plot" – quite literally two or three pages of a scenario of instructions which the electricians follow as meticulously as the conductor of the orchestra follows the musical score.

When most experienced artistes go to a club they take up a lot of rehearsal time with the sound and lighting: after all, people who have paid their money are entitled to see and hear properly. So when a fuse goes (as happens) it can be something in the nature of a major disaster.

So you've got a good house, the lighting and sound are right, you reckon you might get away with the script, you remember that there are people sitting virtually behind you. . . . What's left to worry about?

The drunk and the heckler. In a theatre the lights go down, attention is focused upon you – and off you go. Clubs are not the same. The cabaret is only part of the night out: if you want to ignore it, you can. Yet, again, it's very much up to the draw of the artiste. People have come to see the star attraction, and if the lighting and sound and material are OK, then the audience are likely to be on the artiste's side, so *they* deal with the hecklers to a large extent. *They*, the bulk of the paying customers, don't want their evening ruined, so *they* are the people to turn on a nuisance at a neighbouring table.

At a party or in a pub, there's often the solitary drunk who wants to show off. If he's on your side, urging you on – fine: but the truculent drunk (rare, thank God) can be a bother to deal with if he ignores the urgings of the others present. One trouble for me is not only that I'm not a good ad-libber (although I'm a bit better at it than I used to be, from sheer experience), but when people shout at me from an audience it's often difficult to hear what they're bawling: after all, they haven't got a mike, so all I can hear is an incomprehensible gabble – and if I can't hear the heckle how can I answer it? Even worse, when I *do* hear a heckle, how can I answer it? For I usually don't work out a witty riposte until three hours later on the way home. But at least I've got the answer for the next time – except that it's then a completely different insult!

But I must be fair: I've been lucky with audiences (touch wood), and as I say, the occasional bore irritates me far less than he does the customers: like mutterers or munchers of crisps in a theatre. And after all, loud conversations during my act (as distinct from heckling) can be accidental: people forget that they're *not* in front of the telly in the sitting-room.

And let it be remembered that in the old Music Hall days (even apart from that night at the Glasgow Empire), gallery audiences could be very unpredictable on a Friday or Saturday night. I recall one Saturday on tour when the gallery was in a right old mood. Nosmo King came on, wearing evening dress, smoking a large cigar, told some rather sophisticated tales – and had nuts and bolts and rivets thrown at him. His cigar trembled so much it might have been a fan. Waiting in the wings, I was also trembling (and felt very sad for Nosmo who was a fine performer and very much a father-figure to me). Yet, when I followed him, I got away with it – maybe in my old brown suit they felt sorry for me, or maybe they'd run out of rivets. (If they had, they certainly didn't throw money instead!)

And one thing's for sure: when it comes to drunkenness and bad manners, the West End can sometimes present its problems, especially when a *nouveau riche* nobody thinks that because he's bought two bottles of champagne he owns the establishment.

There was the night when I went with my brother, Sidney, to see Tony Bennett at The Pigalle – and a party at the table behind us talked (loudly and in French) all the time he was singing. I was white with temper: one thing you hate as a pro is to hear people chatter when another artiste is on. People "shush-ed", but the French party ignored them. They may have been having a jolly time, but it was sheer bad manners.

After one song I got up to remonstrate with these people, wondering as I did so if "*Ceinture haute, s'il vous plait*" was a fair translation of "Belt up, please".

As I rose to my feet, and by a mad coincidence, a number of things happened simultaneously . . . There was a "black-out" (the stage went dark for a minute between numbers) . . . I turned to return to my seat . . . A waiter at a "neutral" table opened a bottle of champagne . . . The cork hit my nose . . . I raised my hand in a defensive reflex . . . In my natural clumsiness I hit the base of the bottle, so agitating its contents and changing the direction in which it was pointing . . . The champagne *whooshed* out of the neck of the bottle like a burst water main in miniature – and the French were drenched! With my usual display of bravery I fled to the loo, and was later told by Sid that while I may have missed the best part of Tony Bennett's show, the French party got the (unintentional) message: dripping wet, they sat out the rest of the show in seething silence . . .

In a theatre, because of the footlights, the audience can see you, but you can only sense them: you judge how well you are doing by the laughter and applause (or lack of it) and the *feel* of either captivation or restlessness. Cabaret is different: if people are bored, you not only sense it – you usually see it. And I'll never forget the party of men in Manchester who didn't applaud, boo, smile, laugh – you name it, they didn't . . . except sit wooden. It really threw me, and when I came off stage I asked Dennis to see if he could find an answer. He did: it was a party of non-English-speaking German commercial travellers who'd come to the club hoping to see a sensual strip show!

Back to 1969 . . .

In August I did a series for ITV, *The Frankie Howerd Show*, and to my surprise and delight (I really *was* a-mazed!) three honours came in November. The Grand Order of Water Rats voted me Show Business Personality of the Year, and I was again in the Royal Variety Show. (By now Bernard Delfont was actually phoning me with jokes to tell at his expense, and I thought: "Any more of this and he'll be charging me for them!") The third honour was the first of my two Radio Industry Club awards as TV Personality of the Year.

I also made a film, *Carry On Up The Jungle*.

Now when I'd made *Carry On Doctor*, one of the cast was Joan Sims. She played a character who was deaf and to whom I was married at the end of the film – the ceremony performed by a deaf vicar. This took place on the very last day of shooting – and when Joan and I got together for the scene we both, suddenly and inexplicably, started to laugh . . . and laugh . . . and laugh. There was no special reason for it: as with Richard Waring in *Charley's Aunt*, there was some mad chemistry at work – so we just stood there, hooting. Since laughter is infectious, the director and crew joined in. . . . People came from other sets to discover what was happening – and they joined in! The place was a shrieking chaos.

Then Peter Rogers, the producer, arrived – and he wasn't laughing. He tapped his watch significantly and said: "We've got to be finished by 5.30."

But it was no use. Things got worse (if possible) and in the end the scene had to be faked: they filmed me, then Joan and somehow fused the shots into a composite scene.

When it was over I said to Joan: "One thing's for sure: you and I can never work together again, much as I adore you." Yet who did I find playing opposite me in every scene in *Carry On Up The Jungle*? You've guessed it – Joan Sims.

Before shooting started I said to her: "We were lucky to get away with it last time. So we really mustn't laugh this time."

We went before the cameras for the very first scene – and again some invisible force triggered off the hysterics. We just stood there, screaming and screaming with laughter. In the end we managed to get through the film, but I said to her: "This time it's definite: we'll never work together again." (Nor have we.) "But I love you as a person, so even if it's impossible to work with you, I'll marry you."

Another great burst of laughter. "Married? Can you imagine us ever having even one second of serious passion?"

"That's true," I admitted. "And how would we ever get through the wedding ceremony?"

"Especially if you had Richard Waring as best man," she added.

So that was that. . . . But before making *Carry On Up The Jungle* I'd done the pilot for a show called *Up Pompeii!*.

SEVENTEEN And So – Up Pompeii!

The *Up Pompeii!* script was by Talbot Rothwell, author of the *Carry On* films. When I read it I laughed out loud – very rare for me. Not only did the basic situation tickle me – the slave involved with the lecherous intrigues and would-be infidelities of the aristocrats of ancient Rome – but it had been devised with me specifically in mind, and contained what I considered to be splendidly broad and corny gags, both visual and spoken, in the best *Carry On* (i.e. Music Hall) tradition. For the *Carry On* films were, in my view, a logical progression from the old Music Hall: indeed it's significant that the one began at about the time the other died. So by virtue of its Music Hall and *Carry On* origins, *Up Pompeii!* seemed to me to contain the basic ingredients of popular British humour: cheeky, cheerful, seaside postcard bawdiness designed for a relaxed belly-laugh.

Yet it wasn't designed as a film or for the theatre, but for TV. As I said to the BBC: "Can we get away with it? Is it going too far for the small screen? For people's drawing rooms?"

"Don't worry about that," said "Thing" at the BBC. "Will you do a series?"

"Don't worry" meant that since the series had been designed for me, *I'd* carry the can: not "Thing" . . .

I thought hard. I'd done *Carry On* films, but this was for

television, where my reputation was reasonably spotless. I may have had my cheeky moments, but was this going to be too rich for the viewers' blood? After all, it was full of busty girls and mildly saucy dialogue and innuendo, and sexy (if comic) situations.

"Look," I said, "I'm prepared to take a gamble – but a cautious one for a change. Let's make just this pilot, and see how the audience reacts. If the viewers like it – OK, I'll do a series."

So I did the pilot – although suffering a certain unease, for I still retained the imprint on my psyche of a very "pure" upbringing as churchgoer and Sunday School teacher. So while I had no objection to healthy vulgarity – after all, I'd been a great fan of Max Miller and was myself a product of the Music Hall – would *Up Pompeii!* be going over the top? Of course, "cleanliness" and "filth" are to a great extent matters of individual interpretation, for although the extremes, like black and white, are easy enough to define, it's the grey area in between that causes the confusion of controversy – where does the grey end and the black (or white) begin? In other words, when does vulgarity become filth?

Anyway, the public and critics in the main *did* like *Up Pompeii!*, among the exceptions (predictably) being a certain self-appointed lady censor who was reported as saying: "Sordid, cheap, and a disgrace for a man of Howerd's undoubted talent."

But since the general response was favourable, and the country didn't suddenly wallow in toga-clad orgies, I agreed to do a series of six. Although there were lines I insisted on cutting out because I reckoned there was no way of putting them over except as filth (one, I recall, was about something "falling off"), my early misgivings soon disappeared. The humour was broad, but hardly corrupting. Indeed, the best Press notice we ever got was in the *Catholic Herald* which said that *Up Pompeii!* was a very clean show. Very moral.

And it was, of course. The series was a send-up of sex:

demonstrating that obsession with it is silly and ludicrous. It was a mildly satirical send-up of the absurdity of the permissive society with its cheerless provincial orgies and wife-swapping in glum hamlets. And the shows were basically very moral in themselves in terms of their sexual content – in a nutshell, although everybody wanted it, nobody got it!

We all know that laughter is cleansing and deflating. The tragedy of Nazi Germany was that nobody dared laugh at Hitler. Here we can make jokes about Harold Wilson, Margaret Thatcher and even the Royal Family. In a healthy world we must be able to laugh at ourselves, at others, and at all our weaknesses – and that includes certain aspects of sex. In my opinion, to debunk, to ridicule, is a far more effective method of criticism than fulmination. (Or, for those less intellectual than me, "doing your nut".)

People always have the prerogative of switching off or turning to another channel. Yet there is always a minority of people who want to stop a show that most viewers find perfectly acceptable. *Up Pompeii!* was a godsend for people who loved writing anonymous letters of outrage. Before postage went up to six and a half pence you should have seen some of the mail the BBC received about the weather forecasts – especially references to high ridges of pressure! And as for the isobars . . .

Anyway, the BBC couldn't have had many complaints, otherwise *Up Pompeii!* would never have been re-screened, then followed by a second series that was also re-screened . . . *And* made the charts every time. (Mind you, I was tempted to write a letter of complaint myself when I discovered that although the episodes were re-screened in their entirety, I only received half-fee by way of repeat money!)

The word-of-mouth controversy itself helped, of course, and I often wonder if our self-appointed censors realise that by howling "Ban this evil film/book/play" they often create or stimulate an enormous interest in something that might quietly have died a death if it weren't for their hysterical condemnations!

Mind you, although I expected criticism, and although

the antis were a small (if vociferous) minority, I genuinely didn't want to cause actual *offence*. My attitude is that if I have any value at all it's to try to entertain people, not to insult, outrage or shock them. I'm there (I hope!) to provide some temporary escape from life's grimmer realities. This philosophy doesn't suit everyone, of course. There is a need for tough spirits like Johnny Speight who doesn't care whether he offends or not (although the stuff he's written for me has never been in that mould). In fact he has said to me: "Frankie, your trouble is you worry too much about being liked." And it's true: I do. I have no desire to upset people. Some may call this moral cowardice, but I fail to see it that way – with the Eric Morecambes and Tommy Coopers and Ken Dodds, I like to think of myself as a clown, not a missionary.

It's not wrong to offend if you think you're right to do so: if that's what you want and are happy with a clique following in the Lenny Bruce sense. It's a matter of attitudes.

There has always been room for different types of comedians. Sid Fields, for instance, was funny and clean; Max Miller was funny and outrageous. You paid the money at the box-office of your choice. Just as you weren't forced to see Max (or, later, shows like *Oh! Calcutta*), so a TV set has a choice of channels plus a knob marked "off".

Of course, I didn't want people to switch to another channel when I was on because, as I've said, I didn't want to have offended viewers. But as it turned out the BBC told me that few viewers switched over. Mind you, they didn't tell me how many had switched on in the first place – but I gathered the show was a success.

Important to me as a performer was that I played *Up Pompeii!* in a manner that I feel further developed my TV technique. It was part broad Music Hall, but modified for the intimacy of television. This much I'd learned via *That Was The Week . . .*, and the breakthrough series Galton and Simpson had written for me. So we tried to give the show an intimate quality, with my starting off by directly addressing the audience in the famous (or infamous) Prologues. This technique continued during each episode with me *coming out* of the story from time to time to make asides to the audience and to send-up myself, the people in the studio, the script, the show and the other performers. It was, in a way, a development of what I'd done in mad impulse during *Tons of Money* all those years earlier, only this time was written in as an integral part of the scripts. (I swear it!)

Also the show contained a lot of corny jokes – deliberately. For instance, in one episode, in a game called Bingus, the prize was a Grecian urn. So the line: "What's a Grecian urn?"

Answer: "A hundred drachmas a day."

Groans from the audience at the corniness of the gag – but then I turned to them and said: "Look – it might be old to you, but it's new in these days – AD 54!"

That was the point of including the gag – for me to come out of the show *to make a joke of the joke* – and I was really furious when one critic waxed indignant on the lines of: "Is this the standard of humour we've descended to: what's a Grecian urn?" . . . He'd missed the entire point of the joke (if any).

So it was no accident, or lack of talent on Talbot Rothwell's part, to include these very old Christmas cracker gags which I called "groan" jokes. Indeed, at the beginning of the first series I'd encourage the audience to groan so that I could turn to them and say with arch indifference: "Oh, please yourselves!" or something. But we found it didn't work: it came over as sounding too contrived. Then we fixed it for two or three actors to be sitting in the audience to groan when a particularly bad joke was made, so that I could say: "Oh, shut your faces!" or whatever. But they also sounded forced, and in the end such artifices proved unnecessary – the audiences were quick to do their own, spontaneous groaning. . . . But let no one think that we didn't know they *were* groan jokes, introduced to give me an excuse to come out of the show.

So each episode was played by me on a variety of levels, which baffled quite a number of viewers. Sometimes I'd step out of the show, at other times I'd pretend I was playing this corny rubbish with a grim and manic determination, as if tackling *Othello* – and at times I gave the impression of rising above it all: the bad jokes ("What did you expect – wit?"), the cast's disgusting lechery, and particularly an audience which insisted on reading into my lines double meanings that I didn't (supposedly) intend (An outraged: "You filthy lot!").

We performers all enjoyed the series (although you'd be amazed at the sweat of rehearsals getting everything just right, including those "spontaneous" asides). What confused some members of the public was that they didn't realise that we were playing it tongue in cheek, no matter the dramatic intensity with which (so it appeared) we performed certain scenes.

Anyway, it seemed to have been the most successful TV series I'd done so far (although I may yet end up as a busker outside the *Crossroads* motel – and for real!). But before we knew of the response to *Up Pompeii!* (i.e. before the six recorded episodes were screened), the BBC asked me to do the second series. I said: "No, let's wait until we know how well these go down," and I also insisted that the shows weren't screened until after the nine o'clock news – if the children weren't in bed by then, it wasn't my fault. It will doubtless come as no surprise to you to be told that subsequently, everywhere I went, more kids seemed to have seen *Up Pompeii!* than grown-ups, and I had more fan letters about the series from children than from anyone else.

As I've said, *Up Pompeii!* certainly created discussion, because it was a return, via TV, "of your friend and mine – the old British Music Hall-type humour", and I was told that the then boss of the BBC, Sir Charles (now Lord) Hill, anxiously asked his wife for her views after the first episode was shown. She (bless her) said she thought it very funny.

And so, of course, apart from the dubious matter of vulgarity, there are times when comics are *always* bound to upset *someone*, even devoted fans.

Away from *Up Pompeii!* there was a classic example for

me during *A Funny Thing Happened On The Way To The Forum*. At the end of the first half Jon Pertwee had to make a quick exit from the other actors milling around him. Since this was early Rome, his line was "Unclean! Unclean!" and hearing this old cry of the leper the crowd parted to let him go. It was a simple script contrivance for a quick exit.

A week later I got a letter from a woman who said that she had long been a fan of mine, but was appalled. She'd taken her husband to the show for his birthday, and was I aware that he was a leper? We and the rest of the audience may have thought the cry "Unclean! Unclean!" to have been hysterically funny, but she and her husband didn't. It was in the worst possible taste, and neither she nor her husband would see or listen to me again . . .

What could I do? Only write back and say that we hadn't meant to be unkind; that I hadn't written the show, and didn't even speak the line. That I was just a member of the cast . . .

But that's one of the problems of being a star of a production: one gets all the criticisms from the public as though one had written it, cast it, directed it, acted every part, and paid the salaries.

Certainly you can't allow for having a leper in the audience on his birthday. By the same token, if you extended the woman's argument, you'd never make a joke about any disability (e.g. my "deaf" pianist), or religion or race or colour or politics or thinness, fatness – and so *ad infinitum*.

The secret, I hope, is not to be vicious. But to avoid every possibility of upsetting someone, somewhere, would mean that you'd never have any script left. The number of times I've made a mother-in-law joke, and have had indignant letters saying: "How dare you! I've got the most wonderful mother-in-law in the world!"

Carry the argument to its logical conclusion and you couldn't ask: "Why did the chicken cross the road?" – some earnest animal lovers would demand: "How can you make fun of God's harmless creatures that some unthinking and cruel person permitted to wander at large on the highway?" . . . and so on. I do my best. I try not to be hurtful (and if I'm upsetting anyone reading this book – apart from the diabolical quality of the prose – may I say here and now that I'm genuinely sorry).

So the artist must always expect some criticism, no matter how popular a show, and I've received my share.

Anyway, I did do another series of *Up Pompeii!*: a total of fourteen episodes in all. No more. But with the repeats it meant that the various *Up Pompeii!* episodes were seen a total of twenty-eight times on TV, and gave the impression that I'd spent years doing nothing but *Up Pompeii!*. (Funnily, viewing figures showed that more people saw the repeats than the original screenings.)

The trouble about *Up Pompeii!* was twofold. First, I got saddled with an image, and when I later appeared in other things people still expected me to be wearing a toga; secondly, I acquired the reputation of being the country's most outrageous comedian: a reputation I certainly had not aimed for – I preferred to think of myself, certainly on TV and radio, as a "family" entertainer. Although a send-up record, called "Up, Je t'aime", that I was to make with June Whitfield, was to be banned by the BBC for being too saucy.

Up Pompeii! also had the dubious credit to some degree of changing the patterns of TV viewing in New Zealand, Australia and Canada after it was shown in those countries. Until then their TV had been very tame, but when *Up Pompeii!* was shown, and accepted, others thought they'd go one better – or worse – and I've since seen shows on TV that are almost beyond belief. And at seven-thirty in the evening, too!

The irony is that outspokenness has progressed so much in the past few years that if you saw those *Up Pompeii!* shows today they'd have the controversial impact (sexually) of *Noddy in Toyland*. Standards change: just as *Hair*, with the cast taking off their clothes in a thirty-second dim-out, gave way to the full-frontal romps of *Oh! Calcutta*. And consider the explicit dialogue and sexual scenes you get in films these days, and the dialogue and descriptions in books.

So these things must be considered in the context of their times: and in its time many people thought *Up Pompeii!* was television's sauciest comedy series.

What tickles me are the extraordinary double-standards TV has towards language and sex. For instance, in *Up Pompeii!* (screened latish in the evening), I might have been sitting on the bench for the Prologue, and someone would come along and say: "Hist! Hist!" and I'd reply: "Who is?"

But to actually say "pissed" is mild stuff, even when it's screened before children's bedtimes – as long as it's in a straight play. It's OK for Drama – you call it "Play of the Month" and seem to get a special dispensation. (Odd how I've heard of "dirty" comics but never "dirty" actors – at least not on stage!) Similarly you can talk (and in intimate detail) of every combination and permutation of sexual perversion, if it's on a Sunday evening religious programme. Or if it's a documentary with a psychiatrist in the studio.

Even in cabaret I'd never dream of starting my act with: "I was lying in bed last night with my mistress . . ." yet in a play you'll see them actually *in* bed *and* simulating the sex act. As I've said before, there's always the switch on the TV set (although I *can* understand that psychologically, people find something that's acceptable in the cinema or theatre an unwelcome intrusion when it's said or seen in their own drawing rooms). The point I'm making is of TV's odd double-standards where comedy is concerned . . .

To jump ahead a bit, two years later – in 1972 – the BBC wanted to do another *Up Pompeii!* series, but unfortunately Talbot Rothwell wasn't available, and since his style was so highly individual, it was reckoned that without him the show couldn't be written. A pity, but understandable: writers like Rothwell, Sykes, Galton and Simpson and Speight might have their imitators, but you can't match the originals with their unique sparks of genius. So the formula was adapted for a different series, *Woops Baghdad*, but its weakness was that a *mélange* of writers were used, so the standard of scripts was uneven and varied, and there was also, inevitably, a lack of proper continuity.

Mind you, the series was reasonably successful – but it lacked that Rothwell touch.

Because the humour and situations were broader than in *Up Pompeii!*, and because the girls wore even scantier costumes, it was decided to screen the series even later – at ten-fifteen. Now as you know, TV companies put out trailers of their top shows – little ads, as it were. The trailers for *Woops Baghdad* contained scenes with me and these girls in their skimpy bits and pieces that served as clothes, and with a sample of saucy dialogue – but some were shown at five-forty-five, between the end of the children's programmes and the early evening News! . . . So this time, rather than miss the kids, it drew their attention to it!

To jump further ahead for a moment: I was in Australia for a series of concerts when *Up Pompeii!* made its impact over there. I was virtually unknown Down Under except for this series – and when I got off the plane people truly expected me to be wearing a toga. The trouble was that I'd made *Up Pompeii! four years* earlier (it takes time for cans of film to travel on a slow boat to Sydney), and so I found myself confronted with an image I thought I'd finally shaken off. When people said: "Will you do some bits from *Up Pompeii!*? The audiences will love it," I had to explain that I'd completely forgotten the lines by now. But as far as the Aussies were concerned *Up Pompeii!* was a new show, so at concerts people would shout: "Where's your toga?"

I'd do a cabaret at a night-club with a stage as big as a pocket handkerchief, and the audience expected three pantechnicons filled with scenery and a cast of hundreds to turn up for a performance of *Up Pompeii!*. When it was realised that this wasn't to be the case, they wondered: "So what *can* he do?" – unaware that I'd knocked around for what seemed like hundreds of years as a comic before *Up Pompeii!* was dreamed of. They were quite surprised to discover that I could do an act with just a pianist and jokes that weren't *all* as old as ancient Rome!

Two clubs found a clause in my contract (which I'd overlooked) stipulating that I *must* appear in a toga. I said: "How can I stand for an hour in a toga doing an act about Harold Wilson and my misadventures with a kangaroo on Sydney Bridge? It doesn't make sense."

"Couldn't you at least do the Prologue in a toga?"

I was adamant: "No toga," but wherever I appeared in Australia (and New Zealand) and a photographer was around, he'd find half a dozen pretty girls, drape them in sheets as slave girls – and this strange procession would follow me round the streets.

I said to one such cameraman: "Look, Digger" (I think it only courteous to pick up a few local phrases when abroad, don't you?) "Look Digger, I've no objection to being photographed with pretty girls – far from it! – but do they always have to wear sheets?"

A long pause for thought. Then, hopefully: "Eiderdowns?"

Back to 1970. In January I attended the *Evening Standard* Drama Awards, and received two unexpected honours. One: I was promoted to the top table next to Sir Laurence Olivier whose speech contained the flattering reference that from watching me he'd learned a lot of what he knew about playing comedy. These kindly words may have represented one of his greater acting performances, but from then on I called him Larry (although never in his presence).

The second honour: I was presented with a silver key to celebrate my twenty-one years in show-business. (Actually the award was a few years late – I'd started my professional career in November 1946 – but I made no reference to the fact: apart from embarrassing Max Aitken, a silver key is a silver key, and I didn't want him to take it back with vague promises of keeping it for my twenty-fifth!)

I made three *Up* films: *Up Pompeii!*, followed by *Up The Chastity Belt*, then *Up The Front* – and the first two were among the top ten at the British box-office. Talbot Rothwell wrote *Up Pompeii!*, while Galton and Simpson did *Up The*

Chastity Belt, but despite the financial success of this second one, I wasn't all that happy with it. The trouble began when the producer, Ned Sherrin, came in one day to say that a continuity girl had been timing the film and it was too short.

I said: "Eh? What? Too short? I read the script through in the office with Galton and Simpson and it's too long. In its present form it'll run for three hours."

"This girl's very good and very experienced," Ned assured me.

So Galton and Simpson went away and wrote more stuff, all of which had to be filmed on a very tight budget (my cut was to come from a box-office percentage), and the result – in terms of length – could be compared to the recent six-day Russian presentation of *War and Peace*. So out came the scissors, and the people in the cutting room ended up neck-deep in discarded film. As I say, the finished picture did well, but I still think that the problem of editing these miles of film down to just an hour and a half of screen time inevitably resulted in a bit of a hotch-potch.

Films, cabaret and TV shows kept me busy during 1970 and 1971. Then, early in 1972, two more flattering awards: the Variety Club of Great Britain again voted me Top Show Business Personality of the Year, and the Radio Industries Club for a second time elected me TV Personality of the Year. So without being in the *Guinness Book of Records* class of award winners, I've been lucky with my share of professional honours (however undeserved).

It was also early in 1972 that I made *Up The Front* with Zsa Zsa Gabor, Stanley Holloway, Hermione Baddeley and Dora Bryan, and it was during the filming of this that I was invited to attend Liz Taylor's fortieth birthday party in Budapest. (Richard Burton was making his *Bluebeard* film there with Raquel Welch.) Since we were working to a very tight schedule (as ever!) I didn't think I'd have time to go, especially since I appeared in almost every scene in *Up The Front*. But Ned Sherrin graciously said: "You can have Monday morning off."

With what was intended as heavy irony: "You're too generous. Are you sure you can spare me for that long?"

"Not really," said Ned. "But we'll shoot some scenes around you. Just make certain you're back by lunch time."

Big deal! However, on the Friday night I had a cabaret to do, and so got in very little sleep before reporting at the crack of dawn at Heathrow for the flight to Budapest. We took off to discover that the Continent was shrouded in heavy fog – and this, added to my basic fear of flying, did my nerves no good at all. For hours we circled airport after airport, with me sitting eyes shut, trembling and sweating as though suffering a severe bout of fever – until we finally landed at Munich where I had to be almost carried from the plane. (Fortunately I'd remembered my mother's advice to always wear clean undies on long journeys.) At the airport, during refuelling, passengers and baggage were carefully searched (bombs? drugs? dirty books? I'll never know) then we flew on to Hungary.

I was a bit wary about visiting an Iron Curtain country, but to my surprise everything at Budapest airport was extremely informal: even people who'd got into a muddle with their visas were whisked through. There was a car to take me to my hotel – which was seething with journalists – and in my bedroom I found a sideboard on which stood rows of bottles of pretty well every drink you could think of. There was also a card which stated that its bearer was a guest of Richard Burton, so should be supplied with anything he might want (almost!) but that the tab went to Burton. (It took my memory back to the card I used to be given for tea and doughnuts on the Herne Bay pier during Sunday School outings!)

So when I tidied myself up I thought: "There's no point having a drink up here all on my own; I'll go to the bar and use the card."

I travelled in the lift with Racquel Welch, and half-way down it jammed. There are worse things in life than being stuck in a small lift with Racquel Welch, I promise you.

So we had a cosy chat, and I was almost sorry when the lift continued its journey.

Because of the fog delay, I found festivities already in full swing, and clutching my card I went into one of the bars – which proved to be full of newspapermen. I saw that while wine was cheap, stuff like Scotch cost about £1 a tot, and reckoning that it would do me no harm to keep in with the Press, I insisted on plying them with round after round of drinks, as though there was no tomorrow. . . . "Have another, ladies and gentlemen . . . No, I insist . . . Make them all doubles, my good man . . . Sure you wouldn't prefer champagne?" – and so on. To this day there must be members of the Press who remember me as Flash Frankie, Last of the Big Spenders – without realising that it was Richard Burton's money that I'd been spending!

Finally I left the Press and joined the private party the Burtons were holding at a restaurant in another part of the hotel, complete with gipsy band. Richard had his family over, and at one point they started singing Welsh songs to the accompaniment of this Magyar orchestra – and the effect was somewhat odd, to say the least. Then, by way of a patriotic counter-demonstration, Princess Grace of Monaco led the other guests in a rendition of *Frère Jacques*. And do you know, the Welsh song and *Frère Jacques* and the Hungarian gipsy music suddenly blended together in a curious harmony. It really was extraordinary: almost as though it had been deliberately orchestrated and rehearsed.

Then Liz and Richard came round the tables to chat, Burton clutching a tonic water and at his most charming and unassuming best.

Now I hadn't had much sleep the previous night, I was further exhausted by that flight through the fog, I'd had a few tots with the Press – and I was never much of a drinker at the best of times. All this, plus the strong dark wine at the party (at least I think it was wine: in the candlelight I didn't know what glass – or whose – I was picking up), resulted in the worst hangover I've ever suffered in my life. My skull was an elasticated globule of throbbing pain, my mouth felt as though a family of Arab goatherds had just moved out, my stomach was an agony of noisy protest at the treatment it had received, while my limbs had turned to rubber. I've never faced death as fearlessly as when I awoke the morning after that party.

At lunch I had a long chat with Princess Grace – at least I think I did! But I was determined to see the town, and that afternoon went on a guided tour of Budapest. It's a beautiful city – at least I think it is!

I summoned some reserve of strength for the big do on Sunday night – the birthday proper, and I might mention here that one of my problems had been to know what to buy Elizabeth by way of a present. It was general knowledge that Richard Burton was to give her a diamond the size of a modest iceberg, so how do you compete with that? Answer: you don't even try. I discovered that Liz was very fond of St Laurent silk scarves, so Betty got me some.

Anyway, the dinner was a glittering, almost Royal occasion, and when it was over Elizabeth asked me and some other chums to the Burton suite, and we sat around chatting: people like Princess Grace, Ringo Starr, Racquel Welch, Michael Caine . . . (That's me – Francis Howerd – darling of the jet set!) It was very pleasant and relaxed, but more booze flowed, I didn't get to bed until two a.m., and when I had to get up at daybreak to catch the plane back to London, the accumulation of food and wine and lack of sleep really hit me.

What should have made matters worse was that the fog came down again: but I was in such a state of euphoria inspired by alcoholic and physical exhaustion, I hardly noticed. Via Zurich I got to London, where a car was waiting to whisk me to the studio. I arrived at two p.m. (which wasn't bad, considering), somehow managed my make-up, and tottered on to do a scene with Hermione Baddeley: she playing the *madame* of a house of ill repute (what TV Drama would call a brothel) behind the lines during the First World War, and in which I somehow found myself. Now Hermione was, of course, both a great actress and a superb pro: she waltzed through the scene without bother. Me? I didn't know if I was coming or going. Sweat – one hundred per cent proof – bubbled from me as I staggered on to deliver lines and make gestures.

No – I exaggerate. It *was* bizarre, and I certainly did pour sweat, but I, too, was a pro in my fashion, and so without suggesting that Paul Scofield couldn't have played the scene better, I did manage to summon enough residual strength to put in a reasonably good performance. It wasn't easy – indeed, it was bloody murder as it drained reserve strengths from both mind and body. But I managed, without disgracing myself or the production, and when it was over at six o'clock I collapsed into my car and said to Dennis: "Let's get home – where I'm going to sleep for twelve solid hours."

Which I did – and awoke in the morning feeling some sense of pride. For despite the demands of that exotic weekend in Budapest I had not only survived, but had willed myself through four hours of arduous filming at the end of it.

The appreciation I received for this? After all my blood, tears, toil and sweat (to coin a phrase), the film in the camera proved to have been faulty, so the previous day's material had to be shot all over again!

At this stage, towards the end of the film, Zsa Zsa Gabor arrived from America to play Mata Hari, and aware of her reputation for volatile unpredictability, I didn't know what to expect – or how to cope. Sure enough, she *swept* full of self-assurance into London Airport with a great publicity fanfare – but when it came down to the nitty-gritty of actual work, away from the brittle glitter of the flash-bulbs, she proved to be a very nervous and highly-strung individual. Compared to her, I was positively phlegmatic!

Among other considerations, she was accustomed to Hollywood's leisurely style of takes and re-takes, absenteeism and temperament – nonsenses we couldn't afford on the tight schedule of *Up The Front*. As pros, we learned our lines, rehearsed, then bingo! – after a couple of takes it was in the can (barring accidents). After all, we were only making a *modest* epic, not *The Godfather* or *Gone With The Wind*.

Sensing her bafflement at the non-ballyhoo, hard work, professionalism of it all, I took her to my dressing room and said: "You're nervous. So let's rehearse our scenes here. On our own. *Hmmm*?" (I might add that she was between husbands at the time.)

Now I know that I'm a fine one to talk of others being highly strung, but at least I have some knowledge of the time-and-motion methods of British film making, and had been on this particular production for five weeks (apart from one Monday morning off). Also, despite my own incertitudes, I do have a capacity for making others relax. So we did rehearse in my dressing room, I calmed her down a bit, and when she wasn't happy about lines I assured her that we'd rewrite them to suit her style better.

In the end she quite enjoyed herself, and put in a very good performance. Once she'd unwound, and accustomed herself to the sharp timing of our sort of film making, she proved to be an absolute charmer and genuinely (i.e. non-publicity handout) funny.

I remember saying: "You must give many interviews."

"*Ach*," she replied, "in seven languages."

"Seven?"

"Seven," she assured me. Confidentially: "Mind you, darlink, all lies!"

And I thought: *How marvellous to be able to lie in seven languages: I find it difficult to sustain a conversation in one.*

Her sister, Eva, came over and I took them to the White City where I sponsored for charity a greyhound called Up The Track. Now I'm no gambler, but I thought these girls would bet in thousands. Not a bit of it. They lashed-out forty pence a race between them and were absolutely thrilled to end the night sharing a two-pound profit.

They came back to my place where I'd stocked up with a bottle of local supermarket champagne. Not only am I not a champagne person, but my lack of dexterity caused me to pop the cork in such a manner the stuff exploded over Zsa Zsa's dress (which must have cost hundreds of pounds), then dribbled down her nylons into her shoes. Instead of the expected hysterics, she was superb: "I'm not going to waste it, darlink. I've always wanted to drink champagne from my slipper". . . . And she did.

Zsa Zsa and I got on very well, and there were even suggestions that I might become husband number seventeen (or whatever number was then next in line), but she stipulated: "Darlink, I must have half your bank account." When I countered: "Darlink, I agree – in exchange for half your diamonds," we decided it would be better to remain "just good friends" (as we say in the trade).

EIGHTEEN It *Was* a Nightmare

Not long afterwards I went to Los Angeles and visited the Gabor home where Zsa Zsa's mother also took a great shine to me. "I love 'eem very much," she confided to her daughter. (The trouble was that although she had even more diamonds than Zsa Zsa, she was even more reluctant to share them!) While in Los Angeles I was invited round by Bob Hope. He was full of gags and wisecracks – even though he spent half the time on the telephone discussing complicated business deals. James Stewart was also there. He loves to play the piano – and did so, despite a barrage of Bob Hope insults. Then Alice Faye arrived, and we all ended up around the piano singing songs from her old films. (Fortunately the house was well isolated from its neighbours.)

I got on well with Bob, who had been born in Eltham, although he left the year I arrived (doubtless scared off by the opposition). I also met other old chums out there, including Laurence Harvey – who was extremely tense and plainly very ill.

Now when I was in *Way Out In Piccadilly* the stage doorman came to my dressing room one night to say that a "Mr Milland" wanted to see me.

"Milland?" I shrugged. "OK, show him up." And up he came: a quiet, distinguished, diffidently polite Ray Milland.

"I don't want to intrude," he apologised. "I just wanted to say how much I enjoyed the show."

"Intrude? I'm thrilled," I assured him.

"I hate to bother you . . ."

"Bother me!" I squeaked. "I'm absolutely delighted. I've been a fan of yours for years. I can even remember waiting outside the theatre for a glimpse of you after the Royal Show of 1946. I've admired you as an actor since way back. So please sit down."

"As long as you're certain I'm not in the way . . ."

This enormously famous star is so self-effacingly modest, he's an object lesson for the rest of us in show-business. We sat and talked, then went to dinner, and he came back to my place where we chattered and nattered, and he told me some great stories about Hollywood. One I particularly remember . . .

At the beginning of the war he'd wanted to enlist in the American Air Force, but was turned down. None the less he thought that if he learned to fly he'd be accepted, and so took private lessons. Then (ironically) he starred in a film called (I think) *Wings* and since it involved the use of real aircraft he asked if he could have a flip in one of them. After some consultation it was agreed: "OK – but remember that you and the film are insured for millions of dollars, so go with a qualified co-pilot."

Which he did. And it was a jolly little zoom around the sky – until the failure of the plane's single engine. As Ray put it with what I fancy must have been some understatement: "It was a trifle harrowing."

They swerved and swooped, and did whatever other gyrations you perform in an aeroplane – but the engine failed to come to life, and the plane spiralled lower and lower . . .

Finally the co-pilot said: "There's nothing for it – you'll have to jump."

Ray, wearing the parachute he'd found aboard the aeroplane, looked down at the ground some hundreds of feet below, took a deep breath, began to lever himself from the cockpit – then heard the co-pilot yell above the noise and wind: "It's OK – I've got it."

Despite the engine failure, he now had sufficient control over the plane to glide it down safely.

People rushed up, and in a great Babel of confused sound told Ray how worried they'd been. He raised a restraining hand. "No need to get into a flap," he assured them. "I had my parachute. In fact I was just going to use it."

At this a member of the film crew fainted: he went down frozen solid, like a plank. When they revived him the question: "What's wrong?"

"Wrong?" he croaked, "Wrong? That wasn't a real parachute: it was a prop."

Whereupon Ray Milland fainted.

Anyway, while in Hollywood, I thought I'd play a joke on Ray. I telephoned him, and in an assumed voice asked: "Ray Milland?"

"Yes."

"Who is your favourite English comedian?"

"Frankie Howerd."

I was astounded. In my normal voice I asked: "How did you know I was over here?"

An equally astonished: "Is that you?"

"Yes . . . But how did you know I was in Hollywood?"

"I didn't. I thought it was a journalist. I was asked a question, and I answered it."

"I'm immensely flattered," said I. (And I was. I'd expected him to reply: "My favourite English comedian? . . . Let me think . . ." Instead of which out he popped with "Frankie Howerd.")

So with that joke misfiring (albeit in the nicest possible way!) I said: "Look: I'd like to see you. I've been given a script for a film, *The House In Nightmare Park*, and wonder if you'd play in it."

"Now there's a coincidence," he replied. "I've just been sent a copy of the script, and I think it's very good. I'd love to do it."

Nightmare Park was written by Clive Exton and Terry Nation; it had a strong cast that included Hugh Burden and Kenneth Griffiths. The plot involved me as a Victorian ham actor (yes, I know – the role was a natural), invited by a wicked uncle (Ray Milland) to his rambling mansion where he proposes to kill me before I can inherit the family fortune. So it was a comedy-thriller, and very gruelling for me. For one thing, I was in every scene; for another it demanded an enormous amount of physical action: being chased up and down the stairs by this maniac (Ray Milland) with an axe; crawling on my hands and knees through foggy swamp; tripping over logs; falling down stairs – even a scene in a snake pit. But when I'd read the script I was happy to accept the role – once again I thought: "Well, it's only acting, isn't it? It isn't real life . . ."

So there was the scene where I was chased around the house with an axe until I lock the madman in his bedroom. I was to lean against the door with a great "Aaah" of relief – then the axe comes crashing through the panelling from the inside of the door.

"How do we play this?" I asked the young Australian director, Peter Sykes.

"It's a matter of split-second timing," he said. "The door is really only thin board, so we've fixed it that when you lean against it with that 'Aaaah' of triumph, we release a spring and this axe slashes through, just missing your ear."

"Won't the axe bend or break?" I asked. "Even if the door is only thin board cunningly painted."

Sykes was puzzled. "Bend or break? Why should it?"

"Well, what is it, after all? Cardboard? Rubber?"

Sykes was appalled. "We've got to have realism, Frankie. It's an axe."

"An-an-an-an-axe . . . An *axe*? You mean a real . . .?"

As my voice trailed away, Sykes nodded matter-of-factly. "An axe."

I swallowed hard. "I see . . . Fine . . . An axe . . . But excuse me . . . Just one minute. May I enquire just where I am precisely?"

Sykes, patiently: "You lean with your back against the door, exhausted."

Me: "I see. Then my head hits the panel of the door. As it does, the axe comes through."

"Yes. It's so timed that if you hit the right spot it'll miss your ear and stop just short of your shoulder."

I licked my lips. "I don't want to question your genius, Peter, but since I've got my back to the door how do I know that my head will hit it in the correct position? After all, if the axe is fixed on a spring, I must be mathematically accurate to the fraction of an inch."

"Indeed you must," he agreed.

"*So how do I do it?!*"

"We'll make a mark," he replied cheerfully. "A tiny mark on the door. Hit that with the exact centre of the back of your head and we're all right."

I said: "H-hold on. It-it may seem to you to be an anatomical absurdity, but my eyes are at the *front* of my head."

"Mmmm . . ." Pause for long and careful thought. Then: "You must *feel* the mark."

"You can't feel a mark," I howled.

"Let's rehearse it," he suggested. "On camera. Just to see how it goes."

"All right."

Everything was got ready. When the moment came I locked the door, fell back against it, and said "Aaaah!" It was then that I discovered, to my absolute horror, that the rehearsal included the axe!

Whooosh! The bloody thing smashed through the door and I could literally *hear* the air as this razor-sharp monstrosity swished down to stop within a millimetre of my shoulder.

"My God," I croaked, pouring sweat. "That was a bit of a liberty. . . . But it was on camera, you cunning old villain so at least it's over."

Sykes shook his head. "No good."

"No good? *No good?*"

"You didn't look frightened enough, said the Antipodean wonder boy.

"*Not frightened enough!*" I shrieked. *Not frightened enough?* When the axe came through I was petrified! Paralysed!"

"That was the trouble."

"What was?"

"That you were paralysed. You went all numb. So it didn't show on your face."

I could have choked him!

"Now this time," he said – but at that moment I saw a nurse in the background complete with first aid kit and a glass of brandy. I thought: What am I doing here? I must be raving mad!

And the very implication of her presence caused me to involuntarily fall back against the door and cry "Aaaah!" And *whooosh!*, through the door came that damned axe, this time cutting through my jacket deep enough to draw blood. Another quarter of an inch and it'd have had my collar bone.

I yelled: "That's it! That's me lot! I'm not going through that again. If you want to kill a comic I can give you a long list of candidates."

"No," said Sykes soothingly. "That's it: a perfect take."

"A good job you didn't shoot the bottom of my trousers!" I muttered. "Now, where's that brandy?"

The nurse said: "I'm sorry, but Ray Milland was so frightened he gulped it down in one!"

This was meant to be a comedy – but it went on like that day after day. In the next scene Ray Milland was supposed to be chasing me with this blasted axe . . . I fall over . . . And with legs spreadeagled he makes wild, slashing sweeps at me with the axe, just missing (it was hoped!) my vitals.

"It's got to be timed to split second," said Sykes.

"It's that word 'split' I don't like," I retorted.

"Well," he conceded, "since the shot involves only the lower part of your body, we'll put the stunt man in."

"Thank God for that," I said. "But I tell you what: instead of a glass of brandy, that nurse should have a needle and cotton handy."

So to the scene in the snake pit. "We've allowed three days for it," said Peter Sykes.

"Three days?" I queried. "Just to shoot me and a few plastic snakes?"

"It's a bit more elaborate than that," said Sykes, not looking at me.

Suspicious by now, I asked: "Just how elaborate is it, pray?"

Sykes appeared almost embarrassed. "Well . . . You see . . . The thing is that the snakes aren't dummies. They're for real."

"*Real?*" I screamed. "*Real?* You mean I've got to spend three days in a pit with real snakes? Bugger that for a lark! I'm off . . ."

"Calm yourself," said Sykes. "After all, you're only acting."

I seemed to have heard that before. "Only acting!" I grabbed his shirt. "Look mate: I know we're only acting. You know we're only acting. Ray Milland and the others know we're only acting. *But do the bloody snakes know we're only acting?*"

"They've been de-fanged or de-poisoned or whatever . . . I think."

"You *think*?"

"Look," said Sykes contritely, "you're not really walking out, are you?"

I shrugged. "You know I'm not. But just make certain those reptiles are well fed *before* shooting. Right?"

So into the snake pit where I was in a proper state, I can tell you, as these serpents were brought in. Sykes made one concession: the beasts included a cobra, which reacts to sudden movement with a sharp *splat!* – and you've had it. So as a great favour he had this creature striking at me from behind a sheet of "invisible" glass. As for the rest, they were all over me. Extraordinarily, they were brought to the studios by a couple who kept a house in Chiswick filled with the horrors, and transported them to the studios by tube in plastic shopping bags!

Since snakes like heat and light, the temperature of the set – at least my part of it – was raised to boiling point, and the lad who'd helped bring the serpents to the studios came down into the pit, began to drape them round me and said: "All that can happen is that if you make them nervous they'll bite you."

"*Me* make *them* nervous!" I screeched.

"Sssh!" said the lad. "You must keep calm. Don't frighten them. Just wind them round you, like towels. They love the warmth and contact of the human body."

"Look mate," I replied. "It's very kind of you – but I can think of better companions for a bit of a cuddle."

It really was a horrid sensation: these reptiles slithering behind me, above me, below me – and all over me . . .

Then Peter Sykes ordered: "We must have complete silence. No vibrations. I'm advised that vibrations make them nervous."

In a quavering whisper I asked: "What about me? I'm supposed to be clomping around with heavy boots or fighting them off with a tennis-racket. What about me?"

"You're different," he said airily. "You're acting."

So the crew had to be still and silent in order not to upset the snakes, while I blundered around among them. Somehow there seemed to be a lack of logic somewhere.

After a while I grew rather fond of these snakes, in a way. No, "fond" is too strong a word. I discovered that far from being cold and slimy, they were warm to the touch, did appear to have individual personalities – and when nervous didn't bite me (thank Heavens!) but just slithered off towards the greater warmth of the studio lamps. What I did feel towards them was a curious admixture of terror and compassion, for at times they seemed to be even more scared than I was.

But if the heat kept the snakes happy, it didn't send me into paroxysms of rapture. I must have lost pounds in weight, and on the third day in the pit the point came when I had to say to Sykes: "Look cobber" (another word from my Australian phrase book), "you've shot enough film to keep Kodak in business for a year, so can I get out of this blasted pit? . . . *Please?*"

When filming was over the crew came up to congratulate me for my endurance and "bravery" during the axe, swamp, snake and other scenes. "Brave?" I replied. "I must have been out of my tiny mind."

After all this unintended method acting, I was grateful the film received the first *unanimously* good Press I'd had for a picture in a long, long time. You expect, naturally, some divergence of opinion, but as I recall it, not one critic panned *The House In Nightmare Park*. So although it may have been a real nightmare for me, it was worth it in terms of the end product – although I still have no aspirations by way of taking a snake as a pet. (Asp . . . Asp-irations . . . Oh well, please yourselves!)

I ended 1973 by going back to panto at the Palladium for the first time in many years; as Simple Simon in *Jack and the Beanstalk*, with Alfie Bass and Dora Bryan. (And it was ten years since I'd done panto at all – at Coventry.) *Jack and the Beanstalk* had also been the first panto I'd ever played – at the Lyceum Sheffield, in 1947 – and, ironically, was probably the last to be staged at the Palladium (although I hope I'm wrong). For such spectacular shows are enormously costly to mount these days – around £100,000: a fortune when you consider their limited runs, from Christmas to Easter. It's sad, especially for the kids.

We started off with record advance bookings, and what with matinées and evening performances, it was very hard work, as such shows always are – you arrive at the theatre fairly early and don't leave until eleven at night. To add to the discomfort, at the time the Number One dressing room at the Palladium had no windows: Eric Morecambe described it as "Hitler's bunker", and it was almost true: I'd finish late, eat late, sleep late – and so for three months barely saw the light of day, especially when most Sundays were occupied with charity and other concerts. I was like a comic pit pony.

The show began as a success. I say "began" because *Sunday Night At The London Palladium* had been revived on TV – but for two consecutive weeks wasn't transmitted because of bomb hoaxes at the theatre, and this had its effect on people who would have come to see the panto: they stayed away. During the run we ourselves had a total of twelve such hoaxes: a record for any theatre, I'm told. Each time it entailed evacuating the place while the police searched, and I wonder if the mindless individuals who made such calls realised that group bookings at pantomimes include coachloads of men, women and children who are physically handicapped. It was absolutely dreadful for these unfortunate people to have to be carried from the theatre, then – the search over – brought back in again. The idiots who made such telephone calls should have been there to watch it. The usherettes were wonderful, and as the audiences went out and then returned I'd sit on the edge of the stage trying to make cheerful chat. And, of course, these hold-ups added to the length of everyone's day.

Then the three-day week was introduced. This meant that money was short, which didn't help business. Next came a rail strike and this, bad for business in itself, also affected the coach trade – the vehicles were requisitioned for more vital transportation. The panto proved to be a tough old time all round – and to add to our problems, power cuts were ordered: no lighting outside the theatre, and a forty per cent cut on stage. It really was like wartime theatre again in many ways – only this time I was on stage, not among the audience.

At the time of writing, it marked my last West End show – and I wish that outside influences hadn't made it memorable for the wrong reasons . . .

In July 1974, the Turks invaded Cyprus, and the Ministry of Defence telephoned to say that they wanted someone to go out there quickly to entertain the troops at the British bases. What with wives and children having been evacuated back to Britain, and movement on the island restricted because of the fighting, the lads were extremely browned-off. So would I go? In August I flew to Cyprus with a concert party that included Julie Ege, Lois Lane and the Avons.

Travel around the island was by United Nations helicopters. Oddly, despite my dread of flying, I didn't mind these machines so much. For one thing, I'd got used to them in Borneo. For another, on that sort of concentrated tour one's too tired to be aware of the flying. You get off the helicopter, and since the lads are waiting to welcome you, and there are mikes and cameras, you're immediately on stage. Then the actual concert – and back into the helicopter for the next visit. Mind you, it takes it out of you, especially in the heat of August in Cyprus, and I'm not a young boy any more (not even a young man!).

So what with one thing and another I'd slump in my seat and doze off, almost unaware of the actual flying between stops. But that's what such tours are all about, and they're immensely worthwhile in terms of the pleasure they give (one hopes!). We performed for the United Nations troops as well as our own lads – on tennis courts and football fields, and in canteens: anywhere we could find an audience. There were also amphitheatres, and by coincidence I found that I'd used one of them eighteen years earlier during the EOKA troubles. (If any of the material was the same, that was also coincidence!)

At one point we had to go through Nicosia airport, which was in no-man's-land. Because of the unpredictability of the fighters screaming through the sky, it was thought that despite the helicopter's UN markings, it would be more prudent to make the journey by coach. It was an eerie experience, for parts of the airfield were held by the opposing sides, and we drove through a narrow corridor between them, hoping to God that they'd recognise (and respect) the United Nations flag fluttering from the bonnet. At the end of the corridor there was a solitary Canadian look-out to try and spot unfriendly critics on either side!

The airport itself was a shambles of destruction – smashed planes, the debris of ruined buildings, the runways pockmarked with giant potholes. . . . A sad, sad sight as one recalled how a few weeks earlier Nicosia had welcomed thousands of happy holidaymakers . . .

Our route took us closer to the Turkish lines than to the Greek, and the major escorting us said: "This is a very tricky situation."

"I'm not altogether unaware of the fact," I replied.

"I know you're a comedian, but for goodness sake don't try any practical jokes – like pulling faces at the Turks, or making gestures at them. They may not appreciate your sense of humour, and so open fire."

I assured the major that the last thing I was in the mood for was the making of funny gestures – but to be on the safe side I dropped horizontal on the floor of the coach in case the expression on my face, even in repose, represented an obscene gesture by Turkish standards!

What did throw the Turks was Julie Ege. They were so amazed at the incongruity of this gorgeous blonde slowly driving past, they nearly dropped their guns in pop-eyed astonishment.

When we got into Limassol it looked very sad and desolate, even though a tiny fun fair was open and a few little children were on some roundabouts. It was there I heard about a truly extraordinary man. Although the town had been out of bounds to British troops during the fighting between Turks and Greeks, and its citizens, warring among themselves, were prepared to shoot at anyone who wasn't on their particular side – an unarmed British Military Policeman used to stand calmly at a crossroads in the city centre directing traffic! Apparently he was very well known in Limassol, and despite the hatred and battles raging around, he'd earned the respect of both factions, and such was his personality that he kept the traffic flowing at that intersection as calmly as if he were a bobby at Oxford Circus. I never knew his name, but he certainly deserved a medal.

When I first went into show-business I assumed that the comic's life was always concerned with laughter. Or, put another way, that it was a "jolly" profession. Over the years I've realised how wrong I was. It's precisely because comedians are expected to bring a little joy into people's lives that they are so regularly called upon to visit, and attempt to cheer, people who, for one reason or another, are in trouble. We are asked to visit hospitals, orphanages, the incurables and the old, or to do charity shows to help such people. And, naturally, most of us are happy to help whenever we can. It's a way of *giving back* a certain something – and the irony is that while comedians are associated with laughter, we probably see more suffering than anyone else outside of the medical profession and social services.

We try to create laughter – which is something more therapeutic than many people might suppose. I know from experience, when I've been down, how grateful I've been to laugh at something or somebody.

Recently I visited a home for emotionally disturbed and mentally retarded children. It was really heart-rending: sights that would appal the ordinary man in the street. One kid couldn't help biting herself . . . Another had a dreadful facial disfigurement . . . There was a child that just sat strapped in a cot all day, bouncing up and down, up and down . . . The variety of tragedy was seemingly endless. (And how splendid are the nursing staffs in such hospitals, and how touchingly the children responded to them . . . And how, too, no matter what their condition, all responded to music.)

It's easy to sound pompous about this: to appear "good", to give the impression of a Messiah-complex, as though being a comic means that we were brought into the world to bring comfort and joy via a Divine passport. I feel the answer is to take one's *work* seriously, but not *oneself*.

If there is any propaganda in this bit of sermonising, it's only that most of us have *something* to give back . . .

(Here endeth the lesson.)

NINETEEN Whither Francis?

On my return from Cyprus I did cabaret and club work, taking life as it came.

Then one night I sat in my dressing room at a club, waiting my call and feeling reasonably relaxed since I'd played the club on a previous occasion and knew the audience to be very friendly, and since I'd done this particular act before on the tour I had no worries about the lines . . . But as I sat there I suddenly started to sweat: it just broke out and poured down me. It was really frightening – then, when the stage manager came to say "You're on", I found I literally couldn't move.

"Are you all right?" asked the stage manager anxiously. "Are you ill?"

"N-no," I managed – for I now discovered that I could hardly talk.

"Do you want to see a doctor?"

"N-no," I gasped. "D-delay . . . things . . . a . . . b-bit . . ."

He went away and told the audience that there was trouble with the lighting and sound, but when he returned half an hour later to ask: "Are you ready now?" I was actually feeling worse, and was shaking like a leaf.

It was agony to stand, but almost as though by some automatic reflex, I made my way to the stage. There were claps and giggles, but standing was now so painful I thought I was going to collapse – until I had the presence of mind to ask for a chair.

So I sat, started my routine – but found myself forgetting bits. Waiting in the wings, Sunny Rogers could see something was wrong, so she came on stage, sat at the piano and hissed prompts to me. Fortunately, the audience thought it was part of the act, so somehow I survived to the end. But when it came to taking my bow the pains in my stomach were so excruciating I had to stand bent and with my legs astride to help combat the agony.

Next day I did see a local doctor. He made various tests and said: "There's nothing physically wrong with you. You're suffering from a spastic colon, which is a purely nervous condition." Now that may have accounted for the stomach pains, but it did not explain the sweating and speech trouble and the forgetting of lines.

I decided I needed a rest, but before I could take one I was committed to two TV Specials; one with Bruce Forsyth, the other with Pet Clark. They were very difficult to do, because I now had this awful dread of not remembering the script, and for both shows I had to struggle through the night to learn simple routines that I'd normally have mastered in a couple of hours.

When I actually recorded the Pet Clark show I managed to get through it, but I was in a highly-strung state and did in fact forget some of my dialogue with Pet. Fortunately, from the show's point of view, the recording proved to be overlong and some stuff had to be cut, anyway. All I could do was to write to Pet and the producer to apologise.

Then, on the Bruce Forsyth show, I did a Hamlet sketch – and again forgot words and lines. It would have been understandable if it had been new material, but I'd often performed the sketch before. So this involved a number of re-takes, and when the recording was over I was quick to go on holiday.

I came back to London in January 1975, but the rest seemed to have been of no benefit at all – when bookings were offered I found myself making every conceivable excuse for turning them down. I knew I couldn't go on like this, so I summoned up the courage for one more try, and accepted a booking at a club in Devon. I was told that business promised to be very good, which should have encouraged me – but nothing could override my renewed dread of forgetting my lines. And indeed I did forget words, muddled my jokes – and one night told the same gag three times! On the last day of my booking, a Saturday, I spent the entire afternoon rehearsing – yet it was an act I'd done so many times I'd once known it by heart and should have performed it with effortless ease.

When I got to London I went to see my own doctor, who is also a friend. I put it to him bluntly: "I think I'm getting past it."

"You're not senile," he assured me. "Your problem is psychological – just as that spastic colon was due to nerves and anxiety."

"But why should I have these problems?" I asked. "Things have been going reasonably well professionally. . . . Could it be that some old friends have died recently, which has saddened me?"

"It's not that. It's a result of stress and strain – a reaction from something that may go way, way back into the past: an accumulation over the years of fermenting tension. Now it's manifesting itself."

I went home and thought . . . and thought. What was there in the past that could account for my present state? I remembered with a wry smile, my first screaming stage appearance at the age of four . . . how, later, my obsessiveness to perform had been stronger than my nervous terror of appearing in public – and then it hit me!

Now that the obsessiveness had gone, there was nothing to stop the basic fear from coming through. It was finally taking over.

I thought: "Well, if I'm getting nutty, and unable to perform properly, the best thing to do is retire gracefully. I've had a good run, so perhaps I should leave the profession before it leaves me – as happened once before."

I talked to Val Guest about it – told him how I felt I was

not up to it any more. He wrote me a long letter, which I cherish, in which he said that many artistes go through this period – even that great comic, Will Hay, for whom he'd written scripts, had had the same problem. . . . It was a strangely comforting letter, for one is often inclined to think that a certain condition only happens to *you*.

But I continued to put off shows, began to wonder what I'd do with myself for the rest of my life – then received a letter reminding me of a promise I'd made to do a charity performance for a children's home, how pleased they were that I was coming, and how they were all looking forward to it. I started to think up an excuse, for I simply couldn't face the thought of a stage and of doing an hour's act in front of two thousand people. . . . Then I realised that I'd promised, that it was for a charity, and that it was too late for them to find a replacement. In the circumstances, not to make an effort would have been worse than cowardice: it would have been a dirty trick to play.

So I went, with Dennis and a pianist, sitting huddled in absolute silence at the back of the car, dreading the outcome, trembling with nerves as I imagined that sea of faces . . .

After what seemed to be an eternity of shivering in the wings, my stomach a solid knot of fear, I braced myself, took a deep breath and walked on.

Generous applause . . . I started my patter – and after half a dozen words a little girl in the front row squealed: "You're the man on telly with the funny face! Hello, funny face! . . . Funny face! You're going to make me laugh, aren't you?"

The audience hooted, so did I – and all my tension suddenly vanished. Just like that! It was extraordinary, but the sight of the innocence and happiness of that giggling child brought some strange chord of response from deep down inside me – almost an awareness that someone trusted me to bring them some needed measure of joy.

She came and sat by the side of the stage, chattered away, and by the time I'd finished it was almost as though I was part of a double act!

They say you should never perform with animals or children – but this little girl truly saved me. In some remarkable fashion, she was the unwitting therapeutic agent that caused my self-confidence to come flooding back in a snap-of-the-fingers instant.

Don't ask me the whys or the wherefores . . . All I know is that I will always have occasion to be grateful to her.

As a result of that strange incident, I came to feel that perhaps I wasn't quite ready to go out to pasture, after all. Instead I'd jog along for a few more years, but at a nice, quiet pace.

A nice quiet pace indeed! Fate got the whip out and ever since has been driving me along at a frenzied gallop (I'm thrilled and delighted to say!). In recent months I've done TV series in Australia, Britain and Canada, and have had offers of all sorts of other work, including films and plays. (This book had better end now, because I'm getting quite breathless!)

So Ladies and Gentle-*men*: while all autobiography is by definition an exercise in arrogance and ego, I sincerely hope I haven't bored you.

Because there's an old show-business truism, passed to me when I was young in the business: "Audiences will forgive you practically anything, except boring them."

One final word: as readers will have gathered, my childhood ambition to become a saint resulted in spectacular failure – although it would be arrogant to believe that I acquired instead a monopoly of sin. (Just let's say that I've had my share.) So I suppose that the best that could be said of me is: "He means well."

But then, don't we all?